# ONE WEEK LOAN

# Working with Offenders
## A guide to concepts and practice

**Rob White and Hannah Graham**

WILLAN
PUBLISHING

Published by

Willan Publishing
2 Park Square
Milton Park
Abingdon
OX14 4RN

Published simultaneously in the USA and Canada by

Willan Publishing
270 Madison Avenue
New York
NY 10016

First published 2010

ISBN   978-1-84392-793-8 paperback
        978-1-84392-794-5 hardback

British Library Cataloguing-in-Publication Data

A catalogue record for this book is available from the British Library

Project managed by Deer Park Productions, Tavistock, Devon
Typeset by GCS, Leighton Buzzard, Bedfordshire
Printed and bound by T.J. International, Padstow, Cornwall

# Contents

# List of boxes, case studies, figures, innovative practices, scenarios, stories from the field and tables

## Boxes

## Case studies

# Figures

# Innovative practices

## Scenarios

## Stories from the field

## Tables

# List of acronmys and abbreviations

AIC         Australian Institute of Criminology
AOD         Alcohol and other drugs
APF         Action for Prisoners' Families (UK)
ASPD        Anti-social personality disorder
BBV         Blood-borne viruses
DTTO        Drug treatment and testing order
CALD        Culturally and linguistically diverse
CAT         Convention Against Torture and Other Forms of
            Cruel, Inhuman or Degrading Treatment or
            Punishment
CBT         Cognitive behavioural therapy
CC          Community corrections
CCTV        Closed circuit television
CEDAW       Convention for the Elimination of All Forms of
            Discrimination Against Women
CERD        Convention for the Elimination of All Forms of
            Racial Discrimination
CMD         Court Mandated Diversion
CNI         Criminogenic Needs Inventory (NZ)
CPTED       Crime prevention through environmental design
CROC        Convention on the Rights of the Child
CSC         Correctional Service of Canada
CSO         Community sector organisation
DTO         Drug Treatment Order
DUI         Driving Under the Influence
EBP         Evidence-based practice

| | |
|---|---|
| EU | European Union |
| GLM | Good Lives Model |
| GP | General practitioner (Doctor) |
| HCV | Hepatitis C virus |
| HDC | Home detention curfew |
| HMIP | Her Majesty's Inspectorate of Probation |
| HMP | Her Majesty's Prison Service |
| ICCPR | International Covenant on Civil and Political Rights |
| ICPS | International Centre for Prison Studies |
| IDU | Injecting drug user |
| IMP | Individual management plan |
| IOM | Integrated offender management |
| KPI | Key performance indicator |
| LS/CMI | Level of Service/Case Management Inventory |
| MI | Motivational interviewing |
| MOU | Memorandum of Understanding |
| NGO | Non-government organisation |
| NIC | National Institute of Corrections (US) |
| NOMS | National Offender Management Service (UK) |
| NSW | New South Wales |
| OD | Overdose |
| OH&S | Occupational health and safety |
| PACT | Prisoner Advice and Care Trust |
| PAM | Professions Allied to Medicine |
| PAR | Prison Action and Reform (Australia) |
| PEaT | Prisoner education and training |
| PROP | Post-release options program |
| PTSD | Post-traumatic stress disorder |
| REBT | Rational emotive behaviour therapy |
| RJ | Restorative justice |
| RNR | Risk-need-responsivity model |
| SASH | Suicide and self-harm |
| THC | Tetrahydrocannabinol |
| TPC | Transition from Prison to Community Model (US) |
| UDHR | Universal Declaration on Human Rights |
| UN | United Nations |
| UNODC | United Nations Office of Drugs and Crime |
| VCS | Voluntary and community sector |
| VIP | Victim impact panels |
| VIS | Victim impact statements |
| WA | Western Australia |

# Acknowledgements

We are very thankful for the insightful contributions of Diane Heckenberg and John Cianchi; their practicality and analytical critiques have been influential in shaping this book. Also, the majority of the statistical tables throughout are a result of the investigative skill of Michael McKinnon, who assisted us with data compilation. We are grateful too for Imogen Jones' enthusiastic hands-on approach to being a research assistant in the latter stages of this project.

The incisive discernment of Rob Canton should be acknowledged for the value of his feedback in helping to further improve the breadth and depth of this text.

In our quest to infuse front-line practice wisdom into all facets of the book, many practitioners in the correctional and community services in Tasmania, Australia, were consulted along the way. This list includes practitioners studying in the criminology and corrections program at the University of Tasmania; staff in the Tasmanian Prison Service, IOM Unit, and Community Corrections; and drug and alcohol workers at the Salvation Army Bridge Program. Special thanks to all those prison officers and community corrections workers who talked with us about their experiences in the workplace as practitioners. We want to acknowledge the value of all of these voices from the field, the ones at the coalface – it is you for whom this book is written.

We are deeply grateful to our respective families. From Hannah: my special thanks to Steve, Jude, and Eli Graham for your encouragement and for imbuing me with a strong passion for justice and community service; I have never underestimated the value of a wise sounding board. From Rob: I wish to especially thank Sharyn for making sure that I know, at a practical level, the difference between work and non-work, and to thoroughly enjoy both.

# About the authors

**Rob White** is a Professor of Criminology and Director of the Criminology Research Unit in the School of Sociology and Social Work at the University of Tasmania.

**Hannah Graham** is a PhD candidate and project officer in the School of Sociology and Social Work at the University of Tasmania. She is currently working on a capacity building consultancy with a residential drug and alcohol service around issues of co-occurring mental illness and substance misuse.

# Chapter 1

## Setting the scene

Right now, I'm in prison. Like society kicked me out. They're like 'Okay, the criminal element. We don't want them in society, we're going to put them in these prisons.' Okay, but once I get out – then what do you do? What do you do with all these millions of people that have been in prison and been released? I mean, do you accept them back? Or do you keep them as outcasts? And if you keep them as outcasts, how do you expect them to act?

(Prisoner, quoted in Uggen *et al.* 2004: 284)

### Introduction

This book provides a theoretically informed guide to the practice of working with offenders in different settings and for different purposes. Our intention is to offer practitioners and academics a useful and usable introduction to this type of work. Accordingly, we have concentrated on outlining the general skills, concepts and knowledge that are necessary to work with diverse groups of offenders. It is our hope that this will provide a platform upon which specialist intervention, in areas such as working with violent offenders or those with a mental illness, for example, can be built.

The emphasis in this book is on practice, on the 'how to' component of working with offenders. The practice of working with offenders, however, rests upon a foundation of philosophy, principles and policies, each of which informs how we do what we do. A practical guide, therefore, is at one and the same time a guide to those key concepts that shape how practice occurs at the applied level.

The book offers a unique perspective on working with offenders in that it incorporates three key elements.

- It cuts across specialisations insofar as it attempts to consolidate generic competencies and knowledge from different occupations (for example, social work, psychology, criminology) and different types of agencies that work with offenders (prisons, community sector organisations). For example, the book considers the nature of work in both institutional and community settings in criminal justice. As part of this, it includes case studies and comments from correctional officers in prisons, and workers in community corrections and community sector organisations, about the content and nature of their work.

- The book examines and draws upon what is happening in a number of different jurisdictions, and especially those of England and Wales, the United States, Canada, Australia and New Zealand. Each jurisdiction has its own unique character. Some have provinces, others have states and territories, still others have a combination of national and local governments. We have tried to 'cherry pick' what we feel are some of the better examples of good practice from many different places. The book also provides different types of data, including descriptive statistics, from various jurisdictions and presents this information in comparative tables. All of the chapters also contain stories of innovative practices, including examples drawn from Europe, Asia and the Middle East as well.

- The book is written with practitioners in mind, with theoretically informed discussion of principles and practices. In essence, the book provides an analysis of 'what is' and a guide to 'how to'. Each chapter therefore concludes with two key features. The first, a further reading section, is oriented towards concepts and the 'why' questions of practice. It includes reference to commentaries, analysis and research studies. The second lists key resources, alerting readers to appropriate manuals and handbooks, and the 'how' questions of practice. This includes reference to evidence-based examples of good practice and specific intervention models.

The chapters are structured around a dual focus of workers and their environments, and the nature of the offenders with whom they work. The condition and situation of workers is considered in the context of the condition and situation of offenders, and the dialectic or interaction between the two. As part of this approach, both generic and specialist models and interventions are described and analysed, including discussions of the nuances and differences in their application to divergent work roles and workplaces. The book is intended to be relevant and familiar to those already working in the field, as well as to introduce contemporary principles and practices to those wishing to do so in the future.

This chapter provides background information and an outline of broad trends within corrections. It is very much a setting-the-scene chapter. As such it describes imprisonment trends, participation rates in community corrections, and the character and attributes of offenders generally. We begin, however, with an acknowledgement of the central two problems that perennially beset those who work within this field.

## The core problems of corrections

For sake of brevity we will, for present purposes, merely identify the key problems of corrections rather than tackle them in any kind of depth. For those working in the field these are more than familiar; for those studying criminology and corrections, they are central to any meaningful contemporary analysis.

### Problem 1: Prisons fail

This problem relates mainly to the phenomenon of imprisonment. Basically, the problem is that prisons, as an institution, fail (see Mathiesen 1990). Prisons fail in a number of significant ways.

- They fail to prevent future offending/recidivism.
- They fail to protect and preserve human dignity.
- They fail to use taxpayers' money effectively.
- They fail to address the causes of crime.
- They fail to deal with the consequences of crime.
- They fail to acknowledge the complexities of victimisation and criminalisation, and the offender/victim nexus.
- They fail to facilitate autonomy and self-determination.

The failure of prisons also, necessarily, means that much of what happens in post-release situations also fails. That is, what occurs in the prison, and the impact of imprisonment itself, have a negative effect on what subsequently lies ahead for the offender, and for those who work with offenders within a community setting.

The challenge, therefore, is to figure out a way to make prisons 'work' successfully (across various evaluation criteria), to come up with realistic and positive alternatives to imprisonment (which has major implications for community-level resources), and/or to reconsider the corrections project in its entirety. One thing that is clear is that major social change is needed. Otherwise, there are and will continue to be a lot of people doing a lot of work, for very little social pay-off.

The failure of imprisonment has been noted often, by many different people, and over a long period of time. For example, Foucault (1977) observes how the voices of prison reform were essentially the same from one century to another. He comments: 'For a century and a half the prison had always been offered as its own remedy: the reactivation of the penitentiary techniques as the only means of overcoming their perpetual failure; the realization of the corrective project as the only method of overcoming the impossibility of implementing it' (Foucault 1977: 268). In other words, over many years the failure of the prison was seen to reside in the failure of prison reform. The key demands of prison reform, too, have been the same: the principal aim should be to change the behaviour of prisoners in a positive way; by methods that involve classifying them according to specific individual needs and traits; in a regime that rewards progress towards rehabilitation; that involves work as an obligation and a right; that includes education and general social improvement; supported by suitable professional staff; and with access to help and support during and after imprisonment. Such demands resonate today much the way they did almost two centuries ago at the birth of the modern prison.

For some writers, the fact that prisons fail is in its own perverse way a sign that they are succeeding (see Foucault 1977; Gosselin 1982; Mathiesen 1990). That is, the role of the prison is in fact symbolic and political, rather than rehabilitative and deterrent. As long as the institution fails, it reinforces the stigma of offending, of offenders, and of the lower social orders, and thereby serves to prop up the hegemony of those at the top of the social hierarchy. It is a perfect scapegoat for the ills of unequal and socially divided societies.

We will return to the question of prison failure in the last chapter, when we once again discuss the phenomenon of recidivism and how a rehabilitation agenda is crucial to reducing the likelihood of offenders recommitting crimes and returning to prison.

*Problem 2: Offenders are victims too*

A second core problem of corrections is that, generally speaking, it does a bad job of dealing with the fact that offenders are usually simultaneously both offenders and victims. In other words, those most likely to be subject to intervention by the state and prosecuted as 'criminals' are also among the most vulnerable, marginalised and victimised groups in society, for example:

- For indigenous people, colonialism has tended to equal marginalisation, dispossession and criminalisation.

- Young women (and men) suffer abuse at the hands of others, then are brutalised by uncaring and unforgiving systems of justice when they 'act out' (either through illicit drug use or by engagement in criminal activity such as assaults or sex work).

- Many who suffer from co-morbidity end up enduring the harsh realities of punishment systems, but not dealing with their mental illness or substance abuse while in the hands of the state.

The fact is that the vast majority of offenders who are actually processed by the state and branded as criminals have complex needs and face a wide range of complicated social, economic and political issues. The expression 'the rich get richer and the poor get prison' (see Reiman 1998) is factually accurate, but nonetheless needs to be fleshed out by consideration of the myriad obstacles that most offenders have had to grapple with in their lives.

Consider the fact that women, despite comprising over half the population, constitute a small percentage of the prison population. Given the relatively low number of women who are incarcerated, female prisoners tend to be housed together regardless of official 'security' status (for example, high, medium, or low). Many contemporary programmes and services tend not to cater to the specific needs of women as women, insofar as the system as a whole has a masculine bias in its structure and programming (Alder 1997). Historically, where there have been women-specific programs, these were more than likely to be built upon conservative and limiting assumptions regarding proper 'women's work' (for example, as domestic servants or housekeepers) and ideal notions of 'femininity' (for example, to act in more passive ways, and to dress in particular ways) (see Smart 1976; Easteal 1994). To cater for the special needs of female offenders once they are in the system requires the introduction and evaluation of a wide range of programs dealing with issues such as sexual and other forms of abuse, employment, education and personal empowerment (Cameron 2001).

The failure of prison is in part simply a reflection of the failure of the criminal justice system to accommodate social justice issues within its purview. Punishment is seen as a central driver of the system (even if modified by language that stresses rehabilitation, treatment and reparation). Consideration of the social circumstances and life opportunities of the punished has rarely been of paramount importance, even if courts, police and corrective services occasionally allude to such in their deliberations and intervention policies. Yet, even if based on pragmatic considerations, it is evident that addressing the failure of corrections is fundamentally a matter of addressing the underlying causes and structures of alienation, the struggle for subsistence and having to endure the pains of abuse and ignorance.

## Offending and rehabilitation

Unemployment, poverty and declining opportunities continue to directly affect the physical and psychological well-being of people in our communities. Such social problems are entrenched at a spatial level, and are increasingly concentrated in specific locations within our cities. This is sometimes referred to as a process of ghettoisation. The social costs of marginality are inevitably translated into the economic costs of crime.

### The social context of offending

The social costs of marginality are also transformed into behaviour that is officially defined as 'anti-social' and 'dangerous'. All of this is bound to have an impact on the self-image of marginalised people and their efforts at self-defence in a hostile environment. The pooling of social resources and the construction of identities that are valued by others (if only one's peers) finds expression in a range of cultural forms, including various youth subcultures, 'gang' formations and criminal networks (Hagedorn 2007; Cunneen and White 2007).

There is, indeed, a strong link between the *socio-economic status* of individuals (and communities) and the incidence of *criminal offending*. Offenders who are deepest within the criminal justice system, especially in prisons, disproportionately come from disadvantaged situations and backgrounds featuring low socio-economic status and highly volatile family relationships.

This is a cross-national and cross-jurisdictional phenomenon, as evidenced in a wide variety of reports, research studies and discussion papers dealing with socio-economic status and offending patterns (White and Perrone 2010). Some recent and relevant examples of this literature include:

- Australia (Vinson 2004)
- New Zealand (Papps and Winkelmann 2000)
- United States (Michalowski and Carlson 1999)
- Canada (Kitchen 2006)
- Scotland (Scottish Executive 2005)
- England and Wales (Office of the Deputy Prime Minister 2002)
- France (Fourgere *et al.* 2006)
- Spain (Buonanno and Montolio 2008).

While the specific conditions and influences that mark the relationship between socio-economic hardship and crime vary (depending upon factors such as local neighbourhood social cohesion, state interventions to address mass unemployment and the nature of law enforcement), overall there is a strong positive correlation. This holds for cross-country comparisons as well as nation-specific analysis (Fajnzylber *et al.* 2002).

Socio-economic status has a number of interrelated dimensions that in conjunction create the conditions for disadvantage and offending behaviour. Poverty, social inequality, unemployment and poor housing, among other debilitating factors (such as child abuse and neglect) are directly linked to greater propensity to commit certain types of crimes and engage in particular sorts of anti-social behaviour (see Karmen 2000; Baldry *et al.* 2002; White 2008a).

The literature in this area demonstrates that disadvantaged background is disproportionately linked to the following:

- Offending behaviour
- Engagement in anti-social conduct
- Heightened perceptions of threats to safety and increased fear of crime
- Greater incidence of victimisation.

The processes accompanying the relationship between disadvantaged socio-economic status and the incidence of offending indicate the following trends:

- The homogenisation of offenders, which results as they pass through the gatekeepers and filters of the criminal justice system, such that the most disadvantaged (who essentially share the same social characteristics) are those who occupy the most places within prison.

- The multi-directional influence of factors, such that (for example) unemployment leads to crime, crime leads to unemployment, and the reciprocal and exacerbating influence of such factors on each other.

Theoretical explanations for the link between socio-economic status and the incidence of offending point to:

- *Structural factors* – such as the overall state of the economy, levels of unemployment generally, welfare provision and so on, and how the dynamics of the labour market are reflected in the 'warehousing' capacities of the prison.

- *Situational factors* – relating to the personal characteristics of offenders relative to their opportunities in the competition for jobs, and how marginalisation and the attractions of the criminal economy contribute to offending.

- *Factors relating to social disorganisation* – as manifest at family and community levels, as for example when the intergenerational effects of the unemployment-criminality nexus translates into less knowledge about ordinary work and concentrations of similarly placed people in the same geographical area.

In summary, there is a complex but demonstrated relationship between low socio-economic status and offending. This relationship is reinforced under contemporary corrective services regimes insofar as prisons and community corrections do not have adequate resources, trained staff, effective programs and variety of services to counter the social disadvantages that weigh so heavily on those who feature the most within the criminal justice system.

### I hate rehab

The rejuvenation of 'traditional' concepts such as restoration, reparation, rehabilitation and recognition has major implications for how practitioners and theorists respond to issues relating to punishment, treatment and general responses to offending and offenders. The resurgent interest in 'rehabilitation' is manifest in the adoption of language among government authorities and by non-government agencies that includes reference to 're-entry', 'resettlement', 'reintegration', 'recovery' and 'desistance'. Offenders themselves tend to hate rehabilitation, at least as it is perceived and experienced by them.

> Many people who are currently or were formerly in prison embrace the self-change, empowerment, and desistance perspective. They hold negative attitudes toward the concept of rehabilitation and correctional treatment programs. In general, the distaste for such programs is linked to a sense that these interventions involve things being 'done to' or 'prescribed for' passive recipients who are characterized as deficient, ineffectual, misguided, untrustworthy, possibly dangerous, and almost certain to get into trouble again. Although people who have been incarcerated often believe that some staff members or other outside parties and some types of programs can be helpful, their effectiveness stems from the potential they offer for empowering participants rather than trying to compel them to change. Most argue, 'No one else can rehabilitate you. You rehabilitate yourself'. If there is distaste for correctional treatment programs among people under correctional supervision, there is even stronger antipathy toward interventions tailored to actuarial risk assessments. (M. Kay Harris, quoted in Ward and Maruna 2007: 15)

If offenders are to help themselves, then they must be convinced of the benefit of 'walking the walk' of rehabilitation. In part, this depends upon the programs in which offenders are engaged. Some types of intervention are more likely to foster empowerment and accountability than others. Such projects provide a framework within which offenders can reflect upon and make the changes necessary to forge a new life. They are positive and forward-looking. Others are perceived as intrusive and authoritarian. These tend to be more about containment and about institutionally responding to specific problems. Limited horizons, however, tend to yield limited results.

Rehabilitation of offenders is not only about putting the right program elements in place or choosing the right approach. It is also about philosophy and the politics of intervention generally. How we understand the issues has a major bearing on how we view suitable intervention methods and what it is that we are trying to achieve. Person-centred practice and future-oriented interventions may encourage the development of programs and interventions outside the box, as illustrated in Innovative practice 1.

The history and operation of correctional systems (and their image and reputation as portrayed in the mass media and movies) reinforce the notion that not much good can come about by placing someone within such a system. Given the social background of offenders, it is hardly surprising therefore to also find that most reject the basic premise that somehow 'good' can flow out of a 'bad' situation. This

---

### Innovative practice 1

### The ride of their lives: the prisoners' Tour de France

In June 2009, a very special Tour de France transpired involving 194 long-term prisoners, 124 prison officers and prison sports instructors, and a 2,400 km (1,500 miles) race from Lille to Paris. Stopovers were scheduled for seventeen different towns, each of which has a prison. This Tour is a controlled 'race' – like a rolling prison – with staff cycling alongside prisoners and absolutely no sprints or breakaways (Fournel 2009). The race had an official finish line but no rankings, fostering teamwork and a sense of accomplishment, as Sylvia Marion, a senior prison official, explains: 'We want to show them that, with some training, you can achieve your goals and start a new life' (quoted in Reuters 2009).

The initiative attracted bemusement and surprise, as well as questions from some conservative quarters such as 'Aren't they supposed to be in prison for punishment?' Yet Sabrina Belluci, director of the French National Institute for Victims' Aid and Mediation responded to this question by supporting the reintegrative venture: 'At a certain moment, you have to consider these people, these individuals, these prisoners as people who might one day once again take up the path of society, of community life. I believe that victims understand that very, very well' (quoted in Kelley 2009).

Le Tour de France des prisonniers is groundbreaking in that it offers a reintegration initiative like never seen before – one that fosters self-esteem and teamwork, encourages health and fitness, and rewards endurance and good behaviour with the possibility of sentence reductions. Each of the cyclists has been incarcerated for some time, serving sentences of between five and ten years. They ride to feel alive, as well as to regain their lives.

is especially so when the 'good' is framed by institutional processes that offer the promise of something being done *for* or *to* you, rather *by* you.

Working with offenders thus requires more than just expertise. It demands commitment to social and personal change that is transparent and convincing. If offenders are not rehabilitated and their circumstances substantially altered, then they will likely reoffend. The goal is to facilitate a pathway for offenders to be productive and active citizens. In this there is nothing particularly unusual about offenders. Likewise, there is nothing particularly unusual in individuals resisting others who tell them what to do, prescribe a course of action for them, or offer to 'fix the problem' for them. The last thing anyone needs is to work with someone – in this case the field practitioner – who is patronising or overbearing. On the other hand, there is often a need for some type of incentive to undertake rehabilitation. Coercion is not always a bad thing, after all.

## The world of working with offenders

The world of offenders is one populated by disadvantaged people, with experiences of chronic poverty, low levels of literacy, mental health and general health problems, chaotic family circumstances, low job participation, high levels of interpersonal violence – and the list goes on. A lot of ruined lives and people with sad stories end up in the criminal justice system. Rarely are people of privilege treated the same way or in the same institutions.

The work settings and the demands on workers with offenders are similarly complex and varied. Working with offenders is hard work. It is certainly not work for the faint-hearted or the work-shy. It takes professionalism. It takes commitment. It takes reflection. It is work based upon building relationships and using all manner of communication skills. Complex problems demand complex methods of work, and innovative problem-solving strategies.

The world of offenders and of those working with offenders is also a crowded world. As shown in Table 1.1, prison populations are steadily growing, as are the number of people within community corrections.

The concept of *imprisonment* is not the same as that of *custody*. In determining total numbers of people in custody we have to be aware that there are, for example, six different types of custody in Australia. These are:

- Prisons
- Police stations
- Juvenile detention centres
- Immigration detention centres
- Military prisons or guard houses
- Secure facilities in psychiatric hospitals.

These are overlapping and interconnected systems of custody. For example, asylum-seekers ('illegal immigrants') may be held in prison if other more appropriate facilities are not available; offenders in the defence forces may also be found in prison or police custody;

**Table 1.1** Comparative prison populations by jurisdiction

| Jurisdiction | Prison population total[1] | Date | Prison population rate (per 100,000) |
| --- | --- | --- | --- |
| Australia | 27,615 | 06/2008 | 129 |
| Canada | 38,348[2] | 2007/2008 | 116 |
| China[3] | 1,565,771 | 12/2005 | 119 |
| Denmark | 3,448 | 09/2008 | 63 |
| England and Wales | 83,392 | 11/2008 | 153 |
| France | 59, 655 | 07/2008 | 96 |
| Germany | 73,203 | 08/2008 | 89 |
| India | 373,271 | 12/2006 | 33 |
| Israel | 22,788 | 03/2008 | 326 |
| Italy | 55, 057 | 06/2008 | 92 |
| Japan | 81,255 | 12/2006 | 63 |
| Mexico | 222,671 | 09/2008 | 207 |
| New Zealand | 7,887 | 06/2008 | 185 |
| Nigeria | 39,438 | 01/2007 | 28 |
| Russian Federation | 891,738 | 11/2008 | 629 |
| Scotland | 7,893 | 11/2008 | 152 |
| Sweden | 6,770 | 10/2007 | 74 |
| United Arab Emirates | 11,193 | ?/2006 | 238 |
| United States | 2,293,157 | 12/2007 | 756 |

*Notes:*
1 Total = the number in penal institutions, which includes pre-trial detainees.
2 This figure is the average daily population, including young offenders.
3 Figures for China are for sentenced prisoners only. According to official statistics, a further 850,000 are held in 'administrative detention'.
*Source*: Adapted from Walmsley (2009).

and mentally ill offenders are not infrequently transferred between prisons and psychiatric hospitals according to their state of health and their manageability.

Imprisonment generally refers to instances where an offender has been officially sanctioned by the court and, as part of the court disposition, has been sentenced to a period of enforced detention. Custody, on the other hand, includes both instances of imprisonment and cases where movement of the individual is restricted prior to courtroom adjudication or departmental determination of legal status. For example, being taken into police custody can involve a person being held in a police lock-up for a set period of time without judicial involvement. Or, to take another example, unsuccessful applications for bail are usually accompanied by the holding of an accused person in *remand* custody; that is, to await trial in a secure facility (rather than remand on bail).

Table 1.2 shows that, on average, one in five people who are incarcerated are actually being held pre-trial on remand. It is possible therefore to be held in custody in at least three different ways: in a police jail, in a remand centre, or in a prison. Our concern in this chapter is with the last of these – the prison.

**Table 1.2** Comparative pre-trial/remand imprisonment data by country

| Type of data | England and Wales | United States | Canada | New Zealand | Australia |
|---|---|---|---|---|---|
| Total pre-trial/ remand population | 13,402 | 475,692 | 10,794 | 1,754 | 5,581 |
| Comparative rate (per 100,000 national population) | 25 | 159 | 34 | 41 | 27 |
| Percentage of total prison population | 16.5% | 21.2% | 31.5% | 21.4% | 21.6% |
| Date of data collection | 30/9/2007 | 30/6/2006 | 2004/2005 | 31/7/2007 | 30/6/2006 |

*Note*:
For Canada the figure represents the average daily population, including young offenders.
*Source*: Adapted from Walmsley (2008).

The prison rate varies according to such factors as the availability of alternative punishment or rehabilitation approaches (for example, community-based corrections or work programs), local and regional 'law and order' politics (for example, from the more punitive to those that stress reconciliation or mediation), and the nature of actual criminal activity and the cultures that sustain this (for example, violence associated with legal availability and use of guns).

The gathering of prison data requires that the 'counting rules' are the same for each jurisdiction. For example, the data might be based upon the number of people in prison on a particular day, or as averaged out over a particular month. When making comparisons between jurisdictions it is also important to bear three things in mind:

- The actual *number* of people who are in prison.
- The *rate* of imprisonment in relation to overall population size, usually measured in terms of per 100,000 population.
- The overall *trend* in imprisonment rates, whether this be upwards, downwards, or reasonably stable.

Analysis of these three areas generally provides a good indication of the differences and similarities between jurisdictions. In global terms, prison populations have grown significantly in many parts of the world since the 1990s, particularly in the advanced industrialised countries such as the United States and in Europe (as shown in Figure 1.1, see also Walmsley 2008). Punitive sentencing legislation, such as the 'three strikes and you're out' laws in the United States, and tougher anti-drug laws generally, explain part of this trend upwards. On the other hand, imprisonment rates also hinge upon whether countries adopt neo-liberal policies or state-guided interventions in matters of economy and social welfare. Comparative study has shown, for example, that countries with relatively high welfare spending relative to gross domestic product have relatively low imprisonment rates (Cavadino and Dignan 2006; Pratt 2008a, 2008b).

We also have to acknowledge the impact of 'public(s) opinion' on the overall orientation and operation of the criminal justice system, including corrective services. The media in particular, as well as specific political and community leaders, can have a major influence on how policy is developed, which institutions receive which amounts of funding, and what the key mission of government agencies is to be.

The impact that police practices, and courtroom and sentencing practices, have on prisons is manifest in a number of ways, for example:

- The number of people charged with offences, and the seriousness of the offences.

- Changes in legislation, as in the case of the setting of minimum penalties for certain offences or introduction of mandatory sentencing.

- More use by the judiciary of harsher sanctions, such as custody, as a response to public pressure.

The highly political nature of criminal justice issues also has implications not only for the number and type of people who are sent to prison at any point in time, but also for how the prison system itself may respond to the attention placed upon it. Figure 1.2 compares rates of incarceration with political elections in England and Wales over twenty years, demonstrating rises in prison populations before and after each election. This may, in part, be the influence of law and order politics and 'tough justice' policy approaches that are popular in election years.

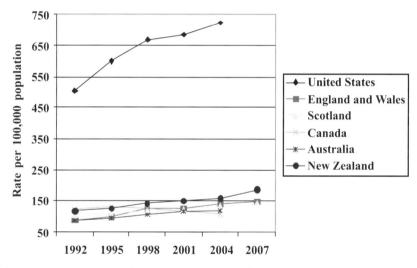

**Figure 1.1** International comparative rates of incarceration, 1992–2007
*Source*: International Centre for Prison Studies (2009).

The composition and size of the prison population is influenced by two things:

- The number of offenders being sent to prison.
- The length of time for which they are sent to prison.

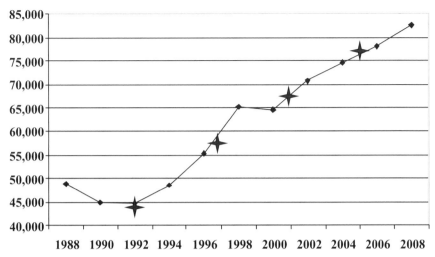

**Figure 1.2** Incarceration rates in England and Wales – a twenty-year trend of the total prison population

✛ = Election year: completion of a General Election in England and Wales.

*Source*: Ministry of Justice (2009a).

The extensive use of 'short' sentences means that a large number of offenders can be processed through the system without necessarily contributing to an overall growth in the prison population. This is because there is a balance between 'entry' and 'exit' numbers. Differences between short-term and long-term prisoners imply different management practices. For the latter, correctional administrators are faced with particular management, engagement and provision of services, which are not relevant for the former.

Who is in prison, for how long, and for what reason – all have implications for how the prison administration might respond from a program and custodial point of view. They also have a major impact with regard to issues such as 'overcrowding', an issue that in the end is out of the immediate control of custodial administrators but is driven by other parts of the criminal justice system.

A further difficulty for correctional administrators is that separate arrangements need to be made for 'remand' and 'sentenced' prisoners.

- *Remand* offenders include those who have been sent to gaol by the courts before they have stood trial. This happens when at the initial court hearing a judge or magistrate denies bail, and the 'accused' person is remanded in custody until the time of their trial.

- *Sentenced* offenders are those whom the court has found guilty of an offence, and who have formally been sentenced to a term of custody.

For various reasons, including both ethical and practical concerns, accused persons should not be held in the same facilities as sentenced offenders. One implication of this is that if remand custody is used more frequently it can have a substantial effect upon the total prison population. This is so even when the number and length of time for 'sentenced' prisoners is reduced.

## Who is who, and who works with whom

The kinds of issues covered in this book traverse a wide range of work domains. This further reinforces the importance of having a holistic view of systems and of people, and the many and varied things that go into working with offenders in a practical way.

At the centre of the exercise is the offender. Offenders come in many different shapes and sizes, notwithstanding the shared social background of most offenders. They vary greatly in terms of types of offending, and in regard to particular social profile. Consider the 'typical' sex offender in Australia, for example. In recent years there has been a significant rise in the number of offenders charged with sex offences. Many of those prosecuted and convicted for these crimes go against the broad norm of the average typical offender. Specifically, they tend to include middle-class, white, older men who have strong academic or educational backgrounds. For corrective services, these types of offenders pose a number of challenges, not least of which is in regard to prison gerontology. Prisons are filling up with old men, and in many cases the institutions are not equipped to deal with older person problems and changes.

The usual corrections landscape is also filled with many people who have been sexually and physically abused, who have some kind of substance abuse problem (whether alcohol or illicit drugs or both), and who have developed a criminal history from an early age. Most offenders (that is, those who have been formally processed in the criminal justice system) are men. More men than women are engaged in violent offences.

17

Many offenders have themselves been victims of circumstance and targets of criminal behaviour, and practitioner interventions are generally directed at dealing with their complex needs in some way. However, offenders are in prison or on community-based orders precisely because they have harmed someone or something else (such as a business or private property). The place of victims in their lives is an issue of great concern (as is the related issue of victim rights generally). As we argue in Chapter 10, rehabilitation that 'works' must also incorporate consideration of how offenders understand what it is they have done, and the harm that they have perpetrated. While the focus is on offender rehabilitation, the substance of rehabilitation ought to include victim concerns.

As summarised in Box 1.1, there are many more players in the criminal justice system than just offenders and those who work with offenders. This, too, makes life complicated and interesting for offender and practitioner alike. For those who end up working or living within a prison, the world around them is dramatically different from that of the ordinary person. It is a world that can change lives.

As implied in *Stories from the field* 1.1, the experience of working with offenders is not just about professional practice and institutional missions. It is a world in which things happen, and a world in which emotions are often heightened. For practitioners, a key aspect of working with offenders is the affective or emotional aspect. Coping with fear, danger, hope, trust, incivility and bravery is integral to much of the work. It is for this reason that working in a total institution often reshapes the psyche and emotional universe of the person who trains to become a correctional or prison officer. A large part of this process is learning the emotions of the job (attitudes and behaviours) as well as the technical aspects of the job (dealing with particular situations or particular inmates). It is a process of becoming and of being (see Crawley and Crawley 2008). Similar processes exist with regard to community-based practitioners, albeit with different kinds of expectations and work-related pressures. In all cases, nothing changes the fact that each practitioner works with an involuntary client (Trotter 2006).

## Paradoxes and controversies

There are many tensions involved with the theory and practice of working with offenders – between generic and specific needs, between

---

*Box 1.1*

*Key players in the criminal justice system*

- **Prisoners**
  *Profile: socio-economic background, biography, skills, capacities*
- **Victims**
  *Interests and engagement: individuals, communities, businesses and action groups*
- **Correctional staff, prisoner support, tradespeople**
  *Nature of work in a secure environment: culture, roles, managers*
- **Official visitors, outside services coming in, volunteer workers**
  *Outsiders coming in: purposes, mission, roles*
- **Parole board, community corrections, outside services assisting with transitions**
  *Assessments and transitions: services, participants, restrictions*
- **Families, children**
  *Nature of contact: living in or visiting occasionally*
- **Media, politicians**
  *Sensational: making the issues, making the news*
- **Prison activists** (PAR, APF, Justice Action, Sisters Inside, Penal Reform International)
  *Multiple hats: advocates, critics and service providers*
- **Oversight bodies**
  Ombudsman, occupational health and safety, coroner, anti-discrimination commissioner, children's commissioner, administrative appeals tribunal
  *Public accountability: does anything ever actually happen?*
- **Academics and researchers**
  *Independence, access and critique: who pays the piper names the tune?*

---

academics and practitioners, between principles and practices, between system imperatives and situational remedies. At the core of these many tensions, however, is the flipside of the 'prisons fail' argument with which we opened the chapter: that is, 'What is it that prisons actually do?' The answer to this is controversial to say the least.

According to some, the dramatic fall in the American crime rate in the 1990s demonstrated the positive association between crime and the probability of imprisonment. In simple terms, it is proposed that

### Stories from the field 1.1

### Working with offenders will change the way you look at the world

Working with offenders will change the way you see the world. It may impact on your sense of humour, you may become cynical and find humour in morbid and horrific events, but this will help you deal with things. Fear not, though, it's not all bad!

It is the middle of the night and about six hours into a yard jack-up (a yard jack-up is prison lingo for a riot). You are on watch at the front of the housing accommodation block. An inmate well known to you walks out of the staff office that has been broken into. He is wearing a correctional officer's hat and carrying a torch. He looks at you and says, 'Well, you can't really come in so I s'pose I'll do your job for you'. He walks off and starts to conduct a cell check.

Cell checks are conducted every half an hour to ensure the safety and well-being of inmates during the night. So picture this: in the middle of a riot an inmate wearing a correctional officer's hat is walking around the unit doing cell checks.

Two hours or so after this the inmates break into another office and pull out a safe. They are laughing and taunting the staff about the fact that they are going to find 'treasure' in the safe. The staff laugh back at the inmates and tell them that it only contains a supply of chocolate bars. The inmates jeer and laugh; they spend the next ten minutes trying to 'crack' the safe unsuccessfully. One of the inmates picks up the safe to move it somewhere else, he drops the safe and the door falls off. The inmates gather around to check out the treasure contained within, only to discover that it is full of chocolate bars.

An inmate is furious that he has been given crumbed fish for his evening meal. He swears at you and rants and raves and demands another meal. You try to explain to him that the kitchen is closed and it is a physical impossibility for you to get him another meal. He continues with his outburst and tells you that he is allergic to fish (he is not allergic to fish); he understands that you can't access the kitchen and demands that you make him some tuna sandwiches. You tell him that tuna is fish; he calls you a liar and tells you that you are stupid. You get him some tuna sandwiches that were left over at lunchtime and tell him to enjoy.

It's Christmas Eve. Two correctional officers dress up in fancy dress, one as a Teletubby and the other a big yellow dog. The officers take a nurse around the prison for the evening medication round. The costumes cause a stir; all of the inmates find it amusing and make comments in jest to the two staff. They come to an inmate who has a history of mental health issues; to put it bluntly, he is odd. The officers open the door, and the inmate is confronted by a big yellow dog, a Teletubby and a nurse. He looks at the two staff and is apparently unfazed; he looks at the nurse and says, 'Your new hairdo looks strange.' The nurse is standing next to a six-foot-six yellow dog and a six-foot Teletubby, and her hair looks strange. Go figure!

Prison officer

the greater the likelihood of imprisonment, the lower will be the rate of crime. This argument has been used in relation to the US, England and Wales, and Australia and New Zealand, and is particularly popular among conservative politicians and/or those pushing a law and order agenda (Saunders and Billante 2003; Burnett and Maruna 2004). The 'prisons work' argument also has enormous implications for community corrections, as does the question of 'what works' as this relates specifically to community-based penalties and programs (Raynor 2002).

Critics of this position argue that prisons do not deter future offending, and that they are more likely to increase recidivism than diminish offending behaviour. Moreover, as one study in Canada has illustrated, where criminal law is the same across the country but administered provincially, it has been found that crime rates do not predict incarceration counts (Sprott and Doob 1998). Imprisonment itself can help to entrench a criminal career; and a more productive and progressive alternative is to put the stress on developing rehabilitative programs (Burnett and Maruna 2004; Ore and Birgden 2003). Prisons 'work' to incapacitate large numbers of people for a temporary period of time. However, in the longer term, they create an ever increasing pool of alienated individuals with few prospects for the future, and little hope in their lives. Prisons 'work', as well, as a key breeding ground for crime and anti-social behaviour.

## Conclusion

The intention of this chapter has been to set the scene for what it is like to enter into the world of working with offenders. There are several crucial issues that underpin interventions that involve coercive controls over an individual. These include whether or not such interventions actually 'work' the way they are meant to, and if they generate the kinds of outcomes that are socially desirable. They also include considerations that pertain to the background and activities of individuals as both offenders and victims.

The chapter has provided a sense of how governments across different jurisdictions are responding to offending and offenders. This is most visibly manifest in imprisonment rates, although this is only part of the story of criminal justice intervention. As subsequent chapters will demonstrate, much of what occurs in criminal justice takes place in communities outside of secure facilities. Indeed, there are many different players and stakeholders in criminal justice, and working with offenders is by its very nature a very complex and challenging area in which to work.

Perhaps the biggest challenge is how to bring together distinctive philosophies, principles and practices into an integrated form of intervention, and to do so under circumstances where system imperatives (containment and control) and ideological conflict within institutions (punitive versus rehabilitative orientations) create inherent difficulties in undertaking a coherent approach. At the centre of these social processes, too, are humans with their own particular needs, strengths, visions and desires – the offender, and the worker. Working with offenders is thus an ongoing project rather than a mission to be accomplished. It is this that provides its dynamism and its rewards, as well as its frustrations and failures.

## Discussion questions

1 Identify or list specific organisations, services and units or teams in the criminal justice and corrections landscape that might be considered 'key players' (see Box 1.1) in your local area or region.
2 Incarceration rates are a significant concern in western jurisdictions like the US, England and Wales, Canada, New Zealand and Australia. What are the main 'types' (criminal offence types, offender demographics) of offenders currently being sent to prison?
3 Growing amounts of people are being placed on remand. What types of practical, operational or ethical issues does this raise for remandees and also prison authorities?

## Further reading

Green, S., Lancaster, E. and Feasey, S. (eds) (2008) *Addressing Offending Behaviour: Context, Practice and Values*. Cullompton: Willan Publishing.

McNeill, F. (2009) 'What works and what's just?', *European Journal of Probation*, 1(1): 21–40.

Penal Reform International (2001) *Making Standards Work: An International Handbook on Good Prison Practice*. London: Penal Reform International and the Netherlands Ministry of Justice.

Uggen, C., Van Brakle, M. and McLaughlin, H. (2009) 'Punishment and social exclusion: national differences in prisoner disenfranchisement', in A. Ewald and B. Rottinghaus (eds) *Criminal Disenfranchisement in an International Perspective*. New York: Cambridge University Press.

White, R. and Perrone, S. (2010) *Crime, Criminality and Criminal Justice*. South Melbourne: Oxford University Press.

## Key resources

Australian Institute of Criminology (2009) *Australian Crime: Facts and Figures 2008*. Canberra: Australian Institute of Criminology.

Glaze, L. and Bonczar, T. (2008) *Probation and Parole in the United States: 2007 Statistical Tables*. Washington, DC: US Bureau of Justice Statistics.

Tavares, C. and Thomas, G. (2008) *European Statistics in Focus: Crime and Criminal Justice*. Luxembourg: Office for the Official Publications of the European Communities.

United Nations Crime and Justice Information Network, available online at: www.uncjin.org/.

Walmsley, R. (2009) *World Prison Population List, 8th edn*. London: International Centre for Prison Studies.

# Chapter 2

# Key approaches to offender rehabilitation

What would prevent offenders from re-offending?

> Something to do with self-progression. Something to show people what they are capable of doing. I thought that that was what my [probation] officer should be about. It's finding people's abilities and nourishing and making them work for those things. Not very consistent with going back on what they have done wrong and trying to work out why – 'cause it's all going around on what happened – what you've already been punished for – why not go forward into something ... For instance, you might be good at writing – push that forward, progress that, rather than saying 'well look, why did you kick that bloke's head in? Do you think we should go back into anger management courses?' when all you want to do is be a writer ... I know that you do have to look back to a certain extent to make sure that you don't end up like that again. The whole order seems to be about going back and back and back. There doesn't seem to be much 'forward'.
>
> (Probationer, quoted in Farrall 2004: 74–5)

## Introduction

This chapter provides a foundational overview of the major principles and perspectives in criminal justice and offender rehabilitation. It begins by discussing therapeutic justice and its implications for correctional practice. Four propositions regarding the nature and dynamics of justice are introduced. Among the intervention approaches that are discussed are models that make reference to the assessment of 'risk-need-responsivity', and the 'good lives', 'social recognition' and 'restorative justice' approaches. The strengths and weaknesses of these various approaches are discussed. The chapter concludes with a summary of key concepts, such as giving and forgiveness.

Offenders come into contact with corrective services *via* a criminal justice pathway that usually includes the following types of elements:

- Caution – informal, formal
- Charge – arrest, summons, bail
- Monetary penalty – fines, restitution orders
- Other non-custodial orders – restitution orders
- Fully suspended sentences
- Community supervision or work orders
- Custody in the community – home detention
- Custody in a correctional institution – full-time incarceration, periodic detention
- Juvenile options – restorative justice forums.

The strength and intensity of engagement with the criminal justice system is determined by a wide range of factors, including the sentencing practices of courts (see White and Perrone 2010). For workers with offenders, however, regardless of the specific law and order agenda and particular social climate, a focus on rehabilitation has been of enduring concern. That is, even in periods when rehabilitation has not been part of, or emphasised as central to, the overt institutional rationale of criminal justice, practitioners have nevertheless recognised its continuing relevance as a core concept underlying intervention practice (see, for example, Raynor 2002).

Today the rejuvenation of 'traditional' concepts such as restoration, reparation, rehabilitation and recognition has major implications for how practitioners and theorists respond to issues relating to punishment, treatment and general responses to offending and offenders. The resurgence of interest in 'rehabilitation' is manifest in adoption of language referring to 're-entry', 'resettlement', 'reintegration', 'recovery' and 'desistance'.

The rehabilitative orientation is evident in the development of new institutional measures, such as therapeutic jurisprudence and problem-solving courts, that provide for a more holistic and rehabilitative focus for criminal justice intervention. These interventions usually take place at the front end of the criminal justice system. Discussion of these occurs in the early stages of the chapter, then enabling other types of interventions to be understood in light of the continuum of criminal justice and corrections. Concern about rehabilitation is also evident in widespread discussion about the sheer number of ex-prisoners re-entering their communities and how the process of transition to a non-crime future might be facilitated. These interventions generally occur at the tail end of the period of criminal justice intervention. Offender-centred programs and strategies are also being developed that attempt to provide a consistent and coherent intervention across the institutional lifespan of offender engagement. This is expressed in the language of integrated offender management, case management and throughcare principles.

Practitioners need to be embedded in the criminal justice process from the point of early contact through to final detachment of the offender from the criminal justice system, and different sets of practitioners need to be working with each other to achieve common goals. This is precisely what models of intervention and offender management (called 'integrated offender management' – IOM – in Australia and New Zealand) are trying to achieve. That is, greater attention is now being given to a holistic approach in working with offenders, and this is institutionally being recognised in processes and practices that attempt to work with the offender in a consistent way across different parts of the criminal justice system. Underpinning the use of IOM and offender management intervention frameworks are various interrelated rehabilitation models. These models, in turn, are reflective of and contributors to new ways of thinking about justice and the practical doing of justice.

## Thinking about justice

Developments across the criminal justice system (including the police and the courts) and evolution in the way interventions are delivered have a number of implications for how 'justice' itself might be conceptualised. The purposes and strategies guiding how we do punishment, respond to victims and deal with offenders are many, and are frequently in conflict (White and Perrone 2010). Out of the myriad perspectives and approaches to justice, however, there are certain key principles that we believe are especially pertinent to practitioners motivated by a rehabilitation ethos.

Accordingly, we have devised four propositions about justice that reflect what we feel should be the key philosophical drivers of justice as a form of practice (summarised in Box 2.1). These propositions reflect both contemporary developments in the criminal justice field at an institutional level (such as the establishment of therapeutic or problem-solving courts) and broad normative theories pertaining to criminal justice (see especially Braithwaite and Pettit 1990 for their discussion of republican theory).

---

*Box 2.1*

*Four propositions about justice*

The philosophy of justice is the driver of justice as a form of practice.

**Proposition 1: Justice ought to be an active process**.
- Emphasis on participation – of victims, of offenders, of advocates, of families, of communities.
- Emphasis on doing something – repairing harm, addressing the wrong.
- Emphasis on addressing issues – collaborative problem-solving.

**Proposition 2: Justice is about maximising liberty**.
- Emphasis on maximising liberties, choices and autonomy – of victim, of offender, of community.
- Emphasis on maximising status, capacities and self-worth – by enhancing control over one's own destiny and bolstering one's standing in the world.
- Emphasis on self-determination – making decisions about one's own future and one's own life and one's own community.

**Proposition 3: Justice deals with the whole person**.
- Emphasis on the human rights and dignity of the person – of victims, of offenders.
- Emphasis on each person as having capacity to do good – it is acts that are socially condemned, not people.
- Emphasis on acknowledging the distorting effects of harmful acts on ordinary people – histories of abuse may engender futures of offending.

*continued*

---

27

> **Proposition 4: Justice has temporal and spatial dimensions**.
> - Emphasis on the past, present and future lives of individuals – learn from what has gone on, and recognise that what we do now has consequences.
> - Emphasis on potentials and what might be, rather than a fixed state – forward-looking and possibilities, with new knowledge and skills opening up new pathways and alternative horizons.
> - Emphasis on the local – what we do in our own backyard (family, neighbourhood, workplace, community) counts and is particularly meaningful.

The adoption of rehabilitative frameworks to deal with offenders stems from diverse pragmatic ('what works'), fiscal ('what is cheaper in the short and long term') and ideological ('human rights should be central') concerns and motivations. Rehabilitation is neither necessarily a 'radical' option nor an indication of a system in reform. Rather, it always takes place within the context of specific political and institutional factors that offer space and opportunities, to some extent, for rehabilitation practices to take place. One such development is that relating to the rise of therapeutic justice – a development that necessarily involves both cross-institutional linkages and professional collaborations across the board. Many of the philosophical and practical emphases outlined in the four propositions in Box 2.1 are now embedded within this particular mode of judicial practice.

## Adopting a therapeutic framework: non-adversarial approaches to criminal justice

Therapeutic jurisprudence provides an answer to the perennial problem of how to manage and understand the complex social problems that regularly arise in law courts. It is a legal term that describes criminal justice, and more specifically, court initiatives that focus on therapeutic interventions to rehabilitate an offender by addressing the underlying social problems contributing to their offending. It forms a framework to aid understanding of the implications of court decisions in the life of the offender and the efficacy of interventions recommended by the court. It also entails an extension of the methods and approaches available to the court in responding to offenders. In brief, therapeutic jurisprudence has been described as an interdisciplinary contribution to the law's healing potential to increase well-being (Winick 2000).

The specialist courts that adopt this therapeutic framework are often called 'problem-solving' or 'problem-oriented' courts, because they represent a move away from traditional adversarial court processes and instead endorse a collaborative case management model of diversion. The criticisms and frustrations that gave rise to therapeutic justice include 'frustration with traditional approaches to case processing, rising case loads, increasing prison populations, and difficulties in providing adequate and effective interventions' (Freiberg 2007: 2). Court lists are burgeoning beyond belief in many western jurisdictions, as are incarceration rates, and court-mandated diversionary measures are increasingly being seen as a valid alternative for special populations who should not have been caught in the revolving door in the first place. Problem-solving courts tackle diverse social problems, including mental illness, intellectual disabilities, substance misuse, homelessness, extreme poverty, sexual offending, and domestic and family violence, as well as offering specialist therapeutic courts for specific cultural and ethnic groups of offenders, for example, indigenous offenders.

Therapeutic jurisprudence can also sometimes be referred to as 'collaborative justice', which recognises the important role of therapeutic treatment providers and their partnership and active formal involvement in the criminal justice system. Rather than offering static one-off pre-sentence reports, for example, social workers, psychologists, counsellors and other support workers can offer an informed opinion to guide the decision-making of the court about rehabilitation. They have a place at the table alongside prosecutors and lawyers, as well as the defendant/offender themselves, which has considerable implications and a transformative effect on the types of language and communication used in court. The agenda driving the court process is working with a person holistically towards outcomes that balance the best interests of offenders, courts, victims and the community. Collaboration is, therefore, required across disciplines and service types in the administration of justice to achieve lasting outcomes. The mechanics and dynamics of collaboration are vitally important, and we will return to these topics in greater depth in Chapter 9.

King (2006) asserts that problem-solving courts are a better alternative to law and order campaigns, and yet they are not 'soft' on crime but are instead 'smarter' on crime. Offenders are made to take responsibility and accountability for their actions – and they are answerable directly to the court (King 2006). Offenders do not escape consequences of their actions; the subsequent interventions are simply more targeted towards addressing their health, welfare and criminogenic needs.

Drug courts are a useful illustration of therapeutic justice in action. These are particularly popular – there are over 50 of them in the United States alone, and most jurisdictions in Australia now have them. Moreover, they are establishing themselves in the criminal justice landscape on the basis that they seem to work. For instance, there has been a 32 per cent reduction in recidivism among drug court participants in New York, which is quite significant in light of the fact that recidivism rates are usually quite high (Rempel *et al.* 2003). Thus, one positive element is that drug courts 'reduce the number of future victims of crime by promoting offender rehabilitation' (King 2006: 9). There is a relational component of these courts, the depth of which is highlighted in the following observation:

> Drug courts and court diversion programs can also generate powerfully moving stories – stories of healing, overcoming adversity, reconciliation with family and friends, and the gaining of a productive and happy life that contributes to community wellbeing. Bringing these stories of hope to the community should be an essential part of raising community awareness about the value of these programs. (King 2006: 10)

Drug-related offending is an area that is perceived to be a perennial problem containing a cyclic chicken-and-egg type of nexus. Thus, stopping this destructive cycle presents a good news story long overdue in the criminal justice and health and welfare sectors, and is of manifest benefit for the local community.

Warren (1998, cited in Rottman and Casey 1999) compares the main elements of traditional courts and drug diversion courts, and uses this as the basis to illustrate differences between the traditional court approach and the approach adopted by problem oriented courts. This is shown in Table 2.1.

For practitioners, the importance of recent developments is that they take seriously the assumption that what happens in the criminal justice system, particularly in the courts, can influence the behaviour of those who appear before them. As Birgden (2002: 182) notes:

> First, the way the law is implemented and operates can either increase, decrease or have a neutral effect on psychological

**Table 2.1**  A comparison of traditional and therapeutic court processes

| Traditional court process | Transformed court process |
|---|---|
| Dispute resolution | Problem-solving dispute avoidance |
| Legal outcome | Therapeutic outcome |
| Adversarial process | Collaborative process |
| Claim or case oriented | People oriented |
| Rights based | Interest or needs based |
| Emphasis based on adjudication | Emphasis placed on non-adjudication and alternative dispute resolution |
| Judge as arbiter | Judge as coach |
| Backward-looking | Forward-looking |
| Precedent based | Planning based |
| Few participants and stakeholders | Wide range of participants and stakeholders |
| Individualistic | Interdependent |
| Legalistic | Commonsensical |
| Formal | Informal |
| Efficient | Effective |

*Source*: Warren (1998) cited in Rottman and Casey (1999).

well-being. Social scientists should identify laws, processes and procedures that enhance well-being. Second, the law should capitalise on the moment that offenders are brought before it as a way to start prosocial lifestyles. Third, the law should be a multi-disciplinary endeavour with the relationship between law and psychology being cooperative rather than antagonistic.

It is recognised, however, that these transformative or new therapeutic court perspectives and processes operate within the traditional court legal framework and environment. Cases from specialist courts or lists can be referred back to the general criminal court lists as well. This highlights the significance of court process – a key and somewhat contentious issue between supporters and sceptics of therapeutic jurisprudence. Nonetheless, safeguards are put into place to protect due process and the principles of natural justice and open justice, so that the interventions of new transformative court processes are not a divergence from foundational principles of law and the criminal justice system. To put it simply, law and justice are still attained, but the methods and the means to the end have developed in new directions and are different.

Therapeutic jurisprudence is more forward-thinking than traditional courts because it does not involve one-off retrospective punishments, but goes further by trying to reduce future offending and being a catalyst for change. Within this framework, rehabilitation is intentional and intensive, rather than haphazard or part of sentence planning. It is also far cheaper than putting someone in prison. Non-adversarial approaches to justice are an emergent trend of innovation. Practitioners are fully implicated in their implementation and potential success.

### Justice as active

A major feature of therapeutic justice is that it demands more on the part of the offender, as well as practitioners and court officials. The move towards making offenders an active participant in the justice process is reflected in other ways within the criminal justice system as well. This can be illustrated through reference to three broad approaches to offender engagement: a 'justice' approach, a 'welfare' approach and a 'restorative justice' approach (see Bazemore 1991).

Generally speaking, the first approach emphasises such things as 'responsibility' for one's actions, punishment, control-oriented objectives and a focus on what the offender has actually done wrong. Justice is thus *something that is done to you*. Often this involves the use of incarceration in a prison or detention centre, or stringent penalties of some other kind. The idea is to get tough on the offender, and to punish them for what they have done.

The second approach places the emphasis on the offender, and favours greater use of community-based sanctions, individual treatment services and attempts to re-socialise or address the 'deficits' within the person that are seen to be associated with the commission of crime. In this case, justice is *something that is done for you*. The point of this kind of intervention is treatment, taking into account the vulnerability and special needs of many people who offend.

Most justice systems embody elements drawn from both the justice and the welfare models. The third approach has gained popularity in recent years and emphasises 'restorative justice'. This type of approach wishes to maintain a relationship of respect with the offender while simultaneously making amends for the harm caused. In its more developed form, this approach attempts to weigh up the specific requirements of each case of offending, and to variably respond to each offender in terms of (a) personal accountability, (b) development of individual competencies, and (c) the need for community-based incapacitation (Bazemore 1991; Bilchik 1998). Here, justice is *something that is done by you*.

There may be a tension between 'control and contain' strategies and 'rehabilitative' strategies. So too, there may be differences between interventions designed as prison alternatives, and those related to post-prison transitions. Nevertheless, how corrections workers actually carry out their work will largely be dictated by the dominant service philosophy. Increasingly, too, is the idea that rehabilitation (whether weighted in the direction of treatment or of restoration) is something that can and should be done within a prison setting as well as outside the prison walls. From the point of view of rehabilitation, there are several models or approaches that warrant particular attention.

## The risk-need-responsivity (RNR) model

The dominant rehabilitation model in use today is that based on assessment and action around risk, need and responsivity (see, for example, Bonta and Andrews 2007).

- *The need principle* – the assumption that the most effective and ethical approach to the treatment of offenders is to target dynamic risk factors.

- *The risk principle* – the assumption that the treatment of offenders ought to be organised according to the level of risk they pose to society – the higher the level of risk the greater the dosage or intensity of treatment should be.

- *The responsivity principle* – the assumption that we match the delivery of correctional interventions to certain characteristics of participants, such as motivation, learning style and ethnic identity.

The RNR model utilises psychological testing as a key diagnostic instrument (see Ogloff and Davis 2004; Coebergh *et al.* 2001). For instance, such tests are delivered shortly after a person has entered into the corrective services system. Both prisons and community corrections tend to rely on instruments such as the Level of Service/Case Management Inventory (LS/CMI) developed by Andrews and Bonta (1998) and their colleagues.

The types of criminogenic needs that might be considered under this model may include: emotions, offence-related cognitions, violence propensity, criminal associates, relationships, substance misuse, risk-taking arousal, psychiatric state, impulsivity, gambling, lifestyle balance and ethnic and indigenous culture-related factors (Coebergh *et al.* 2001). The kinds of topics included in LS/CMI surveys range from general risk/need factors such as criminal history (for example, any prior youth dispositions or adult convictions) and educational background (such as whether suspended or expelled at least once), to specific risk/need factors relating to personal problems with criminogenic potential (intimidating/controlling), institutional factors such as history of incarceration (any misconduct/behaviour report during current incarceration), other client issues pertaining to social well-being, health and mental health (such as financial problems), and special responsivity considerations (for example, motivation as a barrier).

*Risks* are typically conceptualised as *static* or *dynamic*. Static risk factors are those risk variables that cannot change, such as previous offence history, lack of long-term relationships, and general criminality. Dynamic risk factors are those risk variables that are amenable to change, such as substance abuse, pro-social and pro-offending attitudes, motivation and mood state.

*Needs* are generally conceptualised as *criminogenic* or *non-criminogenic*. Criminogenic needs are those directly related to offending behaviour, and include things such as pro-offending attitudes, substance abuse problems, and criminal associates. Non-criminogenic needs are aspects of the individual or their circumstances that if changed may not have a direct impact on their propensity to repeat offend, and include things such as low self-esteem and mental health problems.

Criminogenic needs are, in essence, dynamic risk factors. That is, pro-criminal attitudes, lack of employment and substance misuse are the targets for intervention, since it is these that are linked to reductions in reoffending (see Farrow *et al.* 2007).

The *risk principle* refers to the allocation of resources depending upon the level of intervention required. Assessment is made of dynamic risk factors (criminogenic needs) and subsequent interventions are based upon the results of this assessment. The most intensive services are meant to be assigned to those offenders deemed to be at highest risk of reoffending. Thus, 'Risk in this sense implies likelihood of reoffending, judged by taking into account risk factors: that is, those variables associated with populations of offenders which have been found to be more predictive of offending behaviour' (Farrow *et al.* 2007: 18). Assessment is crucial to this process and there are many complexities to this. Just as there are many different tools of assessment (see Chapter 5), there are varying degrees of training required in order to maximise the accuracy and quality of offender assessment.

The third element of the RNR model is *responsivity*. This involves being aware of those intervention styles that are most likely to work with offenders in general and with particular sets of offenders. For example, general types of intervention such as cognitive behaviour therapy and pro-social modelling should be integrated into structured approaches towards offender intervention, although these and other therapeutic methods ought to be evaluated on an ongoing basis. Interventions such as those pertaining to specific types of mental illness, special types of sex offending, and specific types of substance misuse need to be tailored to the particular problem behaviour at hand.

Responsivity also means developing systems of assessment and classification that take into account *variations among offenders* such as those relating to age, gender, ethnicity, and level of maturity, and *factors pertaining to the individual* such as cognitive and intellectual abilities. On the other side, the complexity of responsivity means that practitioners need to reflect upon their own practices, and in particular to be aware of the impact of their intervention methods and styles on offender receptivity.

On the basis of test results, individual management plans are drawn up that reflect the assessed risk level and dynamic risk factors or needs. This provides the template upon which offender profiles are developed, and behaviour is thereafter monitored in relation to what the tests reveal about a specific individual. Individual LS/CMI instruments are generally tailored to suit local conditions, cultures and institutional arrangements. For example, both long and short assessment tools are available, and specific wording of questions may differ according to specific national/regional context.

There is considerable evidence that the risk-need-responsivity model does enhance the prospects of offender rehabilitation generally (see Bonta and Andrews 2007), and the development of standardised testing based upon quantitative surveys makes administration relatively easy and uniform compared to more qualitative and narrative-based methods of offender assessment. However, as recent debates over the relationship (including whether or not there is compatibility) between RNR testing and gender-responsiveness in corrections highlight, there is need for more theoretical and empirical scrutiny of its applicability in relation to certain population groups and for social purposes linked to collective empowerment (Smith *et al.* 2009; Hannah-Moffat 2009; Taylor and Blanchette 2009).

A further critique of the RNR model, however, is that concentrating on reducing dynamic risk factors (criminogenic needs) is a necessary but not sufficient condition for effective correctional interventions. In practice, there are also a range of interlinked issues (Ward and Maruna 2007; see also Morash 2009):

- Eliminating or modifying various dynamic risk factors is extremely difficult. Individuals want to know how they can live a better life, and what the positive rewards in desisting from crime are.

- The RNR model tends to neglect the role of self-identity and personal agency, that is, self-directed, intentional actions designed to achieve valued goals (a 'whole person' perspective).

- The RNR model is associated with a rather restricted and passive view of human nature.

- The RNR model does not appreciate the relevance and crucial role of treatment alliance in the therapeutic process (trust and personal relationships).

- The RNR model tends to be preoccupied with offenders' risk profiles or traits and downplays the relevance of contextual or ecological factors in offender rehabilitation.

- The RNR model is often implemented in practice in a 'one size fits all' manner, which is at variance with the 'responsivity' principle (it is heavily manualised and prescriptive).

In the light of these kinds of criticisms, a variety of alternative approaches to offender rehabilitation have emerged to supplement as well as to challenge the risk-need-responsivity model.

## The Good Lives Model (GLM)

The two core therapeutic goals of the Good Lives Model are to promote human goods, and to reduce risk. The GLM includes the adoption of strengths-based approaches that shift the focus away from criminogenic needs and other deficits and instead ask what the individual can contribute to his or her family, community and society. In other words, how can their life become useful and purposeful (Ward and Brown 2004)?

This approach starts from the assumption that offenders are essentially human beings with similar needs and aspirations to non-offending members of the community.

> One of the key assumptions of positive psychological theories is that all human beings are naturally inclined to seek certain types of experience or human good, and that they experience high levels of well-being if these goods are obtained. Criminal actions are thought to arise when individuals lack the internal and external resources to attain their goals in a pro-social way. ... From the perspective of positive psychology, in order for individuals to desist from offending they should be given the knowledge, skills, opportunities and resources to live a 'good' life, which takes into account their particular preferences, interests and values. In short, treatment should provide them with a chance to be better people with better lives. (Ward and Maruna 2007: 111)

According to Ward and Maruna (2007), we all, as human beings, are naturally predisposed to seek certain *primary human goods*. These include:

- Life (including healthy living and physical functioning)
- Knowledge
- Excellence in play and work (including mastery experiences)
- Agency (autonomy and self-directness)
- Inner peace (freedom from emotional turmoil and stress)
- Friendship (including intimate, romantic and family relationships)
- Community
- Spirituality (in the broad sense of finding meaning and purpose in life)
- Happiness
- Creativity.

*Instrumental or secondary goods* provide particular ways and means of achieving primary goods: for example, certain types of work or relationship. For instance, it is possible to secure the primary good of relatedness *via* romantic, parental or personal relationships among other means.

The term 'good lives' refers to 'ways of living that are beneficial and fulfilling to the individual in that they meet the basic human needs of body, social and self' (Ward 2002, cited in Birgden 2002: 181). In addition to this, it is argued that any new rehabilitation initiative or intervention should incorporate or consider the strengths and good facets of each offender's 'abilities, interests, opportunities and basic value systems' (Birgden 2002: 181). The goal of this model is to display the talents and abilities of the offender in a useful and visible role, giving the person individual agency and a role in which to demonstrate personal community contribution to others. It is an enhancement approach focusing on providing offenders with the necessary conditions (such as skills, values, opportunities, social supports) for meeting their needs in more adaptive ways (Ward and Maruna 2007). The aim is to support the person and facilitate the discovery and development of necessary strengths and new talents that promote living a pro-social life and healthy balanced lifestyle.

Many offenders come from families with a history of offending, have chaotic lifestyles, have problems associated with drug and alcohol use, have experienced significant personal trauma in their lives, and have little positive experience with schooling and training programs. In the light of this, the considerations that underpin applying the GLM of offender rehabilitation include the following:

- Prisoners and probationers as whole individuals are more than the sum of their criminal record. They have expertise and a variety of strengths that can benefit society. Interventions should promote and facilitate these contributions whenever possible.

- At the same time, many prisoners and probationers are likely to have experienced adversarial developmental experiences, and have lacked the opportunities and support necessary to achieve a coherent life plan.

- Consequently, such individuals lack many of the essential skills and capabilities necessary to achieve a fulfilling life.

- Criminal actions frequently represent attempts to achieve desired goods but where the skills or capabilities necessary to achieve them are not possessed (direct route). Alternatively, offending can arise from an attempt to relieve the sense of incompetence, conflict or dissatisfaction that arises from not achieving valued human goods (indirect route).

- The absence of certain human goods seems to be more strongly associated with offending: self-efficacy/sense of agency, inner peace, personal dignity/social esteem, generative roles and relationships, and social relationships.

- The risk of offending may be reduced by assisting individuals to develop the skills and capabilities necessary to achieve the full range of human goods.

- Intervention is therefore seen as an activity that should add to an individual's repertoire of personal functioning, rather than as an activity that simply removes a problem or is devoted to managing problems, as if a lifetime of grossly restricting one's activities is the only way to avoid offending (see Mann *et al.* 2004, cited in Ward and Maruna 2007: 128).

In order to make a more comprehensive assessment of each individual's potential for achieving a good life, workers need to build trust and strong relationships with offenders so that they can better understand their abilities, likely opportunities, deep preferences, and values.

Case study 2.1 explores the opportunity of perceiving prisoners and incarceration as an opportunity for strengths-based rehabilitation through harnessing and building on an offenders' personal capacity and skills.

## Case study 2.1

### The opportunity of offender workforce development in the US

On a practical level, one of the most acute areas of need for the offender, particularly upon release from prison, is employment. It is the primary source of financial capital. On a symbolic and personal level, employment also satisfies one of the most acute personal areas of need to rebuild their identity and find worth in new, socially and legally legitimate places. Work is an important source of social capital as it forms a core value in our society, as it is seen as a form of citizen-like contribution, also offering opportunities for social connections. On an institutional or sectoral level, there is proven benefit in providing offender workforce development and pre-release employment readiness programs, with the *caveat* that they must be appropriate and meaningful. There is a high correlation between employment and the outcome of offender supervision, with one study finding that unemployed offenders were more likely to be breached or have their release revoked, whereas nine out of ten offenders who

*continued*

gained employment completed their supervision successfully (Johnson 2007, cited in McDonough and Burrell 2008). Yet offender workforce development is no easy challenge as there are often major barriers to gaining employment, from stigma through to issues of lack of educational attainment and lost time: 'doing time means ageing' (Shivy et al. 2007: 470).

An interesting collaborative initiative is taking place in Delaware's Probation and Parole Service, targeting both ends of the spectrum of supply and demand and attempting to increase the opportunities for the offender workforce in the competitive marketplace. The establishment of a specific Workforce Development Program for offenders represents the beginnings of a paradigm shift for corrections in the US. The goals of this program are fairly straightforward (McDonough and Burrell 2008):

- Reduced recidivism – defined as reduction in new arrests
- Increased employment of offenders
- Increased earnings
- Increased levels of skills training and education
- Enhanced employment opportunities.

The first phase of the program was outreach and collaboration with vocational program providers in the community, which offer skills development and training in areas as diverse as 'training for commercial driver's license, cosmetology, welding, electrical skills, forklift training, hazardous waste removal, office skills and auto mechanics' (McDonough and Burrell 2008: 73). An analysis was also conducted of the target offender population. The second phase was introduced with a public launch and positive media showcasing the benefits of employing offenders. During this phase the work of probation officers involved began to change, transitioning towards a focus on securing skilled labour positions, liaising with trade unions, running job preparation classes and setting up apprenticeship preparation programs (McDonough and Burrell 2008). A more sustained focus on ongoing workforce development ensures career pathways are identified beyond the immediate imperative of just getting a job and keeping it, embedding prospects for sustainable desistance and long-term success. Complementary to a direct focus on gaining employment, probation officers also established cognitive behavioural therapy classes addressing personal contributing factors like lack of motivation, low self-esteem, fear of failure, social skills deficits, and underlying problematic thinking and behaviour. This program is innovative because it is imbued with practical and multifaceted ways to combat stigma and barriers to employment, adopting a strengths-based approach to rehabilitation and community reintegration.

## The social recognition approach

Desistance theories include both psychological and sociological emphases, and are concerned with those processes (and outcomes) whereby people desist or stop from offending. The concept of desistance as *outcome* is measured predominantly by reconviction data (repeat offending, recidivism). The concept of desistance as *process* is gauged predominantly by narrative data (what individuals feel and perceive, how they make meaning of their lives). The desire and propensity to desist or to engage in offending is linked to both structural and personal influences (McNeill 2009a).

The social recognition approach is one theoretical approach within the broader desistance literature. Barry (2006) examines youth offending from the point of view of diverse forms of social, cultural, economic and symbolic capital. She argues that it is not just the accumulation of capital that preoccupies young people, but also its expenditure.

Forms of capital include:

- *Social capital* – valued relations with significant others. Social capital is generated through relationships which in turn bring resources from networks and group membership (for example, peer groups).

- *Economic capital* – the financial means to obtain not only the necessities but also the luxuries of everyday living, including inheritance, income and assets.

- *Cultural capital* – legitimate competence or status. Cultural capital comes from knowledge of one's cultural identity in the form of art and education and language.

- *Symbolic capital* – an overarching resource that brings prestige and honour gained from the collective, legitimate and recognised culmination of the other three forms of capital (social, economic, cultural). It is, in effect, the 'recognition' received from a group.

In discussing why young people persist or desist in offending behaviour and activities, Barry (2006) argues that achieving social recognition is vital for young people to gain a sense of achievement and social belonging as they move through the childhood and teenage years. This concept refers to the attainment of a combination of accumulation and expenditure of capital that is both durable and legitimate: 'Social recognition suggests that people both recognize the need of others (generativity) and are concurrently recognized in addressing those needs (responsibility). It is this "duality" of recognition that is crucial in ensuring durability and legitimation' (Barry 2006: 159).

The family of origin and one's local community provides the platform upon which capital accumulation grows and develops. In other words, resources and recognition of varying kinds stem in the first instance from what the family and friends can provide. Issues of poverty, unemployment, lack of income, homelessness and so on are relevant here. The potential sources of conventional capital accumulation include such things as family and friends, family and personal income, schooling and further education, and varying degrees of independence and interdependence. These factors become increasingly salient when considering the data shown in Figure 2.1, which indicates that approximately half of all offenders imprisoned for the first time in New Zealand are teenagers.

Young people not only need to gain capital and work with their social support networks, but it is the expenditure of accumulated capital that brings the rewards of individual gratification and social stability. Examples of this include such things as buying your own clothes, engaging in volunteer work, and generally encouraging and

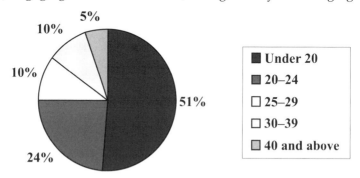

**Figure 2.1** Distribution of age of first imprisonment for offenders in New Zealand
*Source*: Nadesu (2009: 5).

helping others. Barry (2006) talks about the expenditure of capital as including the following:

- *Social capital* – having responsibilities to one's family, partner or children; becoming a parent; giving love, friendship or attention to others; seeking custody of one's child.

- *Economic capital* – 'buying' clothes and other consumables (as opposed to stealing them); spending money on one's house or children; paying taxes and other state contributions.

- *Cultural capital* – contributing towards others' development or welfare through employment, teaching or influence, based on one's own skills or experience; setting an example by one's actions or words; encouraging and helping others.

- *Symbolic capital* – wanting to give of oneself (as mentor, volunteer, worker, for example); wanting to offer restoration/reparation to the community; having responsibilities towards one's house or job.

Social recognition and self-esteem, generally, are built through expenditure of capital (doing something for oneself and for someone else). If this is so, then it also ought to be an important component in the development of juvenile justice intervention strategy. This means addressing the constraints as well as acknowledging the importance of spending what the young person has accumulated in their life.

> Although many offenders talk of restitution to society once they have stopped offending, it may be worth examining the extent to which generativity is rehabilitative for the individual as a result of shame or guilt or whether it is more of a pragmatic desire to give of one's own experiences in preventing similar problems for others. Certainly this research suggested the latter. (Barry 2006: 168).

Thus, for present purposes, it can be observed that through the process of rehabilitation and transition into the community, the individual must be assisted and encouraged to garner and accumulate personal capital in various areas of their life (which goes beyond the narrow focus on the problem of drug use), and then exert the ability to use or spend their capital in the course of a new-found healthy and balanced lifestyle of well-being. The natural consequence or result of this desistance is that the person no longer engages in criminal offending. Overall, the good lives rehabilitation approach and the social recognition theory approach have distinct differences. However, they are complementary and have wider application to rehabilitation than just in the field of corrections (Siegert *et al.* 2007). Both approaches represent clear innovations in practice compared to old or customary approaches involving a primary focus on risk and deficit.

## The restorative justice paradigm

Restorative justice refers to an emphasis on dealing with offenders by repairing harm, and in so doing involving victims and communities as well as offenders in the reparation process. Restorative justice thus emphasises reintegrative and developmental principles and offers the hope that opportunities will be enhanced for victims, offenders and their immediate communities, with the direct participation of all concerned in this process.

Depending upon the specific way in which restorative justice has been institutionalised within a particular jurisdiction – for example, through juvenile conferences, victim–offender mediation, circle sentencing or offender restitution schemes – the focus will generally be on specific events and people (see Cunneen and White 2007).

- *Victim–offender mediation and dialogue* – involves victim restoration, along with active victim involvement, protection of the victim, and meeting of victim needs. Under the guidance of a trained mediator, victims and offenders meet in a safe and structured setting to discuss the nature of the harm committed. Offenders are held directly accountable for their behaviour and must provide assistance to victims in an agreed upon manner.

- *Family group conferencing* – values victim restoration and includes a denunciation, through reintegrative shaming, of the offender's actions. The approach encourages participation by community members (including and especially the friends and family of the victims and offenders) in a meeting, which has the purpose of revealing and discussing the impact of the crime on the various parties. The group decides, as a whole, how the offender can repair the harm done.

- *Circle sentencing (sentencing circles or peacemaking circles)* – emphasises citizen involvement and sharing of power, and community empowerment. The approach involves the creation of a respectful space (literally, a circle of concerned people) in which consensus decisions can be made on an appropriate disposition or outcome that addresses the concerns of all parties. The circles place an emphasis on speaking from the heart, allowing participants to find the best way of assisting in healing all the parties involved and preventing future occurrences.

- *Reparative probation* – has as its main concern victim restoration and community empowerment, with offenders undertaking tasks that directly benefit victims and communities. The person works in the community to perform personal services for victims and/or community services. Often the community services are oriented towards enhancing conditions for disadvantaged or less fortunate people within particular communities.

- *Balanced restorative* – provides victims with the opportunities, as well as the necessary services, for involvement and input, and gives offenders the opportunity to increase their skills and capacities; with connections forged between different community members. It includes an assessment of the offender from the point of view of ensuring community safety, allows for offender accountability for their actions, and works to enhance the competency of the offender while that person is in the criminal justice system.

It is usually the case that the idea of social harm is conceptualised in immediate, direct and individualistic terms – that THIS particular offender has harmed THIS particular victim. One consequence of this is that the emphasis on repairing harm tends to be restricted to the immediate violations and immediate victim concerns, thereby ignoring communal objectives and collective needs in framing reparation processes. Thus, the emphasis remains that of changing the offender, albeit with their involvement, rather than transforming communities and/or changing the conditions under which offending takes place.

Certainly a restorative justice approach would appear to have great potential to effect change in an offender's behaviour and attitudes in a positive direction. This is because it does not exclude people from the community (or, conversely, expose them to a school of crime, as in the case of prisons and detention centres), nor does it pathologise the offender (by placing most attention on their faults and weaknesses).

The restorative perspective is driven by the idea that the offender deserves respect and dignity (they are persons), and that they already have basic competencies and capacities which need to be developed further (if they are not to reoffend). In this framework, the emphasis is on what the person *could do*, rather than what they *should do*. What is important is that the offender achieves things at a concrete level, for themselves, including making reparation to their victim. In the end, the point of dealing with offenders in particular ways is to reinforce the notion that they have done something wrong, to repair the damage done as far as possible, and to open the door for the reintegration of the offender back into the mainstream of society.

The music and drama initiatives described in Innovative practice 2 exemplify a creative response to reintegration, using therapeutic pastimes to help inmates look forward to a different future.

## Practice and policy implications

Together, the theories and approaches outlined above constitute a major overhaul of how people are dealing with questions of rehabilitation and offender desistance. In particular:

- The nature, type and extent of intervention is now being debated in ever greater detail, and the limitations of psychological and social models are being called into question – that is, case management and integrated offender management models are being rejigged to incorporate *strengths-based* approaches and concepts.

- The new-old thinking about rehabilitation and reintegration is premised upon a high degree of *client participation*, client choices and client engagement, since only through this means is lasting 'reform' or rehabilitation to be truly achieved.

- The essential need for *collaboration* and a *constellation of services* has been highlighted across the board of diverse interventions. Accommodation and employment provision are crucial to laying a groundwork upon which rehabilitation and other forms of intervention can take hold for positive purposes.

To extrapolate on these, we might reconsider some of the potentials offered by restorative justice. In some practical circumstances, restorative justice may be effective in providing offenders with greater developmental opportunities, and in ensuring greater victim and community satisfaction and engagement in criminal justice matters. The practices of restorative justice do indeed contain the

*Innovative practice 2*

*Redemption songs: music and dance in prisons*

'Jail Guitar Doors' is a scheme operating in prisons in the UK, teaching inmates to learn new musical skills, using their time inside creatively to cultivate self-esteem and self-expression through music. The scheme is predominantly run by volunteers, including chaplains and charity workers, with one prison governor crediting the scheme as making life behind bars 'that bit less soul destroying' (Gould 2008). This type of music therapy is estimated to make a substantial positive impact on reoffending rates, cutting them from the UK national average of 60 per cent down to as low as 15 per cent in some cases (Gould 2008).

Creative self-expression and teamwork is being promoted through dance in the Philippines. When approximately 1,500 inmates in the Cebu Rehabilitation Centre were recorded dancing *en masse* in standard orange jumpsuits to Michael Jackson's 'Thriller', coordinated by a prisoner accused of mass murder, the performance drew more than 10 million hits on YouTube (Seno 2008). Once infamous for gang violence and a culture of staff corruption, inmates at Cebu have now done performances of 'Sister Act', 'Jailhouse Rock' and 'Radio Ga Ga' (Riminton 2007). Over the three years the initiative has been running, there has been a major reduction in rates of serious violence incidents from once a week to once a year (Riminton 2007). Regular dance performances and increased therapeutic focus have contributed to a move away from a past culture of gang violence and staff corruption, and continue to act as an antidote to negligent levels of overcrowding (up to sixteen in one cell).

seeds for creatively and constructively responding to the injustices of life suffered by most offenders (see, for example, Bazemore and Walgrave 1999; Denckla 1999–2000). At the least, restorative justice implicitly offers recognition that families and communities have an important role to play in trying to grapple with the causal reasons for personal offending. In some exceptional cases, restorative justice also offers young people themselves a pivotal role in the justice process as decision-makers, as well as participating as offenders or victims (see Hogeveen 2006).

In many cases of restorative justice, there is an emphasis on active agency. This refers to the idea that people are to be held directly accountable in some way, and that they are meant to do things, themselves, rather than simply being passive actors in the criminal justice system. Importantly, when they engage in doing something (such as painting a fence), this is generally constructed as being to the benefit of somebody else (a victim of graffiti perhaps). Restorative justice thus involves *acts of giving* as well as *acts of forgiving*. The offending act may be condemned, and respect for the offender maintained, but young offenders are nonetheless expected to repair the harms they have caused.

This aspect of restorative justice – the notion of actively giving of oneself – also features in the other approaches to offending presented in this chapter. Rehabilitation, desistance and restoration are thus construed as being mainly about capacity building rather than personal deficits. The point of intervention is to achieve a result whereby the offender will be seen as a community asset rather than a liability.

> The capacity or capability aspect of rehabilitation directly involves providing individuals with the internal and external conditions necessary to attain valued outcomes in ways that match their abilities, preferences and environments. Internal conditions refer to psychological characteristics such as skills, beliefs and attitudes, while external conditions refer to social resources, opportunities and supports. (Ward and Maruna 2007: 174)

Hence the goal of intervention within these frameworks is to display the talents and skills of the offender in a useful and visible role, giving the person individual agency.

The 'social recognition' theory, the 'good lives' perspective, and the 'restorative justice' approach all acknowledge the dynamic interplay of structure and agency – of how personal choices and personal values are made and experienced within the confines of certain external material constraints. For those working within the criminal justice system, social intervention based upon these approaches has to take seriously the narrative accounts of the offenders themselves. They also have to address those internal and external factors that impinge upon people's sense of self and their place in the world.

By focusing on self-empowerment and self-determination through capacity development, models of intervention based upon the notion of positive strengths operate on the assumption that increases in the positives will naturally result in decreases in the negatives, for example, desistance from offending. In Box 2.2 we distil some of the core concepts that lie at the heart of much of the thinking about correctional practice at the present time. These build upon and in many ways complement the foundational understandings and methodologies associated with the RNR model. We have presented these concepts for doing justice as being sets of related concepts insofar as, for example, there is a strong connection between giving and forgiving, between seeking redemption and aspiring towards a good life, and so on.

Models, concepts and approaches have to be able to resonate with those who are subject to them – our clients – if they are to have adequate practical purchase. So, too, they must bear some relation to how practitioners experience their work and their worlds of work if they are to be adopted and utilised in the most effective ways. At the

---

*Box 2.2*

*Key concepts for doing justice*

Philosophy of justice has to be translated into active participation if it is to be meaningful.

**Key concept 1: Forgiving – giving**
- Strategic use of forgiveness is essential in motivating people to make things right, and to instigate changes in their own life – forgiveness on the condition that they take action in some way, by repairing harm and by engaging in programs and services that will enhance their personal development and well-being.
- Giving is one of the most meaningful acts for humans, and makes us feel good about ourselves and to value the world and others generally – we can repair the damage in ways that make sense and generate pride.

**Key concept 2: Redemption – good life**
- Redemption can be seen as a journey towards self-knowledge and personal fulfilment through better choices. It offers hope – now and into the future.
- Creating a good life is intensely personal, and has elements commonly shared with the rest of humanity. Achieving this is shaped by the economic and social resources available to us as well as what happens within us.

*continued*

---

> **Key concept 3: What works – problem-solving**
> - To address the failures of prison and the inadequacies of justice, the focus has to be on 'what works' in addressing social and moral issues, and in working with people to achieve better lives.
> - Justice is always intertwined with social, economic and cultural issues – a collaborative problem-solving approach is needed if the best outcomes are to be forthcoming.
>
> **Key concept 4: Social respect – self-respect**
> - Social respect is achieved through the combination of acknowledging harm, and giving something to the community, to each other, and to one's self. It is a status conferred upon us notionally, as in the case of human rights, or proactively, as in the case of doing something deserving of beneficial attention.
> - Self respect is about being able to achieve a sense of one's self as being a good person. For all of us, this means dealing with the harms we have received and that we have perpetrated, in ways that allow us to nevertheless continue into the future in a positive way.

very least, however, it is how we think about working with offenders that shapes how we interact with them, and for what purpose.

**Paradoxes and controversies**

As we saw in Chapter 1, there has been a massive growth in incarceration in a number of jurisdictions. Accompanying this growth has been heightened concern about what to do with people while they are in prison, and how best to manage their situations once they have been released from prison. For a prison system that is overwhelmed by numbers and that consequently does not have the resources to devote to rehabilitation, working with offenders basically means containment; the lack of programs and preparation within prison will subsequently also affect working with offenders post-release in the community.

Meanwhile, as shown in Table 2.2, the caseloads of corrections workers in the community are also significant – and growing. The level of resource granted to particular areas of corrective service is

**Table 2.2** Comparative data on persons on probation and parole by country, 2006

| Type of data | England and Wales | United States | Canada | Australia |
|---|---|---|---|---|
| Total persons placed on probation | 146,532 | 4,237,023 | 116,769 | – |
| Total persons placed on parole/ conditional release | 25,600 | 798,202 | 8,132 | 8,983 |

*Source*: Adapted from Australian Bureau of Statistics (2006) and United Nations Office on Drugs and Crime (2008a).

signalled to some extent in how corrective services are evaluated. Thus, from the point of view of performance management, particular measures are used to determine service function (see Scenario 2.1). What gets rewarded (and resourced) institutionally is that which is overtly valued within and by organisational performance measures.

If resources are not forthcoming to ensure an effective community corrections sector, and if intensive supervision and support is not provided in the prisons to those who most need them, then reoffending is guaranteed to stay the same or to increase. To stop reoffending requires a major commitment to changing the life circumstances of offenders. Simultaneously, this also generally means that we need to address the communal relationships and social problems that serve as the launching pad for criminal and anti-social activity. All of this has implications for the nature, intensity and extent of work for those engaged in working with offenders.

## Conclusion

This chapter has provided a summary overview of several interesting and promising theories and approaches to rehabilitation. The renewed interest in such theories and practical interventions is associated, in part, with the recent shift towards therapeutic justice and problem-solving courts. Such an institutional orientation necessarily means that different workers within and across the criminal justice system need to work closely together, and to do so on an agenda that is less about 'justice' as such as about holistic approaches to responding to the complexities of offender lives.

### Scenario 2.1

### What qualifies as quality? The theory and practice of performance

Consider the examples of objectives, standards and performance indicators below. In what ways do these quality improvement measures relate (or not relate) to the theories outlined in this chapter (for example, the RNR model, Good Lives Model, restorative justice)? Are there other types of data or information these performance indicators might be missing?

| Jurisdiction | Objective and standard | Performance indicators of effectiveness |
| --- | --- | --- |
| England and Wales | *Incident management* – incidents are managed effectively to protect staff, prisoners and others and to ensure the minimum disruption to business. Threats are identified and reviewed regularly and contingency plans are in place for dealing with those threats. | ▪ Audit compliance. <br> ▪ Number of accidents and reportable major injuries, dangerous occurrences and diseases to be no more than limit set. <br> ▪ Agreed number and type of contingency plan tests to be run. |
| | *Violence reduction* – establishments maintain personal safety for staff and prisoners and reduce the harm caused by violence, taking necessary action to prevent it. | ▪ Audit compliance. <br> ▪ Rates of serious assaults. <br> ▪ Existence and quality of a violence reduction strategy. <br> ▪ Behaviour management through sentence planning. |
| | *Prisoner's family life* – establishments enable prisoners to maintain close and meaningful relationships with family and friends, while taking account of security needs. Visitors are treated with respect. | ▪ Audit compliance. <br> ▪ An efficient system is in operation for booking visits. <br> ▪ Examination of complaints by family. <br> ▪ Regularity of visits permitted. |
| | *Resettlement* – all prisoners have the | ▪ Audit compliance. <br> ▪ Regularity of |

*Scenario 2.1 continued*

| Jurisdiction | Objective and standard | Performance indicators of effectiveness |
|---|---|---|
| | opportunity to maintain and develop appropriate community ties and to prepare for their release. Provision by the Prison Service in collaboration with probation areas is targeted on the basis of an assessment of risks and needs and directed towards reducing the risk of reoffending and risk of harm. | resettlement and discharge planning meetings.<br>• Consideration of resettlement needs in prisoner induction and allocation.<br>• Records of employment, education, training and accommodation status planned at discharge. |
| Australia | *Efficient resource management* – measuring the inputs per output unit in terms of resource planning and expenses in corrective services. | • Real recurrent cost per prisoner/offender.<br>• Offender-to-staff ratios and caseloads.<br>• Prison utilisation and occupation rates.<br>• Programme costs per offender. |
| | *Provide programme interventions to reduce the risk of reoffending* – corrective services aim to reduce the risk of reoffending among prisoners and offenders by providing services and programme interventions that address the causes of offending, maximise the chances of successful reintegration into the community, and encourage offenders to adopt a law-abiding way of life. | • Percentage of eligible prisoners employed.<br>• Percentage of prisoners enrolled in education and training.<br>• Participation rates in offence-related programmes. |

*Source*: Australian Commonwealth Government Productivity Commission (2009); HM Prison Service (2009b).

## Discussion questions

1  Identify and discuss some examples of therapeutic jurisprudence and problem-solving courts from within your country.
2  What is 'criminogenic'? What types of offender needs and skills should be prioritised in the process of supporting desistance and reintegration?
3  Discuss the relationship between the risk-need-responsivity (RNR) model and the Good Lives Model.

## Further reading

Birgden, A. (2004) 'Therapeutic jurisprudence and responsivity: finding the will and the way in offender rehabilitation', *Psychology, Crime and Law*, 10(3): 283–95.

Byrne, F. and Trew, K. (2008) 'Pathways through crime: the development of crime and desistance in accounts of men and women offenders', *Howard Journal of Criminal Justice*, 42(2): 181–97.

King, M., Freiberg, A., Batagol, B. and Hyams, R. (2009) *Non-Adversarial Justice*. Sydney: Federation Press.

McNeill, F. (2009) *Towards Effective Practice in Offender Supervision: Report 01/09*. Glasgow: Scottish Centre for Crime and Justice Research.

Ogloff, J. and Davis, M. (2004) 'Advances in offender assessment and rehabilitation: contributions of the risk-need-responsivity approach', *Psychology, Crime and Law*, 10(3): 229–42.

## Key resources

Barry, M. (2006) *Youth Offending in Transition: The Search for Social Recognition*. Abingdon: Routledge.

Day, A., Casey, S., Ward, T., Howells, K. and Vess, J. (2010) *Transitions to Better Lives: Offender Readiness and Rehabilitation*. Cullompton: Willan Publishing.

Farrow, K., Kelly, G. and Wilkinson, B. (2007) *Offenders in Focus: Risk, Responsivity and Diversity*. Bristol: Policy Press.

Maruna, S. and Immarigeon, R. (eds) (2004) *After Crime and Punishment: Pathways to Offender Reintegration*. Cullompton: Willan Publishing.

Ward, T. and Maruna, S. (2007) *Rehabilitation: Beyond the Risk Paradigm*. New York: Routledge.

# Chapter 3

# Institutional dynamics and the workplace

My expectations have been exceeded once I concentrated on the work and not the politics of the organisation.
(Probation officer, quoted in Annison *et al.* 2008: 264)

## Introduction

The first two chapters of this book provided background discussions about current trends in corrections and working with offenders generally. From steep increases in prison populations (and simultaneously growing numbers of offenders on community-based orders) to the renewed interest in rehabilitation and emerging intervention paradigms, these chapters laid the foundations for subsequent chapters. In this chapter our intention is to be more practically and practitioner oriented, with particular attention being paid to interpersonal, interdisciplinary and institutional dynamics that shape what is done with whom and why.

This chapter explores issues that workers face every day in their role and interactions with other workers and agencies. Prisons present a unique environment where a strong culture is evident and it is important that this is explored in the context of a workplace, not just from the perspective of offenders. Workers in community settings also face unique challenges and dilemmas, which are considered within organisational and broader structural contexts. Discussions include the gender dimensions of correctional service work, and ways of working with offenders depending upon the residential setting (either within prison or in the community). The interface and interaction between 'inside' workers and 'outside' workers is also discussed.

Underlying the more coercive interventions associated with criminal justice are a series of interrelated, and seemingly contradictory, sentencing principles (see White and Perrone 2010). The aims of sentencing, which are both symbolic and functional, are generally seen to include:

- Denunciation and public reprobation
- Retribution and 'just deserts'
- Incapacitation and community protection
- Rehabilitation and reform
- Individual and general deterrence
- Reparation and restitution.

The mission statements of most corrective services generally try to encapsulate these sentencing aims. For example, the purpose of the Department of Corrections in Queensland, Australia is to provide, in partnership with other key criminal justice agencies, 'community safety and crime prevention through the humane containment, supervision and rehabilitation of offenders' (Corrective Services Queensland 2008: 2). In many jurisdictions, these types of mission statements are accompanied by a description of key organisational values – such as integrity, accountability, respect for others, teamwork and so on.

A close reading of correctional services documents reveals an uneasy combination of basically incompatible objectives. This reflects the ambiguities of sentencing principles as much as an institutional difficulty in sorting out main priorities. Practical difficulties arise when departments have to weigh up issues such as 'rehabilitative services' and 'secure containment' in the context of government pressures to demonstrate 'cost effectiveness'. Likewise, the public images of prison as being 'too soft' (for example, sensationalistic news coverage of television sets and swimming pools) or 'too hard' (for example, ancient prisons with no heating systems) make it difficult to frame a penal response that will satisfy everyone. Objectives relating to rehabilitation, which require intensive and extensive programs and support services for inmates, are seen to contradict the other main current in penal thinking – that is, the prison (or community-based penalty) experience is often viewed first and foremost as punitive in intent, which means that prisoners ought to suffer some types of deprivation due to the pain they have caused someone else. Furthermore, in some cases the emphasis may be on ensuring community safety, through incarceration of those offenders deemed to be particularly dangerous.

In addition to perennial problems associated with how to juggle competing objectives, corrective service authorities also have to deal with 'outside' pressures, such as ensuring that the policies of the government of the day are implemented. This has a direct impact on the specific orientation of a service, and the overall level and type of 'service' it provides to offenders in particular. For example, there are pressures in some jurisdictions to reduce the scope for early release of prisoners by tightening up parole eligibility requirements. Simultaneously there may be greater concern about drug rehabilitation strategies within prison, and with efforts to change prisoner behaviour through psychiatric and training programs. Another example relates to the focus of community corrections – whether this is oriented towards punitive community reparation (such as chain-gang types of work) or rehabilitative ideals (repairing harm in a fashion that maximises victim, offender and community dominion).

Specific kinds of policy prescriptions have a major impact on the environment within prisons and within community-based services. In particular, they can restrict or assist corrective service authorities in terms of their immediate management practices (for example, through the use of earned remission as a social control mechanism) or they can assist in helping to emphasise the rehabilitative potential of a program (by freeing up resources for residential drug rehabilitation). In a nutshell, government policy in areas such as law enforcement and sentencing can have a significant and direct impact on the administration of criminal justice.

## Working in prison

The prison is a very unusual environment in which to work. For a start it is a total institution, in which all activity is closely monitored and all personnel subject to strict rules of conduct. Many within its confines do not want to be there – they are involuntary clients. Some, however, choose to be there, since it is a source of work and income. As a place to live and to work, the prison is inevitably 'artificial' and fraught with tensions.

A key feature of the prison is that it necessarily operates on the basis of deprivation. The nature of deprivation varies from country to country and from institution to institution, but deprivation, at the very least referring to freedom of movement or basic liberty, is central to its mission. The archetypal prison environment violates many of the known principles of social and psychological development. Indeed, it tends to promote norms and practices that legitimate rather than reduce deviance. The pains of imprisonment can be summarised as follows (see Sykes 1958; Mathiesen 1990):

- *Deprivation of liberty* – massive restrictions on movement, and the cutting off of people from their friends, families, and loved ones.

- *Deprivation of goods and services* – a drastic reduction in material possessions.

- *Deprivation of ordinary, loving, sexual relationships* – major physiological and psychological problems that call into question one's sexuality and sexual status.

- *Deprivation of autonomy* – the subjection of the individual to a vast body of rules, regulations and commands that are imposed and total in nature.

- *Deprivation of security* – being thrown together into anxiety-provoking situations of forced and prolonged intimacy with others who in many instances have a history of violent behaviour (including prison officers).

- *Deprivation of power* – the power that the prison wields in controlling both formal and informal benefits and burdens in the lives of the incarcerated.

In this type of context it is not surprising therefore that a unique institutional culture develops and pervades the processes pertaining to how one might work with involuntary clients such as prisoners. Prison culture or prisonisation refers to the adoption of the norms of inmate subculture based on an adversarial relationship between guards and inmates. Generally speaking, behaviour that the institutional authorities view as conformity is viewed by inmates as deviant, and vice versa. Once an individual enters the prison system, they undergo a symbolic depersonalisation transition – they are stripped, probed, re-dressed, and bestowed the status of convict. As part of this process, the individual is required to take on the mores, customs and culture of the prison, all of which are premised upon a basic conflict between inmate and prison officer. The prison setting and prison resources heavily shape prison culture as well.

Facilities, services and programs matter to prisoners, and they heavily influence the dynamics and ethos of the worker–inmate relationship. These can be evaluated on the basis of quality, availability, content of provision and cultural appropriateness, and how well these match both immediate offender and management requirements, as well as international standards (see, for example, United Nations conventions pertaining to prison standards and prisoner rights, Council of Europe standards for the treatment of prisoners, and the Standard Guidelines for Corrections in Australia; for commentary, see Brown and Wilkie 2002; Murdoch 2006; Grant and Memmott 2007/08). Overall levels of resources and quality of facilities affect both prisoners and workers within a prison setting. Drab walls and claustrophobic architecture make for unpleasant places to work, much less to inhabit 24 hours a day, seven days a week.

If we are to understand prison culture we also must look at prison officers – who they are, what their role is, and what they are attempting to do. Working within prisons has become highly complex in recent years, particularly with the introduction of initiatives such as 'integrated offender management'. Prison officers are being asked to perform a wider range of tasks than merely that of turnkey, and this has implications for their pre-service and in-service training, career structures, levels of work-related stress, and general staff relations (O'Toole and Eyland 2005; Crawley and Crawley 2008; King 2009).

The nature of the prison regime itself is a big factor on prison culture and, of course, on prison work and prison workers (see Brown and Wilkie 2002). For example, authoritarian regimes tend to be associated with antagonistic relationships between staff and inmates, high levels of violence (self-harm/suicide, inmate on inmate violence, as well as prison officer to prisoner and prisoner to prison officer violence), and 'codes of behaviour' that are reflected in, and reinforced by, both inmate and custodian institutional practices (see also South and Wood 2006; Carlton 2007; Goulding 2007). Not surprisingly, prisons have also over time been associated with the development of specific language, as illustrated in Table 3.1.

The problems associated with an antagonistic prison environment, and high levels of distrust and dishonesty, make change on either side very difficult (White and Perrone 2010). For example, prison officers who individually adopt a 'humane' approach to their tasks, and who wish to establish a closer more positive relationship with inmates, are invariably exploited by some prisoners. Over time, this can lead to cynicism and disenchantment about the possibilities of reform.

**Table 3.1**  Inside prison words: Australia 2009

| Word | Meaning |
| --- | --- |
| Slots, box, hole | Cell |
| Pups | New officers (because they have not been around long enough to be dogs) |
| Screws, dogs | Officers |
| Tamps, rock spiders | Inmates who have committed sex crimes against children |
| Laggin | Time spent in jail |
| Laggin pills | Medication |
| Buy-ups | Canteen for chips, cigarettes, drinks and lollies |
| Ox, baccy | White Ox tobacco |
| Sallyport | Vehicle bay for entry into the prison |
| Wardsman | Person who cleans the accommodation units or cells |
| Toss a cell | Conduct search of inmate's cell |
| Dogs, rats | Person who gives information to officers or the police |
| Traps, food hatch | Flap in the door for the purpose of meals delivery or handcuffing |
| Round the back | Separation of inmates to a loss of privilege area |
| Brew | Alcohol made in prison from fruit and bread |
| Boss | Officer |
| Shanghaied | Move to another area of the prison against the inmate's will |
| Fish tank | Observation cell |
| Over the fence | Escape from custody |
| Do the bolt | Escape from the prison farm |
| Tatts | Prison tattoos – representations include:<br>• brick walls  = inmate's ability to fight<br>• spider web = has seriously hurt another person<br>• dollar sign on hand = has committed an armed robbery<br>• four dots in a square with one in the middle, on the hand = four dots mean prison and the one dot is the person. |

On the other hand, prison life is also characterised by a sense of the routine and by certain normalised behaviours. Most of the time, for most of the people (workers and inmates), violence does not feature prominently and things run more or less smoothly on a day-to-day basis. While there is certainly an 'us' versus 'them' mentality, in practice staff and prisoners find a range of ways of coexisting, many of which are in effect more collaborative than adversarial. This is further explored in Chapter 6 when we discuss the importance of concepts such as human rights and respect when it comes to good work practice.

It is also worth pondering over the match (and sometimes lack of it) between what both workers and prisoners say about their overall relationship with each other, and how in fact they often function more symbiotically than first appearances may convey. Moreover, as research has demonstrated, a prison where people are dealt with fairly and well, enhancing the prison's overall legitimacy, is a place that is not only more likely to engage people in effective service, but is also likely to be better ordered and more secure (see Liebling 2004). In other words, certain aspects of institutional practice can have a profound influence on staff–inmate relationships, for better or for worse.

Prisonisation is a process that varies according to basic penal philosophy (for example, punishment versus rehabilitation), the nature of local prison conditions (lighting, heating and adequate bed numbers), the historical relationship between the prison philosophy and inmate (control orientation versus helping hand), use of technology (level of surveillance), gender relations and the different ways in which men and women identify themselves (positive or negative association with a criminal subculture and the perceived importance of social status), and operational management (state versus private prisons). The effects of prisonisation on a person's sense of self and behavioural patterns become most striking in their impact upon release into the community:

> When you're in prison, you've no identity … In prison, you're nothing. Especially people doing long term sentences, in my experience anyway, you've no preparation other than they'll say 'here's your stuff' surprise, surprise, I'm experiencing that yet again. When you get a long sentence, your only memories of the outside world is what you remember prior to being in prison. And as for what I call the Rip Van Winkle syndrome, it's like coming awake after 100 years, suddenly you're pushed out … not pushed out, released, and you have to become a passenger, neighbor, pedestrian, customer, all the things I listed, and nobody prepares you for it. (Prisoner, quoted in Howerton *et al.* 2009: 450)

The 'Rip Van Winkle' syndrome the prisoner speaks of is illustrative of what parts of a person's sense of self come alive upon release into the community, where the 'reality' or senses required to survive are completely different from those in a total institution. Reintegration and preparation spoken of above comes to the fore as a mandate for those involved in correctional work.

Working within a prison setting involves working with a great many different other workers, not only with a diverse client group. The breakdown of prison staff in the UK is provided in Table 3.2. By far the largest group of workers within prison is that of the prison officers, whose mandate includes the basic custodial function of security as well as other types of functions.

For prison officers, issues of security and containment are central. Preserving one's safety and ensuring the safety of others, including prisoners, is high on the list of priorities. There are pressures to learn new skills – for example, to become 'case managers' of prisoners – but when all is said and done, job performance ultimately rests upon ensuring positive containment. Officer safety, inmate safety and community safety are paramount considerations that pertain directly to the role of prison officer.

Prison culture from a prison officer perspective varies from that of the inmate although there are important overlaps. From an inmate perspective, prison culture includes such things as an 'us versus them' mentality (based on antagonism), a prisonisation effect (learning the language and behaviour codes) and bringing attitudes and knowledge in from the outside (importation of anti-social and criminal attributes). From a prison officer perspective, prison culture might be interpreted as including elements such as 'protecting us against them' (solidarity with co-workers), pride in one's work (according to sense of mission),

**Table 3.2**  Prison staff in the UK

| Type of worker | Percentage of total |
| --- | --- |
| Officers | 50.7 |
| Operational support (e.g. staffing prison gates) | 15.2 |
| Administration | 15.3 |
| Healthcare | 2.2 |
| Chaplaincy | 0.6 |
| Psychology | 1.9 |
| Industrials (e.g. workshop instructors) | 7.0 |
| Other | 4.0 |
| Operational managers (i.e. governor grades) | 2.8 |

*Source*: Crewe *et al*. (2008: 5).

and taking steps towards professionalisation (through pre-service and in-service training). The very existence of a prison culture, and a prison work culture, can contribute to stress and strain on the part of workers.

Indeed, the process of becoming and being a prison officer has distinctive stages of progression and development (Crawley and Crawley 2008). From an initial interest through to training, and then ultimately being a prison officer, one learns such things as the technical aspects of the job (such as how to undertake a cell search), institutional mission (the rationale for the job you are doing), about prison culture (including inmate resistances) and how best to deal with the emotional side of the job (incorporating attitudes, behaviours and events within a prison setting). There is much to learn, and contemporary prison work has been increasingly professionalised as the tasks have become more demanding and varied in nature.

What is also learned is the best and the worst aspects of the job. The best aspects might include, for example, the ability to be a peacekeeper and to use discretion for positive purposes (Liebling 2004). Wielding a modicum of power in a total institution can have its 'up side' as well as potentially breeding the despot. The worst aspects might include constant on-the-job stress related to having to deal with involuntary clients, including some who are, literally, dangerous individuals, dangerous to be around. Work-related stress also emerges from roster systems that provide for the uneven hours of shift work (since the prison is a 24/7 institution), from staff shortages relative to inmate numbers and program needs, and high levels of staff sick and disability leave due to on-the-job events and/ or stressors. General pay and work conditions (including the physical infrastructure of the prison) are also major factors in job satisfaction and worker confidence and morale.

While the offender is the central client in the prison environment, for prison officers there are other significant players with whom they must often interact as well. Key issues here include how best to relate to 'inside' workers such as health workers and social work staff, and to 'outside' professionals such as drama teachers, chaplains, prison visitors, and drug and alcohol workers; and how best to interrelate with the families of prisoners. For other workers who have to spend time inside a prison, there are frequently questions that stem directly from the nature of their specific occupational focuses. These differ greatly from the prison officer concern with safety and security, and reflect specific task-related emphases. Consider, for example, how non-prison officer positions might construe what is a major question of practice for them, given their respective occupational domains (see Bennett *et al.* 2008):

- *Parole officers* – how best to work within a prison setting, as well as in the community?
- *Drug and alcohol workers* – do drugs in prison make users easier to manage and give staff an easier time?
- *Teachers* – how to tailor teaching strategies and techniques to satisfy the needs of prisoners?
- *Psychologists* – what to do to contribute to addressing racism and homophobia in prisons?
- *Health professionals* – how to deal with a lack of trust from a client group of involuntary residents?

From the point of view of service provision, there is bound to be a tension between 'security' and 'service' objectives (see, for example, King 2009). Each in its own way is essential to the success of the other, since good service provision can diminish potential security issues, and good approaches to security can enable better forms of service provision. Nevertheless, the conflict between the two may well be exacerbated by the entry into the prison context of 'outside' service providers (such as, for example, a non-government organisation which provides input into recreational programs in a centre), which may have quite different agendas and perceptions from the 'insiders', regarding what they are trying to do and what their key priorities are.

The costs associated with providing a safe, secure and humane institutional setting – and furthermore one that provides a comprehensive treatment and educative offering for inmates – are enormous (see Figures 3.1 and 3.2). These costs are compounded by any increases in prison populations, by an increased flow of people into and out of the system, and by longer sentences for offenders generally. Thus, the costs of prison likewise have a major influence on what kind of programs or facilities will be able to be offered in practice, and the overall place of security issues in the life of an institution.

In a period of declining fiscal resources (government budget allocations available to public institutions) and escalating costs, it is difficult to envisage that maintaining services and funding allocations within a correctional institution will be an easy task. And certain groups require even greater than usual amounts of staff attention and resources simply because of their unique situations. For instance:

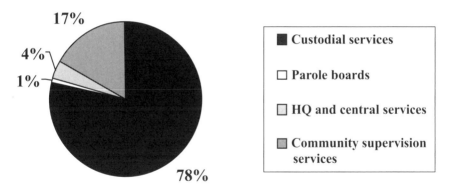

**Figure 3.1** Total operating expenditures for provincial/territorial government adult correctional services agencies in Canada, 2003–04
*Source*: Adapted from Statistics Canada (2005).

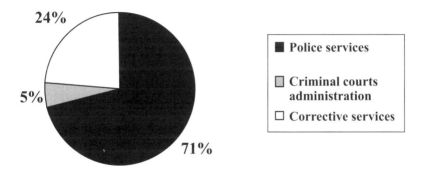

**Figure 3.2** Composition of government expenditure on criminal justice in Australia, 2006–07
*Source*: Australian Institute of Criminology (2009: 105).

- The low number of *women and girls* in the system has implications for the development of specific programs designed to meet their different needs.

- While the number of *sex offenders* is relatively small, their demands on professional staff are very great, including where and how they are accommodated within the broader prison population.

- Services provided to people with *mental illness and intellectual disability* within the criminal justice system similarly requires more attention.

- The issue of *drug use and abuse* also looms large in any program development and service provision.

- There may be chronic and long-term patterns contributing to the current socio-economic status of an offender, for example, *intergenerational unemployment, familial debt and poverty*.

- People who share *religious and cultural practices* that differ from the host country mainstream, and also *foreign prisoners*, frequently experience difficulties relating to language, personal and spiritual obligations, food requirements and racism.

Issues relating to drugs, abuse, educational and vocational needs, psychiatric problems, leisure and recreation, sexuality, and so on demand a high level of professional expertise in addition to the everyday tasks associated with the running of secure facilities. We have to be mindful that specific difficulties and problems are exacerbated in circumstances where the usual 'pains of imprisonment' remain. Furthermore, the concentration of 'hard cases' – that is, already marginalised people – into segregated groups tends to influence the institutional dynamic of prisons in repressive rather than rehabilitative directions. The provision of medical services, mental health services, drug and alcohol services and sex offender programs raise a number of issues pertaining to supervision, care and specialist intervention. Again, adequate provision will cost money.

More generally, the engagement of professionals with a broadly developmental, welfare and treatment orientation can create internal problems within an institution. As pointed out by the New South Wales Ombudsman inquiry into juvenile detention, there is a 'serious division between specialist staff and operational staff in all centres' (1996: xii). The division essentially reflects the difference between 'custodial' and 'welfare' priorities – the relative emphasis each group places upon security versus services. Consider, for example, the prescriptions offered by a youth worker who periodically participates in detention programs in New South Wales:

> If a programme seeks to encourage people to respect others, then the programme must respect the participants. If it seeks to encourage self control then there must be opportunities for this to occur within the programme. If … choice and decision-making are being developed, then there must be opportunities for these processes within a group. These must be genuinely present and not just expressed verbally. (Slattery 2000/2001: 57)

However, these types of intervention may be difficult to implement successfully if adequate protocols are not put in place beforehand: prison officers (who are 'permanent' workers with adult prisoners and youth detainees) and professional staff (including occasional 'guest' workers) need to be clear about their roles and duties in given situations. Also, the philosophical basis of these kinds of approaches, that emphasise choice, opportunity and participation, may appear to run counter to a custodial emphasis on security, restriction and discipline.

The type and style of intervention pose a number of questions for specialist and operational (that is, prison officers) workers alike. For those staff associated with the 'helping professions', such as social workers, psychologists and psychiatrists, there are always going to be difficulties and dilemmas in working with 'involuntary clients' who are legally mandated to receive assistance. In addition to working towards the mandated goal of preventing further offending in the future, service providers are influenced by factors such as available resources, the restrictiveness of the offender's setting, the worker's proficiency in engaging the offender, and the offender's willingness and ability to 'become a client in the complete sense of the term and to utilise the services of the correctional worker to address problems and concerns beyond those specified by the mandate' (Borowski 1997: 359).

Institutional resources, general staff relationships and professional training specific to the demands and context of correctional institutions are all important factors in the nature and quality of the services meant to assist prisoners. For prison officer staff, the issues are likewise complicated by the multiple demands on the criminal justice system as a whole. New methods of working with prisoners – such as 'case management' models that place the focus on the individual detainee, to ascertain factors that contribute to their offending behaviour, and are designed to address their specific needs through development of a defined case plan – have ramifications for the overall management of prisons, and the relationship between specialist and operational staff. Importantly, innovative ways of working with offenders require major shifts in the traditional culture of prisons (which includes management styles, as well as worker attitudes and practices). This is a significant challenge. But the stakes are high: 'While poorly skilled staff may be able to lock and unlock gates, it takes talented and skilled individuals to be able to interact positively with young offenders, care for their welfare and rights, and also maintain appropriate security and safety for themselves and others' (NSW Ombudsman 1996: xvii).

The professionalisation of prison management and staff is a vital part of broader institutional reform.

The introduction of new methods of working with inmates is invariably accompanied by uncertainty, stress and conflict as old ideas and practices are challenged. For example, the attitudes of some prison officers are perceived as an obstacle to efficient service delivery involving outside agencies (White and Mason 2003). This occurs where support staff or welfare workers are viewed as 'do-gooders' that somehow undermine the prison structure, which in turn is perceived to be first and foremost about containment and control.

Consider the evaluation of a program in Tasmania, Australia, involving outside workers working with prisoners inside the prison (White and Mason 2003). A common theme of the discussions surrounding the program was the nature of its status as an 'outside' agency provider, and how this related to the success or otherwise of the service. This was reflected in prisoner comments (see two of these below).

> Working outside the prison structure allows him to do a better job. If Mike wasn't here there would be no one to assist inmates. Mike gets trust from being an outsider. There is nothing left to fill the gap if he goes. (Prisoner)

> Inmates need someone who is on the outside. Mike has no alternative agendas like others, he's open and honest and he has gaol cred. (Prisoner)

It was also reflected in prison services documentation, giving a managerial view:

> For example, one particular inmate ... was a severe self-mutilator and suffered from low self-esteem and a tendency to continually 'mix it' with other inmates, resulting in sanctions imposed and lengthy transfers to the Risdon Prison Hospital.
>
> Mike applied himself diligently [to the prisoner] and slowly won her confidence. We are amazed at the transformation from a troublesome young woman to one talking constantly about a future and looking forward to release from prison, as well as now having a good rapport with staff.
>
> As this programme is totally independent of the prison system the inmates are less suspicious of Mike therefore discussing confidential issues that they would not discuss with

staff so staff wholly support the continuance of this programme and look forward to the valued support of Mike in the future. (Internal document, women's prison, 20.11.01)

However, the 'outsider' status, while beneficial from a service perspective, appeared in some instances to create problems and tensions from a prison operational perspective. As observed above, this reflects a perennial issue within any custodial situation; namely, differences between 'custodial' and 'human service' priorities, and the relative emphasis that is placed on security versus services.

The prisoners valued this particular program and thought it provided a useful non-institutional avenue for inmates to reduce/relieve the stresses associated with incarceration by having someone to talk to and communicate with, and that it enabled them to liaise better with their families and loved ones. It also offered an avenue to release pent-up emotions. However, the prison authorities had mixed attitudes towards the program, due to problems in how it was introduced and implemented, how funding was established and subsequently allocated for the program, differing perceptions among prison officials regarding the status and role of a 'lay' worker within a prison environment, and the perceived lack of reporting and accountability of a prison-funded program. It was notable that the support worker himself was inevitably placed in an ambiguous position due to the nature of the work. On the one hand, to do the job requires certain personal qualities and task-related attributes; on the other hand, these very qualities and attributes may be seen as inappropriate in secure punishment facilities. This is a catch-22 situation that can only be resolved by careful consideration of the philosophical rationale guiding prison management and prison programming.

How custodial staff and professional staff relate to each other, how outside agencies work with correctional officials, and the quantity and quality of resources within the prison environment will, however, all have a major impact on the prison experience. The role and place of 'outside' workers within the prison service is a matter requiring a lot of further thought – such workers are invaluable to the rehabilitative task and the goals of restorative justice.

The kind of occupation you are in and the specific tasks you have been assigned play a major part in how you see your job and how you relate to others within the prison. The other significant divide in terms of prison workforce is that of gender. Prisons are predominantly populated by male inmates. Most prison officers are male. The ratio of male to female workers who work inside a prison varies according to whether or not they are prison officers, teachers, health workers, or other kinds of professionals. Basically men predominate among those who work in the most coercive or hard end of the criminal justice system, as indicated in Table 3.3.

The importance of gender in terms of prison culture is highlighted in *Stories from the field* 3.1. Being a female prison officer carries with it quite distinct challenges, in part stemming from the male-dominated nature of both prison life and prison work.

Table 3.3 Comparative correctional workforce data by gender and country

| Type of data | England and Wales | Scotland | United States |
|---|---|---|---|
| Male | 64% | 75.3% | 66.7% |
| Female | 36% | 24.7% | 33.3% |
| Total number of staff | 51,239 | 4,007 | 419,637 |

*Note*: This data refers to people who are employed in correctional facilities or prison services.
*Source*: Adapted from Bureau of Justice Statistics (2008); Institute for Criminal Policy Research (2009); Scottish Prison Service (2009).

### Stories from the field 3.1

### The challenge of being a female officer in a male prison

Female officers working in a male prison will always encounter a range of stereotypes and attitudes significantly different from those faced by male officers. The number of female prison officers working in a male prison has dramatically increased over the past few years. Females have, in the past, been seen as a risk to the security and good order of the prison. I have attempted to capture the experience and challenges faced by myself and other female staff working in a male prison. This paper is an attempt to explain what is 'normal' for female officers. What is normal is not what is necessarily acceptable.

*Prison*
Prisons are not a normal environment, and as such do not allow people to foster the normal relationships that they would have outside of the prison environment. Within the prison setting there have been two distinct groups of people, them and us, good and bad,

crims and officers. There has been a change over the past few years as we have started to see an increase of 'others' coming into the prison, 'others' including education, therapeutic services and outside support services. The opening up of our prisons has allowed inmates to have more contact with females.

Prisons have their own very distinctive culture and there are also different cultures within different groups of people.

### Prison officer culture

Prison officers that are exposed to danger or to a perceived danger tend to be suspicious of what they see as 'outsiders'. The same could be said for the military and police officers – what people see as closed ranks, or codes of silence, is what these professions use to protect themselves from any outside criticism. Prison officers are constantly on alert to signs of danger, violence and offending behaviour from inmates. Prison officers often become isolated from the general community when socialising. They tend to socialise within their own groups away from other people. This leads to solidarity and a strong sense of belonging among these officers. Prison officers have protection or perceived protection under the code of silence. There is a set of unwritten rules underpinned by an exaggerated need for internal solidarity and loyalty which demands, *inter alia*, that the prison officers do not criticise one another, and do not scrutinise each other's behaviours too critically. Female officers are expected to conform to this code of conduct, but their male counterparts are still often suspicious of their intentions of working in the prison.

### Female officers in a male prison

Despite the increasing number of female officers they are still comparatively rare and simply because of this they will attract the attention of both inmates and male officers. Most female officers will be able to describe the feeling of walking into a yard or areas where there are only male prison officers and having all conversation stop.

In a predominantly male environment in which the majority of inmates are in a state of forced celibacy, this can result in female officers becoming the focus of unwarranted sexual attention. Some of the sexual attitudes can be foreign to some female officers, as they may not have experienced this outside prison. Inmates will notice if you change your perfume, have your hair cut in a different style, wear different make-up or jewellery. Inmates will comment on all these and

*continued*

other things concerning your appearance. Your body image can also take a battering. Inmates have no problems telling you if you have put on weight or your thighs are big. It can be very difficult for some females in the beginning to cope with this criticism. These comments can lead to you having problems with your own self-image. You may also become a sex object for some inmates. It is not uncommon for a male inmate to call you over to a cell door to speak to you and the inmate is masturbating behind the door. Female officers may be told by inmates what they would like to do to them in a sexual way. This can range from 'I want to make love to you' to 'When I get out I am going to find you, tie you up and rape you'. Neither of these two comments are acceptable in any way and need to be dealt with seriously.

These comments to female staff can often be ignored by their male colleagues. I have heard male officers make comments: 'What does she expect? This is a man's prison.' The nature of the sexual comments will often change depending on the female officer's response to it. If she is perceived to enjoy it, it will escalate; she is further devalued and loses her professional credibility. However, if she ignores it or responds icily, she is a tease, who enjoys tormenting inmates by reminding them of what they cannot have. So what is the best way to approach the sexual comments in jail? I have found the best way to deal with this issue is, as soon as the comments are made, to speak to the inmate quietly, one on one, and point out that you do not make comments about what *they* look like, the fact that they may be fat or ugly or other faults they may have, and you don't expect them to make comments about you. This should be done in a direct and firm manner. When inmates are confronted in this non-threatening approach, this will often stop the problem, as females have different ways of dealing with issues. If the inmate has mental health issues, this will be dealt with in a very different way.

There is also the sexual stereotype that you must be a lesbian or hate men. This may be triggered by the female officer's appearance. Most prisons in Australia have rules regarding how you are to wear your hair if it is below collar length. These rules state that you must have your hair tied back. It is often easier to have your hair short, and this leads to the image of 'short hair butch lesbian'. If it is known that the female is single, yet she still rejects the advances of male inmates, it may be assumed that she is a lesbian. This may stem from the underlying belief that women should try and please men, look attractive for them and be available and accept their advances. Rather than viewing the woman's rejection as appropriate and professional, men may feel rejected and reframe it so there has to be something 'wrong' with the woman.

There is also the challenge of maintaining your professional image while working with a large group of male officers. There are relationships between male and female officers. These relationships may be long term or a one-night encounter. They happen and we have to continue to work together in a professional manner. One or both parties may be in a relationship outside prison. I will point out that these things happen but it is not desirable. It is hard enough to maintain a professional standard without being labelled as a 'slut'. Make no mistake, you as a female will be blamed for any problem that comes out of a one-night encounter. The best advice I can give you is DON'T DO IT; it is not worth the trouble it will cause at work.

There are some male officers that still today do not accept female officers in a men's prison. You will hear snide comments; the best thing you can do is ignore them and be the most professional officer you can be. If the comments become harassing or of an unwarranted sexual nature there are processes in place in all prisons for dealing with these issues.

Female officers may also be seen as 'care bears' or at risk of being manipulated by male inmates, much more so than male officers. Because many women have a maternal instinct, it is believed by some that they become easy targets.

Female officers working in a male prison are often territorial. New female staff, especially if they are the only female members of a new recruit group, may find themselves feeling ignored by the other female officers. Female officers are generally a tight-knit group; they may not always be friends but they will share a strong bond. New officers may feel alienated from the main group. Usually the new officer will be accepted by the group, but it may take time. I make no apologies for this; this is the way it is.

I found that one of the most terrifying things as a new officer was walking down the front of the Divisions in the Prison. There were six yards of inmates standing at the wire making comments as my recruit school walked past; but the worst part was the group of approximately fifteen male officers standing at the end of the walkway. No one looked at us, as we walked down towards them.

*continued*

When we had reached about halfway they turned and looked at us, then looked back straight ahead. All I could think about was, I hope my fly in my trousers is done up, and please don't let me trip and fall over. This was the first time I experienced what was referred to as 'Officer Presents'. It was a frightening experience and one I will never forget.

*Guidelines for female officers*

1 *Self-examination* – understand and examine why you want to work in a prison.
2 *Peer support* – use other females and senior officers for advice and support.
3 *Dress appropriately* – be mindful of where you are, and who you are working with. Tight shirts and trousers are not OK.
4 *Be prepared for your intentions to be questioned* – people will question why you are working in a prison.
5 *Stereotypes* – don't be afraid to challenge them; every officer that makes a small change can help break down the images.
6 *Be firm, fair and constant* – always do what you say you are going to do, and never lie to inmates.

*Conclusion*

Female officers have an important role to play in a men's prison. Women can create a sense of normality and balance to an often hostile environment. It is part of the role of female officers to provide a positive feminine image to male inmates. This positive image can only be portrayed to male inmates if a female conducts herself in a positive and professional manner at all times. Some inmates have a history of contact with females that have been all negative; this may have been with family or partners. What we are trying to portray to male inmates is that you can have a friendly relationship with a member of the opposite sex that does not involve violence or sex.

I hope that new female recruits into the prison service go on to become valuable members of a multi-focused team and enjoy the experience of prison life as much as I do.

Geraldine Hayes, Custodial Officer, Australia

Certain social and occupational divisions are important to understanding why and how particular sets of workers tend to act the way they do. For female prison officers there are the challenges of working in what is still very much a male-dominated profession. Non-prison officers likewise have to negotiate their work in the context of facilities dominated by prison officers and their baseline concern with containment.

In summary, working within prisons involves two major competing demands:

1 Meeting prisoner needs – services:
   • *General*: rehabilitation, personal development, community engagement
   • *Specific*: women, sex offenders, mental illness, drug users
2 Ensuring positive containment – security:
   • Officer safety
   • Inmate safety
   • Community safety

Meeting these demands requires many different people, with specialist and generalist skills, working in tandem. Increasingly the work of the prison also incorporates input from those whose primary sphere of activity is working with offenders in the community. It is to this group of workers that we now turn.

## Working within community settings

While prisons receive the press, the more likely place to find offenders is in fact in the community. Prisoner numbers may be growing, but so too is the overall size and reach of the criminal justice system in many jurisdictions. This is illustrated in the graph in Figure 3.3, which shows the number of persons under probation supervision over a seven-year period in England and Wales.

The development of community-based corrections has to be seen in the context of wider developments in the field of criminal justice. Thus, it is important to acknowledge the proliferation of community-based programs and interventions across areas such as crime prevention, diversion from courts, corrections, and post-release programs. In other words, the movement in support of community corrections is related to general tendencies and processes affecting all

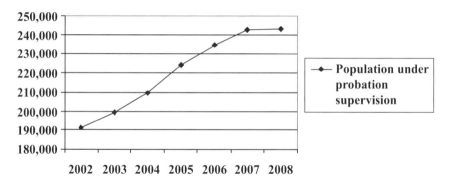

**Figure 3.3** Probation supervision rates in England and Wales – a seven-year trend
*Source*: Adapted from Ministry of Justice (2009a).

parts of the criminal justice system – specifically the incorporation of 'the community' into the criminal justice field at many different levels and in many different ways (see Cohen 1985). Within 'corrections', as a distinctive area of work, there are two general trends of particular note: deinstitutionalisation and decarceration (White and Perrone 2010).

Deinstitutionalisation refers to the shifting of the focus away from institutions and towards community-based options. It involves the use of alternatives to traditional institutional care or imprisonment, and specifically to programs that do not involve locking people up in a detention centre or prison. Nevertheless, they are kept under some kind of control or surveillance in the community itself. The usual or conventional methods of community-based control include things such as probation and community service orders.

Decarceration refers to attempts to remove individuals from the prison environment by minimising the time they have to spend there. While deinstitutionalisation diverts people from prison, decarceration removes them from prison. The term 'decarceration' is also sometimes used in a more generic sense to mean any type of diversionary measure that represents a move away from the use of institutions and which is the opposite of incarceration. The conventional methods of decarceration include things such as parole, day-leave schemes and conditional release orders.

Interestingly, while the prison and community corrections share much in common, they do not always see their mission in quite the same way. Moreover, depending upon the local criminal justice context, and the ways in which offending and responses to offending are configured in politics and policies, several different approaches to community-based intervention can be identified (White and Tomkins 2003). These include:

- *Community incapacitation* – the main emphasis is on concepts of community safety and offender control. This involves intensive monitoring and supervision of offenders in community settings. The aim of community corrections, from this perspective, is to keep offenders under close surveillance and to thereby deter them from reoffending.

- *Community-level rehabilitation* – efforts are made to change offender behaviour in positive ways as well as improve community relationships by use of supportive, participatory measures. The aim of community corrections, from this point of view, is to prevent recidivism through behaviour modification *via* some type of therapeutic or skills-based intervention. The emphasis is on personal development and enhanced capabilities.

- *Restorative justice* – involves the offender in activities intended to repair the harm to victims and the wider community. The aim of community corrections, based upon restorative assumptions, is to restore harmony through the offender doing something for and by themselves to make things better in the community. The emphasis is on improving the well-being of offender, victim and community.

These approaches are both time-bound in that they come to prominence at different points in time and space-bound in that they take hold in different places in different ways. Importantly, these describe broad system tendencies, within which workers have some leeway to do their own thing or to protect their own jobs until things change to match their own expectations. Consider, for instance, one review of recent community corrections history in the United States:

> In the 1970s and 1980s, in response to a more retributive focus on corrections generally, community supervision and parole agencies also began emphasizing the surveillance and punishment aspects of their work. 'Tail 'em, nail 'em, and jail 'em' became an accepted operating norm in some supervision agencies. In the course of studying the dissemination of new approaches to case management and classification in the late 1980s, it was not

uncommon to hear some community supervision staff refer to themselves as 'treaters in hiding'. This characterization suggests the climate of the time with respect to a treatment focus – as well as the conviction on the part of many in the field that treatment interventions with offenders were still an essential element of community corrections. (Burke 2001: 17)

Community corrections workers deal with offenders who have in common many of the social characteristics and complex needs of the prison population (especially considering that many offenders in community corrections are there as part of post-release programs). There are nonetheless differences in the population groups that are worthy of brief comment. For a start, there are proportionately more women offenders under some type of community-based order than in the prison population. This is illustrated in Table 3.4. On the other hand, both men and (in countries such as Canada, New Zealand and Australia) indigenous people (male and female) are over-represented in prisons and in community corrections relative to their population size in the general population.

In a similar vein when it comes to the gender of offenders, there are many more female professionals working as community corrections officers than as prison officers. Furthermore, these workers tend to be better educated and more likely to have university-level educational credentials than prison officers. These factors, too, can be a source of tension between the two overlapping parts of the corrective services.

The circumstances under which community corrections workers perform their work differ from their prison counterparts as well. They do not work in a total institution, but under much more 'normalised' conditions in the community. Many work a nine-to-five job, since there is not the compulsion of shift work as necessitated by a total institution. Issues of containment, therefore, are not issues as such for community corrections workers, even though matters of safety and security still feature prominently. Stress is often associated with high numbers and the intensity of caseloads, rather than length and time of shift.

There are unique challenges to the work that further serve to mark it off from working within a prison setting. For instance, community corrections workers have to learn particular ways of working that involve interviews with offenders, home visits, and group work. Community-based work may involve engagement with offenders in residential care settings, halfway houses and various rehabilitation and

Table 3.4  Offender characteristics in community corrections in Australia, 2007–08

| Type of data | NSW | VIC | SA | WA | QLD | NT | ACT | TAS | Australia (Total) |
|---|---|---|---|---|---|---|---|---|---|
| **Male** | | | | | | | | | |
| Number | 15,141 | 6,259 | 5,208 | 4,211 | 10,896 | 1,015 | 1,196 | 890 | 44,815 |
| Percentage | 84.2% | 80.6% | 81.3% | 77.9% | 79.7% | 88.1% | 85.0% | 79.3% | 81.6% |
| **Female** | | | | | | | | | |
| Number | 2,786 | 1,392 | 1,197 | 1,195 | 2,769 | 137 | 212 | 232 | 9,920 |
| Percentage | 15.5% | 17.9% | 18.7% | 22.1% | 20.3% | 11.9% | 15% | 20.7% | 18.1% |
| **Indigenous** | | | | | | | | | |
| Number | 3,213 | 342 | 988 | 1,723 | 2,528 | 868 | 123 | 133 | 9,918 |
| Percentage | 17.9% | 4.4% | 15.4% | 31.9% | 18.5% | 75.3% | 8.7% | 11.9% | 18.1% |
| **Non-indigenous** | | | | | | | | | |
| Number | 13,952 | 6,726 | 5,388 | 3,672 | 11,138 | 283 | 1,173 | 958 | 43,289 |
| Percentage | 77.6% | 86.6% | 84.1% | 67.9% | 81.5% | 24.6% | 83.4% | 85.4% | 78.8% |

*Source:* Adapted from Australian Commonwealth Government Productivity Commission (2009).

therapeutic communities. The work inevitably requires working with non-government agencies and many different stakeholders, including offender families. A key tension within community corrections is the line between giving direction and support to offenders, and having to breach them for failure to comply with court-ordered or legislated conditions.

Specific types of community corrections are designed with specific purposes in mind. They may be devised as alternatives to prison, as tough but community-based sanctions, and as methods of restorative justice. Examples of these are provided below.

Examples of alternatives to prison (diversion options) include:

- *Boot camps* – often a short period of imprisonment, what the Americans term 'shock incarceration', followed by intensive supervision.

- *Intensive supervision probation* – normally involves intensive supervision, compliance with monitoring conditions (such as urinalysis testing for drugs) and attendance at treatment programs.

- *Electronic monitoring* – occurs in a range of different ways, often within programs known as 'house arrest' or 'home detention'. It basically involves the offender wearing an arm or ankle band that can be electronically monitored (for example, when they leave the house or certain vicinity it sets off an alarm at headquarters).

- *Day centres* – offenders attend a centre where activities related to reducing offending behaviour are conducted.

- *Periodic detention* – strictly speaking not a part of community corrections, this type of measure allows a sentenced prisoner to be at liberty in the community on a defined basis. They are held in custody on a part-time basis only, usually consisting of two consecutive days in a one-week period.

Alternatives to supervision (tougher options) include:

- *Community service* – involves offenders engaging in some fairly extended term of service to the community. It is hoped that the offender will not only repay their dues but also make useful contacts that will serve to reconnect the person to mainstream society.

- *Community-based order* – provides the surveillance and guidance that traditional probation might have provided, but also attempts to go further towards achieving a reduction in the needs or risk factors that seem to propel offenders towards criminal behaviour.

- *Fine option* – this is a community-based sentence where the offender is serving a sentence for default of a fine. In most jurisdictions this order type requires an offender to complete community service as a reparatory act.

Alternatives to retribution (restorative options) include:

- *Juvenile conferencing* – this is based on the idea of bringing the young offender, the victim, and their respective families and friends together in a meeting chaired by an appropriate independent adult (juvenile justice worker or police officer). Usually some kind of apology is made by the offender to the victim, and often the offender has to repair the damage they have caused in some way (for example, through undertaking community work, or mowing the lawns of the victim for a month).

- *Indigenous courts* – these may involve some form of circle sentencing where the emphasis is on community participation. Remedies are sought with the advice of indigenous community elders and the process takes into account special circumstances faced by offenders, cultural practices and the impact of crimes in their communities.

- *Victim–offender mediation and reparation* – involves discussions involving victims and offenders about the nature of the offence, and how best to provide some kind of recompense or reparation for the harm caused.

Working with offenders in a community setting thus applies to many different types of work, informed by quite different institutional principles and criminal justice philosophies. There is nothing inherently progressive or rehabilitative about community-based corrections. In fact, a source of tension is the increasing bureaucratisation of community corrections, alongside the increase in professionalism, with more administrative requirements accompanied by very high caseloads. This is illustrated by the following probation officer perspectives about frustrations in their work role (quoted in Annison *et al.* 2008: 264–6):

It [the job] is far more about case management and administration than actually working with offenders.

I find it sad that the effective work I had hoped to do with offenders will not be possible owing to high case loads, and I can see that most of my time will be spent working with high risk offenders.

The sheer volume of worthless, needless, repetitive paperwork and bureaucracy. It's like ivy – parasitic, and covers and strangles the true purpose of probation.

Yet the content of the work very much depends upon the institutional context and the nature of the approach adopted by community corrections workers. For example, community service as such should not be equated with either rehabilitation or with restorative justice. Walgrave (1999) discusses how in some judicial settings authorities use community service as a punishment (that is, intended to inflict pain), while in other settings it is informed by a rehabilitative objective (as manifest in various forms of re-education and treatment). In further contrast to these approaches, he argues:

> … community service can also be used in a restorative sense, if it is meant to compensate for harm, restore peace in the community and contribute to safety feelings in society … Attention will now be turned to the harm and the restoration of it, including the reintegration of the offender, as this is an important item in restoring peace in the community. (Walgrave 1999: 140)

As we saw in Chapter 2, the most effective forms of intervention are said to be those directed at criminogenic causes (see Bonta and Andrews 2007). Nevertheless, the social context within which these factors become significant is also now seen as a critical contributor to the offending behaviour and cannot be completely ignored (see Ward and Maruna 2007). Research indicates that programs that seek to address offender risks and needs must cut across the full suite of variables known to influence reintegration, relating to intrapersonal conditions (physical, psychological and emotional health, substance abuse and educational levels), subsistence conditions (finance, employment and housing) and support conditions (social support, formal support services and criminal justice support) (Shinkfield and Graffam 2009).

In this regard some jurisdictions are moving to supplement the risk-need-responsivity approach by drawing upon the Good Lives Model in ways that individualise offender interventions according to determined physical, social and psychological needs. This approach introduces a self-management dimension to community reintegration, which focuses on enhancing offender skills to prevent reoffending. Offender management is also underpinned by notions related to therapeutic jurisprudence, which is concerned for the well-being of individuals within the criminal justice system. Together these theoretical models highlight the importance of correctional staff in engaging offenders in pro-social ways, and the importance of adopting strengths-based approaches to re-entry.

The relationship between prison work and community-based work is complex and relates to organisational models of intervention as much as sanctioning practices. What affects the relationship between 'in prison' and 'out of prison' work is also the ratio and balance between use of incarceration and use of community-based options. This balance, in turn, reflects the priorities of the overall criminal justice system at any one point in time.

- Where there is an *increase* in the use of imprisonment, and a *decrease* in the use of community corrections, this represents a significant reliance upon the most harsh and coercive forms of intervention and punishment.

- Where there is an *increase* in the use of imprisonment, and an *increase* in the use of community corrections, this seems to represent a form of net-widening *vis-à-vis* the overall correctional system.

- Where there is a *decrease* in the use of imprisonment, and a *decrease* in the use of community corrections, this indicates greater reliance upon diversionary measures, whether these be restorative conferences or fine default schemes.

- Where there is an *uneven trend pattern* relating to participation across either or both imprisonment and community corrections, this seems to indicate local factors affecting fluctuations in offender numbers, and corrective services and policies that are highly contingent upon immediate political, judicial or operational variables.

These contextual variables have a major impact on the working conditions and task orientation of both those who work in prisons and those who work in the community.

Discussion of community-based corrections and prison-based corrections also needs to take into account the mundane routines and experiences associated with 'the job'. Each sphere of activity has its own work-related flavour and work culture. This takes the form of how people dress (for example, in uniforms or more casually), how they speak with each other (including different forms of humour), the immediate concerns of the job (containment and rehabilitation emphases) and how the work day and work week are organised (ordinary times or shift-based). Working within a total institution also means that certain days are more significant than others in the lives of both workers and offenders, as illustrated in Scenario 3.1.

Finally, before we conclude, attention can be turned to cutting edge examples that are working towards the end of the prison as we know it, and instead fostering rehabilitative cultures that are sustainable and very effective. One example is the case of Bastoey Prison in Norway, described in Innovative practice 3.

## Paradoxes and controversies

The peculiar place of volunteers and 'outside' workers within a custodial setting means that they are immediately vulnerable to system-related tensions and conflicts. These conflicts relate to the existence of very different conceptions of what prisons ought to do, and the role of diverse workers within the prison system. Interesting dichotomies emerge in service provision, for example, professional support staff versus custodial staff, and tensions between 'security' and 'service' objectives.

Yet, while historically there have been tensions between prison officers and professional workers – as well as between probation or community corrections staff and prison officers – the orientation of many corrective services today is towards integrated models of intervention. This means that a vast array of workers across many different domains of activity (for example, from accommodation case managers through to family planning and women's health workers) are supposed to collaborate with each other on an ongoing basis. Moreover, models of intervention such as integrated offender management demand that community corrections officers provide feedback into and work within the prison for at least part of their work role.

## Scenario 3.1

### A standard day and weekends in prison

A standard day in prison during the week can be intensely busy; it feels intense, and there is a frenzied energy.

During the week there is the usual number of uniformed correctional officers plus a modicum of uniformed managers. The 'others' that make up the staffing complement of the prison are from the government health and human services department; there are nurses and their management, admin support, psychologists, the doctor and the pharmacy staff.

There is the Therapeutic Service team, which consists of the senior psychologists and the five psychologists plus their administration support person. There is also a large number of inmate education staff and inmate welfare and support staff. On any given weekday there are up to 51 non-uniformed staff in the prison.

All of these services move from one area to another and see large numbers of inmates in a short period of time. The movement starts at around 0830, it breaks between 1130 and 1230, and ceases for the day between 1530 and 1600.

All of this and the inmates have visits, education, court, video link-ups, health appointments and out-yard activities. Weekdays are frantic; generally on weekdays there are more incidents. These incidents can be anything from self-harm attempts to inmate fights.

In contrast to this, weekends are 'laid back and casual'. The prison feels relaxed and things seem to run smoothly. There is less than a quarter of the movement around the facility.

There is still a small contingent of nursing staff and they run clinics but this is on a much smaller scale than during the week. Inmates in general are more settled and incidents are less frequent. Interestingly the largest incidents, sieges and riots, have occurred on and over weekends, usually 'kicking off' on Friday afternoon.

Prison officer – Australian prison

*Discussion*
How do you think this can be explained? Do you think that this phenomenon could occur in other jurisdictions?

*Innovative practice 3*

*Eco-prisons and environmental conservation projects in Norway and England*

'Prison' conjures up an immediacy of grey, concrete, razor wire, bars, and enclosed spaces. Yet there are emerging examples of correctional facilities that are the very antithesis of traditional notions of prison. Located on an island one and a half hours from the Norwegian mainland, Bastoey Prison is the world's first eco-prison. Bastoey's environmentally friendly incarceration is cheaper because of self-sustainability through organic farming and renewable energy, fewer staff – in the evenings, four staff supervise 115 prisoners – and no guns (Arun 2007). Daily schedules are busy and focused on competency development and hard work tending to animals and cultivating produce, vocational skills training and recreational sports. Prisoners live in unlocked houses under a prison philosophy of 'human ecology' and taking personal responsibility for motivation and positive change (Associated Press 2007).

Prisoners in England are involved in conservation programs turning prisons into eco-havens for threatened species, nine of which are now internationally recognised sites of specific scientific interest (Randerson 2008). Prisoners are supported to rehabilitate prison grounds, while at the same time rehabilitating themselves through therapeutic diversion, vocational skills development, teamwork, monetary reward, and community contribution. Greening activities range from learning horticulture, cultivating wild flower meadows, pond-digging and tending beehives. Leyhill Open Prison in Gloucestershire has 55 hectares of farmland and gardens, with its 'Time, The Healer' garden winning gold at the Chelsea Flower Show (Randerson 2008).

The traditional 'turnkey' role of corrections has been heavily criticised over many years and has profoundly worked against prisoner reform and client rehabilitation. Prison overcrowding and law and order mandates, however, reinforce a more narrow, instrumental and coercive function for the prison – one based essentially on containment and incapacitation. Tensions between and among workers therefore may stem from different situational, historical and contextual causes. Such tensions are nevertheless important to acknowledge and, as best possible, to resolve if working relationships are to be maintained and enhanced.

## Conclusion

This chapter has provided a review of some of the institutional dynamics that shape worker conditions and practices within a prison and within a community setting. Certainly issues of prison culture have a major bearing on the work that occurs within a prison context, but this culture is also significant for post-release interventions as well.

There are identifiable and very specific workplace cultures, and divisions within these cultures. For example, prison officers can sometimes disagree on whether or not and who among the prisoner population is specifically 'deserving' or 'undeserving' of services. The tension between security and service provision within a total institution environment can also spill over into mistrust of outsiders who are seen as vulnerable to prisoner manipulation or unaware of the seriousness of safety concerns.

How people do their jobs is shaped by the actual material work conditions and physical settings of the job. It is also influenced by pre-existing workplace cultures and traditions, and by the professional attributes and training associated with particular kinds of work. If collaboration is indeed a goal within contemporary corrections, then differences in situation and perspective have to be acknowledged and reconciled with broader institutional goals.

## Discussion questions

1 Identify the 'inside' workers and the 'outside' workers at a local prison or detention centre.
2 How does the kind of work one performs at a prison influence how one experiences prison culture generally?
3 What are the key differences in the working situation and working conditions of prison officers and community corrections workers?

## Further reading

Annison, J., Eadie, T. and Knight, C. (2008) 'People first: probation officer perspectives on probation work', *Probation Journal*, 55(3): 259–71.
Drake, D. (2008) 'Staff and order in prison', in J. Bennet, B. Crewe, and A. Wahidin (eds) *Understanding Prison Staff*. Cullompton: Willan Publishing.

Liebling, A. (2004) 'The late modern prison and the question of values', *Current Issues in Criminal Justice*, 16(2): 202–19.

Tracy, S. (2004) 'Dialectic, contradiction, or double bind? Analyzing and theorizing employee reactions to organizational tension in corrections', *Journal of Applied Communications Research*, 32(2): 119–46.

Trotter, C. (1996) 'The impact of different supervision practices in community corrections: cause for optimism', *Australian and New Zealand Journal of Criminology*, 29(1): 29–46.

Ward, T. (2009) 'Dignity and human rights in correctional practice', *European Journal of Probation*, 2(1): 110–23.

## Key resources

Corrective Services Minsters' Conference (2004) *Standard Guidelines for Corrections in Australia*. Corrective Services/Department of Justice in each state and territory.

Klaus, J. (1998) *Handbook on Probation Services: Guidelines for Probation Practitioners and Managers Publication No. 60*. Rome and London: United Nations Interregional Crime and Justice Institute.

Liebling, A., Price, D. and Elliott, C. (1999) 'Appreciative inquiry and relationships in prison' *Punishment and Society*, 1(1): 71–98.

United Nations (2005) *Human Rights and Prisons: Manual on Human Rights Training for Prison Officials*. New York: Office of the United Nations High Commissioner for Human Rights.

# Chapter 4

# Case management skills

If you can get an inmate something they have a right to, that works really well and makes a big difference to your relationship. But what makes a huge difference to your relationship is if you can't get that thing and you return to them and explain why. Because then you get respect.

(Prison officer, quoted in Cianchi 2009: 49)

## Introduction

Case management is a generic term that is used to represent different models of intervention in various settings used by workers in diverse occupations. Here, discussion focuses on canvassing the issues that arise from practice, and unifying or consolidating information to depict what constitutes a holistic and balanced approach to offender needs, risks and aspirations.

The integrated offender management model is first presented in some detail. Offender management or integrated offender management, in this context, refers to a method of practice that incorporates many different practitioners, over the term of a person's contact with the correctional services system, which addresses multiple issues relating to dynamic risk factors. As used here, integrated offender management does not refer to the integration of probation and police oversight, rather to processes and relationships specific to the work of corrective services as such (but which may include a role for the police). The chapter then outlines the essential competencies in case management, and the main practice issues for case managers. Scenarios are used to illustrate the skills needed in complicated situations in working with offenders.

The point of working with offenders is to improve their chances of not reoffending once they formally leave the orbit of the criminal justice system. The intervention goal is therefore aimed at enabling the offender to desist from crime. Given the multiple disadvantages and complex needs of most offenders, this means that offender management has to be inclusive of many different types of assistance, and oriented towards developmental purposes.

Helping offenders basically means providing them with the resources, the programs and the opportunities to forge new ways of living and interrelating with those around them. Institutionally, this is reflected in budgets, expertise and buildings that offer offenders the services and programs they need to address their criminogenic behaviour and enhance their life prospects generally. Organisationally, it means that practitioners have to be able to tap into a wide range of expert knowledge and professional skills if offender needs are to be met holistically. Systemically, provision of this kind of integrated support also demands that workers across the prison/community rift, and across the government/non-government divide, see value in working collaboratively with individual offenders along the total course of the pathway upon which they are to travel.

Case management is about working with individual clients. Integrated offender management is about doing so in a united and collaborative effort – across time, across institutions and across professions. Each dimension is personal, and each is complicated since it constantly involves dealing with the human factor.

## Offender management

At its core, offender management is basically informed by the view of corrections as a problem-solving enterprise. That is, the point of intervention through offender management is to reduce the possibility of reoffending, and to provide a mechanism whereby offenders can be assisted to help themselves, improve their prospects and attain a 'good life' for themselves.

Offender management (commonly referred to as integrated offender management (IOM) in Australia and New Zealand) refers to an integrated system of intervention that covers prison inmates and post-release offenders throughout the total course of their sentence.

It includes those who have been sentenced to community-based orders as well as those who have been incarcerated. The status of the offender, therefore, does not change the overall orientation of the intervention strategy.

Offender management is meant to be a structured approach to reintegration which relies on the use of standard tools to assess and manage the needs of offenders from induction through to final release. In Australia, for example, many jurisdictions use a variation of the Level of Service/Case Management Inventory (LS/CMI) to assess offender needs or dynamic risk factors, risks pertaining to offender behaviour, and the responsivity of the offender to particular kinds of intervention. The LS/CMI is administered within both prison and community contexts, and is the central tool utilised by practitioners in devising an appropriate intervention response for the client. It provides a comprehensive measure of risk and need factors, and combines risk assessment and case management into one evidence-based system.

Once offenders have been assessed, a comprehensive offender management profile is put together. The next step is sentence planning. This is developed from the information based on the assessment processes. In essence, the higher the assessed risk of serious reoffending, the more intensely the offender is managed (Mellor 2002: 4). This is basically an application of the risk principle of the RNR model. Moreover, assessment also takes into account dynamic risk factors and non-criminogenic factors such as those pertaining to social characteristics and lifestyle choices that may influence future opportunities.

This approach enables the criminal justice system to use consistent and objective induction, assessment and offender (sentence planning and management) processes, and to offer a range of effective and targeted interventions matched to offender status, needs and motivation (Mellor 2002: 3; Newbold 2008: 389–91). Sentence planning is a guide for all interactions with the offender, and specifically guides offender reintegration. Essentially, this is a risk-management approach designed to enhance community protection, as well as preventing reoffending (White and Perrone 2010).

The crux of offender management is that each offender ought to be treated on the basis of *throughcare principles* (see New South Wales Department of Corrective Services 2008). These principles are premised on the idea that there ought to be a continuous, coordinated and integrated system of offender assessment, program allocation, service provision, evaluation of program impacts and smooth transition back into community life. Integrated offender management thus describes the total intervention process between and within institutional and community-based settings, which is designed to reduce the impact on a prisoner of the shift from prison to the community (White and Perrone 2010). Within this framework, a sentence plan may be devised to describe the treatment, educational or vocational options available to an offender once needs and risks have been rigorously assessed. Case management describes the process of implementation of the sentence plan, and includes ongoing evaluation and review (see Merrington and Hine 2001).

The term 'case manager' varies depending upon jurisdiction and occupational context. At its most broad level, a case manager is someone who has central administrative authority in regard to a specific client, and who is responsible for tracking the client as they progress through a system. Manager in this sense signals coordinator. This type of case manager needs to build strong relationships and connections with many other different practitioners, as there is an emphasis on the skills of referral, liaison and generally bringing coherence to an interdisciplinary endeavour. Who and how to respond to an offender is driven by the assessment process and by the availability of suitable practitioners who can be called upon to assist in the reintegration process.

In its more specific manifestation, a case manager may also refer to the person who is responsible for the day-to-day interactions with the client. Another term for this type of position is 'caseworker'. Again, much of this hands-on role necessarily involves referral and liaison work, considering the multiple needs of most offenders and the specific expertise required to work with clients with regard to particular issues (such as sex offender treatment or forensic mental health). Even for those who are involved with direct therapeutic engagement with the offender, therefore, there is an element of working with outside professionals.

There may be some misunderstanding about the proper role of the case manager given the differences in how it is used in different corrective service systems, and indeed in the literature more generally. This can lead to role confusion insofar as the emphasis in generalist practitioner work (such as a probation officer) may be construed as first and foremost that of coordinating referrals and establishing outward-oriented links, or as dealing intensively with a client and referring outwards on a selective basis. The complexity of client needs, and thus the variability of what each client may require, adds to this potential confusion over role. This is examined again later in the chapter.

The complexities involved in administering and implementing offender management are illustrated in Figure 4.1, which provides a pathway analysis of an ideal offender management system. Reducing reoffending is not a philosophy – it is a goal. Typically, prison philosophies are pitched at the level of 'incapacitation', 'punishment', 'rehabilitation' or, sometimes, 'restorative justice'. Principles and practices follow from the key philosophy. This is reflected in daily routines, rules and rule-setting, relationships between prisoner and prison staff, criteria underpinning assessment of everyday behaviour, and so on. The structure, and resource priorities, of offender management will depend upon the philosophical orientation of corrective services as a whole. Conceivably offender management could be organised from the basis of a 'containment' philosophy, but it would look very different from offender management from a 'rehabilitation' (or 'restorative justice') philosophy. Detailed practical implications of various imprisonment philosophies in relation to prison structure, organisation, daily routines, expectations, evaluation and so on would reveal substantial differences at the level of practical implementation.

Another element related to questions of philosophy is the increasing centrality of 'human rights' in discussions of prison organisation and processes (United Nations 2005; see also Chapter 6). There are important issues here relating to the security and safety of prisoners *vis-à-vis* management of prison and the human rights agenda. This

*Throughcare processes*:

Coordination by case manager
Continuous review and evaluation

*Offender management*:

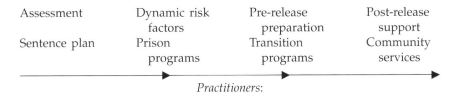

| Assessment | Dynamic risk factors | Pre-release preparation | Post-release support |
|---|---|---|---|
| Sentence plan | Prison programs | Transition programs | Community services |

*Practitioners*:

Prison officers, Prisoner support, External providers, NGOs, Community corrections

**Figure 4.1**   Offender management processes

can be contrasted with the loss of rights perspective, and the notion of civil death (that is, systematic denial of prisoner rights) which seems counter to integrated offender management intentions.

Rather than assuming needs, risks and responsivity, it is important to have a clear idea of the inmate profile at the level of both the individual (age, gender, ethnicity, type of crimes, length of sentence, previous offending) and the subgroup (for example, sex offenders, violent offenders, drug abuse). Resource allocation has to begin where the prisoners are at, as well as be targeted on the basis of length of sentence (under three months, twelve months, over one year, and so on). Alternative sentencing is needed in many cases, especially where, for example, drugs are the issue and problem.

It is also important to look closely at the relationship of sentence planning and case management, and the wider prison environment. The goal of offender management might be to assist with reintegration (and reduce recidivism) by assisting prisoners to 'take responsibility'. Yet, how can they do this in an environment in which there are restrictive prison rules and procedures? Prison is an entirely artificial environment. How can we build into that environment and the prison process greater scope for 'normalisation' and development of personal autonomy (including learning and taking responsibility)? The notion of prisonisation relates to the ways in which the institution itself changes people. How can we modify or change the overall prison culture in ways that enhance a progressive and constructive offender management process?

As elaborated in Chapter 3, prisoners live in the prison. Prison officers, professionals, and support staff (across many service areas, including food preparation and tradespeople) work in the prison. Improving the overall living and working environment is crucial to the possible success of integrated offender management. Prisoner views of their own experiences ought to be taken into account when it comes to planning programs and strategies. It needs to be remembered that the prison, as a home, is also a place where 'bad moods' (that we all get into) can happen and ordinary 'ups and downs' may be either exaggerated or penalised due to the artificial environment. How we deal with these issues will impact upon the success or otherwise of integrated offender management as an approach to offender rehabilitation.

The management of the offender management process itself will generate many and diverse staffing-related issues and problems. The relationship between prison officers and non-custodial staff (especially prisoner support and professional health staff) will need to be worked out carefully. Related to this, it may well be that new divisions emerge between custodial staff who do 'security' and those who do 'case management'. Who has authority and who is seen as doing the 'real work' are matters of occupational culture and executive leadership (King 2009).

How teams are put together in relation to particular individuals, as part of case management, is tricky but needs to be addressed. So too, if throughcare principles are to apply, there has to be a smooth process of transition for the prisoner once they leave the prison – this means outside workers coming into the prison well before the prisoner goes outside. Who is responsible for what becomes important, as does constant liaison between all service providers and custodial staff. Efficient management processes and structures will need to be created.

Another aspect of working together is how staff and prisoners interact. If offender management is meant to provide a stepping stone to reintegration, then it means a possible shift in the relationship between prisoners and those around them. Typically prisons remove responsibility from prisoners, and do so to an extent that is unnecessarily harsh and unproductive, leading to the observation: 'If you want people to behave irresponsibly, don't give them any responsibility, and take away what they have' (Pryor 2001: 4). Given the renewed interest and insistence upon human rights in prison (see Chapter 6), and the declared aim of corrective services in many jurisdictions to treat prisoners with humanity, then it makes sense for those who work with offenders to treat each prisoner individually and to be open to the notion of prisoners taking on greater responsibility even within a highly coercive institutional context.

To put it differently, rather than being treated passively (as someone to punish, or someone to provide treatment for), prisoners need to be encouraged to take responsibility into their own hands (justice as something done by them, themselves). If the latter is accepted, then it is important to have respectful, and to some extent more equal, relations between participants in the offender management process. Related to this is the constructive possibilities of both prisoner mentor schemes and interventions that allow external opportunities for giving – helping others is often a vital step in helping oneself (see Innovative practice 4).

### Innovative practice 4

#### Freely give, freely receive: the value of offenders doing voluntary work for charity

Initiatives enabling offenders to volunteer in charity shops in England have been heralded as a form of 'retail therapy', emphasising skills building and personal development. Both symbolically and practically, this form of rehabilitation exemplifies a form of social inclusion because offenders work alongside community members with pro-social lifestyles and give something back to their community, with a total of 36,000 voluntary hours notched up by offenders in England each year (Leverton 2009). One offender speaks of the importance of trust and building new healthy relationships: 'Meeting the ladies who ran the shop was like a therapy in itself. I saw a completely different side to humanity. Most of them had never had a parking ticket. They asked me questions, which made me ask questions of myself' (quoted in Leverton 2009).

Maruna (2007) argues strongly for voluntary work to be merited with the same therapeutic and rehabilitative value as other more structured cognitive interventions. Benefits for offenders include an improved sense of self-worth, accomplishment and purpose, community mindedness (for example, through helping charities or repairing wheelchairs), putting them 'in the dignified position of being a help-giver rather than a passive help-receiver' (Maruna 2007).

### Essential case management competencies

There are various skills and competencies required of caseworkers, in accordance with an individual's job position. People come to do case management from different professional backgrounds, such as social work, counselling, allied health and so on. Also, with changing models and institutional cultures, a practitioner may find their role changing. For example, a prison officer who may have formerly had responsibilities centred primarily on supervision and security may find their work transitioning into that of correctional case manager with responsibility for dealing with the prisoner as a whole person with complex needs.

Caseworker functions may vary in different settings but all have in common the assessment of clients' needs, strengths and deficits, the development of a comprehensive treatment plan, linkage with necessary services, monitoring of service delivery and participants' advocacy. The list provided in Table 4.1 is by no means comprehensive, nor is it presented in any order of importance. It is a preliminary list of a scoping nature, one that arose out of a whiteboard session in a workshop with practitioners and criminology students when the question was posed 'What makes a good case manager?'

**Table 4.1** Core competencies, skills and attributes of a case manager

| Interpersonal attitudes and attributes | Core skills and competencies | Interventions and tools |
| --- | --- | --- |
| Empathy and compassion | Engagement and establishing rapport | Motivational interviewing |
| Non-judgemental | Role clarification | The LS/CMI |
| Integrity and ethics | Screening and assessment | Psycho-education |
| Flexibility | Reflective listening | Group work facilitation |
| Resilience | Intake and/or discharge procedures | Relapse prevention |
| Discernment and insight | Treatment/sentence planning | Cognitive behavioural therapy |
| Consistency and stability | Goal setting and problem solving | Communication skills training |
| Hope | Risk management | Life skills and recreational/ lifestyle planning |
| Respectful and encouragin | Referral and collaboration | Anger management |
| Sense of humour | Caseload prioritisation | Assertive community outreach |
| Sense of justice | Ethical and legal knowledge around confidentiality, information-sharing, and mandatory reporting requirements | |
| Tenacity and backbone | Managing non-compliance, boundary testing | |
| Motivator | Conflict resolution | |
| | Crisis management | |
| | Coping skills and self care | |
| | Administrative skills and time management | |
| | Professional writing/case notes | |
| | Advocacy, supporting empowerment and client participation | |
| | Aftercare and throughcare | |

Over the next few pages we will explore some of these issues. Specific tools and interventions are covered in greater depth in Chapter 5.

## Approaches to Casework

The development of a comprehensive case management approach should involve elements such as:

- Assessing, planning and brokering services and programs
- Reviewing offender outcomes and compliance
- Evaluating the impact of services and programs
- Designing a process for offenders leaving the system to be linked into community supports and services.

To do this, practitioners need to have a good working knowledge of local resources and agencies, to develop a plan that matches assessments of the client, to liaise with relevant organisations and practitioners, and to continually update knowledge of both client progress and the availability and quality of community partners' contributions. In working with specific clients, case management skills are required such that offenders are active participants in planning and evaluation, they are treated with sensitivity and respect, they are listened to carefully and appreciatively, the limits of confidentiality are clarified, and offenders are offered pro-social models of behaviour by workers. As a process, case management involves a series of identifiable stages (see Merrington and Hine 2001):

1 Screening and assessment (identify needs and risks)
2 Supervision plan (objectives, methods, suitability)
3 Pre-program work (preparation, motivation)
4 During program (support, other issues, progress reports)
5 After program (completion report, follow-up work)
6 Periodic review (needs, revise objectives, alter methods)
7 Final assessment (review needs and risk, seek offender feedback on supervision, assess impact of supervision)

The success of case management depends to a large degree on the practitioner–offender relationship, and this is further discussed in Chapter 6. It also depends upon good record keeping and, especially, the construction of good case notes.

*Screening and assessment*

'Screening' and 'assessment' are used interchangeably, and yet there are subtle but important differences between these two activities that are the mainstay of case management work.

Screening refers to a brief method of determining whether a particular issue, attitude or condition is present (for example, the potential existence of a mental disorder) or is not present (for example, absence or lack of motivation or readiness to change or engage in treatment). It can be undertaken by a practitioner trained to administer a screening tool, but not necessarily qualified to conduct a thorough psychological assessment (which can only be done by a clinician). The aim of screening is to increase the detection of a condition, attitude or state – information that can be used for things like determining who will and won't have access to a pre-release employment readiness program or to help a case manager decide whether the person needs to be referred for a full assessment. Screening for things at the earliest point possible helps with case planning and treatment pathways.

Assessment should be thought of both as an activity, and also as a continuum of activity that happens throughout the length of case management and maintaining a therapeutic relationship with a client. Assessment can be used to monitor various dimensions of a client's well-being, to help a client to discover their strengths and personal capacities for reintegration and rehabilitation, as well as to identify problems warranting intervention or areas of concern. Important critical transition points throughout the continuum of care may include:

- Upon intake
- When a client's situation or state changes, or as a form of progress monitoring reflecting on goal-setting and achievement
- After a crisis
- Discharge planning and aftercare.

Various types of screening and assessment tools appropriate for use with offender populations are listed at the end of Chapter 5.

*Role clarification, client participation and advocacy*

Role clarification is essential to maintaining good boundaries, as illustrated by a comment by a prison officer in an Australian prison (quoted in Cianchi 2009: 46):

> Yes, you can be friendly but not be their friends. I am there for a purpose and they are there for a reason, and if we can keep that in the background for the majority of the time that is good. But if it ever comes to the fore, we have to have an understanding about what part they play and what part we play.

This implies a good relationship, but also the management of offenders' expectations.

It is important that good practice and models of service delivery be informed by the perspective of those it affects – the clients. Ongoing consultation with clients can provide insight into the effectiveness of interventions in the progress of their treatment outcomes. Good practice ensures that client input occurs in the planning, delivery and evaluation of services and approaches. It is important that clients are aware of their rights and responsibilities, to ensure equity and also clarity that can help avoid ambiguity and misinterpretation that may be a component of problematic conflicts in corrective services contexts.

Within the prison or community corrections context, effective advocacy may require some independence; some clients may feel daunted about speaking openly with a person who may be perceived as part of the establishment of which they speak about. Equity cannot be assured unless all parties have a voice and are comfortable in expressing their perspective. Given that those who work with offenders are working with involuntary clients, the question of participation and development of advocacy skills is fraught with confusion and potential conflict.

Research by Rome *et al.* (2002) shows misconceptions among both practitioners and clients about advocacy in the field of alcohol and other drugs. Given that many prisoners are likely candidates for precisely this kind of intervention, it is instructive to carefully consider the issues. Table 4.2 sets out the integrated care perspective on the aims and purposes of advocacy.

Feedback and consultation is vital if case management is to have an interactive and mutually respectful basis. It can be argued that there is little point in achieving well-integrated service provision and excellent partnership if there is insufficient communication and collaboration between service providers and service users – in this case meaning offenders. Advocacy is about informing and empowering the individual client to actively engage in this process of communication and collaboration. Is this possible in what is essentially a coercive service provision context?

**Table 4.2** What advocacy is and is not

| Advocacy is about: | Advocacy is not about: |
| --- | --- |
| • Protecting people who are vulnerable, discriminated against, or difficult to provide services to. | • Creating a substitute for making services more accessible or to bypass user involvement in the planning and delivery of services. |
| • Empowering people who need a stronger voice by enabling them to express their own needs and make their own decisions. | • Avoiding the need to provide person-centred services. |
| • The right of the service user to be heard, and the promotion of a person's rights in an assertive but gracious manner. | • Primarily about making complaints, although advocacy may involve supporting people who want to make a complaint and helping them to do so effectively. |
| • Developing partnership between providers and users of services. | • Subtly putting the pressure on practitioners to comply with client demands due to the presence of an advocate. |
| • Empowering individuals to be active in the provision of their care. | |
| • Being informative and supportive. | |

*Source*: Rome *et al*. (2002).

### Family inclusive practice in case management

An important part of case management is family inclusive practice. Figure 4.2 illustrates the sheer number of children (those under eighteen) affected by high incarceration rates of offenders, many of whom are parents, in the United States. The experience of incarceration can have a significant negative impact on family living on the outside. Families may experience poverty due to the main income earner being incarcerated (see Smith *et al*. 2007).

Prison visits can be a source of stress or even alienation as some families decide not to subject children to the procedures involved in maintaining prison security. Families of prisoners have significant need for clear and up-to-date information – which is often not adequately met, leaving families in the dark and with few services to turn to that will directly support them. An offender's case manager can play a vital role in keeping families informed as well as liaising with offenders about family matters and issues.

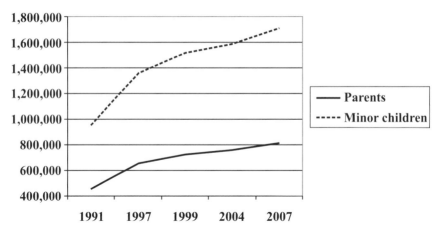

**Figure 4.2** Official estimates of the total number of incarcerated parents and their minor children in the United States
*Note*: 'Minor children' refers to those aged under 18 years.
*Source*: Adapted from Glaze and Maruschak (2009: 2).

Family inclusive practice remains one of the most complicated aspects of holistic approaches to offender rehabilitation in that there is a dynamic interplay and, in some cases, regular change between a person's family embodying the solution as well as the problem. Family conflict and changing family social dynamics can pose challenges for areas such as duty of care, disclosure and obligation, information-sharing and confidentiality. Practitioners have to be sensitive to what is going on in regard to family circumstances, yet not unnecessarily intrude upon the family as such. Another consideration when working with families is the issue of domestic violence, as illustrated in Scenario 4.1.

Discussions of family inclusive work raise a host of issues that go to the nitty-gritty of working with offenders. This is especially so with regard to the provision of a front-line service, and particularly one that is offered in a community context. Consider, for example, the following issues that a community sector organisation may encounter: service opening hours; accessibility for young mothers with prams; buses to and from the service; parking; stigma and public surveillance of who is checking in with your agency; waiting room snobbiness about having to mingle with 'those' kinds of people balanced by real issues of risk and offenders in close proximity to other community members (especially children); receptionist training and awareness of how to speak to clients on the phone and at the front desk. The list could go on – to also include such matters as; in the case of

## Scenario 4.1

### An offender with a history of family violence offending and substance use

You receive a new offender on caseload who has been convicted of family (domestic) violence offences. He has received a twelve-month order. He has been assessed as being at a high risk of family violence reoffending due to a past, less serious, incident with his partner. The police facts state that the victim received injuries to her chest and upper arms and was treated by her GP for ongoing chest pain. It also states that the offender required medical intervention, including twelve stitches to his hands and forearms.

A statement obtained from the victim states that the offender regularly drank to intoxication, and at these times he would become abusive and sometimes violent towards her. She advised that on this occasion he had come home late from the pub and due to his dinner not being hot he grabbed her by the arms and dragged her out of bed, and proceeded to kick her chest while she was on the floor. He then left the room. She heard a loud smashing sound and went into the lounge to find that he had fallen through the glass door, cutting his hands and forearms on the broken glass.

At the first supervision session the offender informs you that he feels he has been treated unfairly by the legal system, as he was acting in self-defence and was not the instigator of violence in his relationship with the victim. He explained that she had attacked him with a knife and he had held his arms up to prevent her from stabbing him in the chest and face. He explained that after she had stabbed his hands and forearms she lunged at him again, so he pushed her in the chest to get her off of him. She then fell to the ground so he pinned her down by the arms until she dropped the knife.

You now have to develop some goals with the offender to address his offending.

*Question*
How do you approach this, given he has advised that he was acting in self-defence, and would never intentionally hurt a woman?

long interventions, the practical value of regular breaks (for smoking among other things); taking time out for reflection; whether to write down information on the spot or to rely upon memory; and so on. How practitioners carry out their tasks, and the immediate surrounds and circumstances accompanying that work, will have an impact on how family friendly and family inclusive the intervention will be.

## Case notes and report writing in the criminal justice system

Case notes are what caseworkers rely on as their official source of documentation (see Scenario 4.2). Recording all actions and interventions with or about a client is essential to effective case management. Written casework information is a means of accountability to the client and the organisation. Case notes also ensure continuity of service, especially for clients who may transition between different workers and areas within a service and between services.

Why are case notes important? Healy and Mulholland (2007: 68) outline several reasons why they are so foundational to professional practice. Case notes are:

- A vital information base for client work

- A way of clarifying the case situation for both the practice worker and the client

- A means by which workers and service users can make visible to others, such as team members, aspects of the social context of the client's needs that might otherwise be ignored

- A method of promoting opportunities for collaborative responses in health and community services teams

- A means of promoting good practice

- A vital information base for the achievement of consistency in social work intervention.

In the event that staff are required to recall information for legal purposes, through attendance in a court of law or to quote a specific intervention or session in a court report, correct recording of information will assist staff to respond in a truthful and accurate manner. If case records are not written objectively they may be deemed inadmissible for legal proceedings due to stringent court standards. Service provision to clients with complex needs may result in extensive dealings with the legal system, and high-quality case notes act as a form of protection for all involved.

## Scenario 4.2

### Report writing in the criminal justice system

Criminal justice practitioners are expected to demonstrate impressive resumés showcasing practice skills, front-line experience, diverse knowledge, and applied training qualifications. An often overlooked but influential and important aspect of criminal justice work is the ability to write. Professional writing reflects a worker's professional opinion, areas where they have exercised discernment or discretion, their values and the motivation for the outcome they are hoping to achieve. Pre-sentence reports are a good example of what is meant by this.

A pre-sentence report is a generic term used to describe a type of report that is used in a lot of different jurisdictions to assist a criminal court of law. Although 'the precise practices vary, broadly speaking, pre-sentence reports provide the sentencing courts with information, advice and assessment about, *inter alia*, the personal and social circumstances of the convicted person as well as about their character, offending behaviour, physical and mental condition, normally leading to an assessment of sentencing options' (Tata *et al.* 2008: 835).

Practitioners from different disciplines in the criminal justice and health fields may be asked to write a pre-sentence report for the court, for example, social workers, clinical psychologists, professional counsellors, and medical or psychiatric practitioners.

*Questions: Are pre-sentence reports neutral or objective? Consider the type of language that is expected in these reports. How would you go about expressing your professional opinion? What types of words or statements should be strictly avoided in a court of law?*

Sentencing and report writing in criminal justice involve political and social dimensions and processes that go beyond the immediate concern of the correction of an offender. Inter-professional working, relative professional status, and the daily working of bureaucracy all influence how these reports are constructed (Halliday *et al.* 2009). In other words, the content of a pre-sentence report will bear some imprint of various factors:

*continued*

- Whether the report writer is employed in the community sector or by a government correctional agency.

- The quality and quantity of information available to the report writer (for example, social workers in England have access to witness and police statements, but social workers in Scotland do not).

- The professional status (and its relativity to other occupations) of the report writer, for example, a social worker as compared to a clinical psychologist or psychiatrist and the social standing of each of these different occupations in relation to the legal fraternity and judges.

- Tensions on behalf of the report writer about which hat to wear when providing advice to the court, for example, balancing a welfare or therapeutic 'hat' with a punishment or correctional 'hat'.

- The policy and political 'flavour' or leaning of a particular judicial officer or court.

- The policy and political flavour or leaning of the current government.

*Questions: What are the kinds of punishment objectives that need to be balanced in the process of sentencing an offender? What types of information about the offender would a report writer need to use to reflect or give advice in relation to these different objectives?*

In a four-year ethnographic study of the inter-professional relations involved in pre-sentence report writing by social workers in Scotland, Halliday and colleagues (2009) uncovered some interesting social processes at work. As mentioned above, participants in the study found that report writing is a professional activity that evokes some conflicting tensions. The researchers found that:

> Social workers still experienced much more ambivalence concerning potential conflicts between the needs of the judge as sentencer and the offender as a subject of social work support ... [Offenders] are the ones with whom the social worker interacts, discussing their life histories, and attempting to seek ways forward to address their offending behaviour ... Often offenders face multiple and complex problems in their lives ... Those who present to the criminal justice social work

teams then, are not only offenders, but are people with needs who evoke responses preoccupied as much with care as with justice. (Halliday *et al.* 2009: 413)

*Questions: Who is the client or 'consumer' of a pre-sentence report? Who is the target audience?*

True to the welfarist imperative of strengths-based rehabilitation to empower clients, therapeutic workers often focus on meeting the needs of the offender. Yet report writing must be done bearing in mind issues of risk management, reducing recidivism (as distinct from purely supporting responsivity and criminogenic need) and promoting community safety and interests. It must comply with the legal dimensions and requirements of the type of professional language and advice that is admissible in a court of law, as well as respecting the legal obligations placed on the worker through things like privacy laws governing the jurisdiction in question. Add to this the social dimension of professional relationships and the study found that all of this becomes a complex process.

Social workers in the Scottish study were insecure or uncertain of their place in the legal system and 'concerned about their credibility as criminal justice professionals. Reports were written, in part at least, as a way of seeking esteem and credibility in the eyes of judges – a motivation that undermined the policy objectives of social enquiry in sentencing' (Halliday *et al.* 2009: 405). One participant stated a fear of being perceived as 'naive', another stated apprehension about the possibility of judges laughing when reading their report (Halliday *et al.* 2009). To overcome this, workers may often endeavour to construct an account or narrative in a way that leads to a 'logical conclusion', revealing personal preferences and hoping to leave lasting impressions through the power of suggestion and a cynical belief that judges 'skim read' reports to get to the point (Halliday *et al.* 2008: 211). In summary, the Scottish research reveals important social factors involved in how, why and for whom reports are written – the human side of criminal justice work.

A final point to note is that pre-sentence report writing is also increasingly subject to a managerial or bureaucratic impetus to streamline and improve the calibre of these reports to comply with a high standard of streamlined reporting, as part of a wider push for quality improvement (Tata *et al.* 2008).

*continued*

> *Question: What kinds of strategies or approaches can a practitioner use to balance the competing demands and social dimensions of criminal justice report writing?*

### Practical tips for keeping good case notes

All records, electronic or otherwise, should be made as soon as possible after the intervention or event to maintain a high level of accuracy. Case notes should always note the date, time and essential details of the contact and any further actions required. All records must be signed in person or electronically. It is important to note only the facts of an intervention or support session, and to avoid any speculative comments based on hearsay or opinions unsupported by documented evidence (see Case study 4.1).

The following tips (adapted from Best Practice in Alcohol and Other Drug Interventions Working Group 2000) may be useful in enhancing your case recording skills:

- Always maintain clear and up-to-date case notes.

- Always tell clients about the presence of client files, where they are stored, who has access to them and why client files are maintained. Clients have the right to apply for access to their files where the privacy or freedom of information legislation allows (dependent on jurisdiction). Write client case notes with the assumption that clients may read them.

- Any written information may be subpoenaed and required as evidence in a court of law. Avoid any statements of opinion, speculation, judgements or value statements about the client.

- Only record information that is considered important to treatment.

- Avoid transporting case files or client notes. You never know when your car will be broken into, your house burgled, or your bag stolen. If you must transport client case notes, for the purposes of clinical supervision for example, only ever transport photocopies of the original documents, with key identifying information blotted out.

- Case notes should be signed and dated. Do not use correction fluid; if you make a mistake, cross it out. If you make alterations at a later date, sign and date them.

- Write what you observe. If you must record interpretations and opinions, provide the evidence that led to the conclusions.

- Don't record suspected psychological or psychiatric diagnoses, unless the diagnosis has been given by an appropriately qualified professional. If this diagnosis is recorded, clearly state how you gained the information.

- When you write about what a client has said to you, make it clear where the information came from. For example, 'John stated that …' or 'he reported that …'

- When a client expresses suicidal ideation, self-harming thoughts or behaviours, or thoughts or behaviours of harm to others, record very carefully all the steps taken.

### Recording information related to case collaboration or referrals

When documenting exchanges of information about a client between your agency and another, record the following in your case notes (from Best Practice in Alcohol and Other Drug Interventions Working Group 2000):

- Who supplied the information (name, title, agency, position in the agency, their relationship to the client).

- How the information was supplied (letter, face to face, fax, email, phone).

- Why the information was supplied (who asked for it and why).

- If any action is planned as a result of the liaison, what is the action, who is responsible for its implementation, and when it will be completed by.

- Whether your client (the agency, or others) are at risk, and what steps are to be taken to minimise that risk.

Additionally, case formulation, or a formal case presentation, is not just important to coincide with screening and assessment or cognitive behavioural therapies. Objectively writing up a case history will be useful for case reviews with the therapeutic team, as well as for any court reports or reports required for other agencies and purposes.

## Case study 4.1

### Writing up client assessment information into a professional case history in case notes

The following information is a hypothetical case study about a male offender. His profile is given in verbatim-style quotes, representing information that has been gained during his initial assessment and court proceedings. Your role is as his alcohol and other drugs caseworker, and he has been referred to you by an integrated offender management case manager in the government Department of Justice.

*Practical exercise: your brief*
As a caseworker, your task is to translate this verbal conversational information into written professional case notes, to a standard that may be admissible to court at a future date, if required. Case notes cannot be subjective, conversational or speculative. They need simply to state the objective facts. Write up a formal case presentation by distilling this information into a formal case history under the given headings: Criminogenic and offending history; Family of origin; Substance use; Health; and Post-release.

| | |
|---|---|
| *Name:* | Jason Michael Smith |
| *Gender:* | Male |
| *Age:* | 30 |
| *Criminal charges:* | Unlawful entry with intent, break and enter |
| | Theft |
| | Resisting the direction of a police officer |
| | Breach of suspended sentence |

Jason Smith was referred to this service on 6 January 2010 by an IOM caseworker, Adam Adamson, who sent you the client's information *via* fax. Therefore, you have gained the following pieces of information from two sources: an assessment of the client undertaken in the week before he was released from custody and from an intake assessment done at this service, completed on 9 January 2010.

• *Criminogenic and offending history*
Jason's first contact with the law was at the age of fourteen years, when he was caught by police stealing things from a local shop. He was given a few cautions by the police, but didn't get into any serious

trouble at that stage. However, he was charged and first went to court at the age of sixteen years.

'Yeah, I got caught out driving a car, doing a few tricks, when I was sixteen. I didn't have a licence, didn't want to be arrested either. I'd been drinking, and acted up a lot for the policeman when he tried to breath test me 'cos I knew it wasn't going to be good. The cops charged me, it went to court, and I got sent to a youth/juvenile detention centre for eight months.'

Jason reoffended again, and was caught at the age of 20 and prosecuted for theft and property related offences.

'They sent me to prison again for a year, but this time it wasn't juvie, it was an adult prison. That was shit … I got caught again for stealing when I was 25, but got off a bit better that time because I'd supposedly been of good behaviour for a few years [laughter]. Yeah, the judge gave me a suspended sentence on the condition that I stopped my wicked ways and was of good behaviour.'

- *Family of origin – information and background*

Jason's parents' names are Tracy Jones and Rick Smith. He lived with both of them for the first five years of his life. His says that his mum and dad split up because they used to argue all the time and his dad would get really violent.

'When they split up, they had one hell of an argument. My dad bashed my mum, broke some bones and her face looked pretty bad too. I f*****g hate him for that. Someone called the police, he got charged with assault, and went to prison. I didn't see him after that, didn't want to. Mum went off the rails for a little while after that, it screwed with her head. She had a few boyfriends, and so we had to move around a bit. All the house moving, moved school a few times. I hated school, wanted to get out of there. F*****g teachers just didn't understand.'

Jason says that he was close to his grandmother (his mother's mother), Sheryl Jones. When things got rough between his mum and her partners, he went to stay with her. This happened a bit throughout his childhood. Unfortunately his grandmother died when he was twelve years old.

- *Substance use*

'I started smoking pot when I was thirteen. But I didn't get onto the hard stuff, Speed, until I was sixteen.'

*continued*

Jason became addicted to the amphetamines and, in order to keep up his habit, he did a lot of burglaries and theft to get the money to pay for the drugs. He says that he finds it hard to cope without them, and would like professional help in order to stop using drugs and prevent any future reoffending. This was the reason he was referred to you for alcohol and other drugs rehabilitation, and will be seeing you on a weekly basis.

• *Health*
'When I was in prison, the doctor there did an assessment and a few tests. They told me that I've got hep C that probably came from a dirty needle; it bloody well scared the shit out of me. A real wake-up call, that's for sure ...'

Now that Jason has been released into the community, he would like professional support to help him know how to deal with living with a blood-borne virus and chronic health condition. A referral to another agency is required in this area, so you have chosen to make a referral to a local agency to provide hepatitis C support.

• *Post-release*
Jason Smith was released from prison on 6 January 2010. One of his bail conditions involves a requirement that he is not to meet up with or have contact with former pro-criminal associates. Jason has said that this may be difficult because a lot of people that he knows come into this category. Now that he is out of jail, he doesn't have a very big social support network.

He is staying with his mum at the moment until he finds a more permanent place to stay for the long term; he is currently looking for a unit. Jason wants to get in touch with and see his two children now that he has been released. The other goal that he has expressed is to find a job in a manual trade.

'I'd like to become a tradie because I'm fairly good with my hands, I hate office paper-pushing type jobs, and 'cos tradesmen earn a fair bit of money too.'

Jason has signed a Release of Information Authority giving his consent for you to make referrals and liaise with other practitioners and agencies involved in his care.

*Exercise*
Now that you have read through his assessment information, try writing this information into a formal case history, as stated in the brief at the beginning.

## Worker accountability and workforce development

An essential part of case management is adequate record keeping and ensuring that what one does is transparent and accountable. Accountability takes a variety of different forms and we underestimate at our peril that which makes the wheels turn. There are different facets to accountability that are important to making the life of a worker or agency easier in the long run.

### Record keeping and client progress

As indicated above, in order to work efficiently you need to keep good records. Good skills in paperwork are even more essential if you want to do a trend analysis, to see how performance is stacking up over time. For example, data needs to be collected on who is going through the system, and how they are progressing as they do so. Record keeping need not be too onerous, however. It may involve the use of *pro forma* sheets consisting of a simple tick-a-box information sign-off.

### External scrutiny

Adequate records and reports are important as well in instances where files are demanded by outside agencies or by clients. Court subpoenas, client complaints and applications under freedom of information legislation may translate into opening up of files for close scrutiny. This means that files have to be professional and complete; otherwise, there is the danger of being implicated in things untoward and possibly ethically corrupt and professionally incompetent. Ombudsmen, official prison visitors, correctional service inspectorates and the like can use investigatory powers to unpack and closely examine what it is that workers claim to do in their everyday practices.

### Resource allocation

When it comes to resource allocation and prioritisation, it is essential to know how to make our work more effective, to put resources where they count. This is especially the case where there is limited staff. For example, measures need to be put into place that allow assessment of who is or is not responsive to particular intervention programs. It is no use wasting time, energy and staff resources on clients who basically do not want to participate in a particular program. Targeting of resources is part of being accountable for those resources. In a similar vein, responsivity is not only about abstract assessment, but could also be as simple as making sure that the worker who best connects with a certain client is the worker assigned to that client.

## Performance indicators and quality improvement

We always work within a specific organisational context. Our work therefore must dovetail with agency philosophy, its business and resource planning, and key performance indicators. Measures of personal performance and measures of agency performance need to be clearly set out, and developmental strategies attached to any kind of staff review process. This is an essential component of the broader quality improvement agenda of an organisation. It is not only clients who can benefit from evaluation of strengths and limitations, needs and risks. Self-assessment is a useful tool to help guide quality practice.

Accountability is not only about reports and performances, but about priorities within certain organisational constraints. For instance, from a management perspective, it is necessary to prioritise resource allocation in the most effective manner (White and Perrone 2010). This might take the form of a *casebank model*. This refers to an organisational method of allocating resources in which non-targeted offenders are ranked in order of level of risk and needs, and as individuals move through the system resources that have been freed up are distributed on the basis of the ranking order. Offenders who are deemed to be low risk and low needs may receive very little in the way of direct supervision or intervention by correctional services staff. Conversely, those deemed to be high risk and high need will be allocated supervisory staff and program support as a matter of priority. They collectively constitute targeted cases, and are thus not considered suitable for the casebank model.

Selection of programs for offenders depends upon the quality of the assessment process, the ways in which offender interventions are prioritised and allocated, and the availability of programs. There may be conflicts over whether to put time, energy and resources into generic programs (such as employment or education) or specialist programs (such as anger management and sex offender). Much hinges upon whether or not trained professional staff are available to offer various types of programs. So, too, unless community-based programs are evaluated and monitored closely, then there is no way of really knowing how a program is assisting an offender or is working to reduce the likelihood of reoffending (White and Perrone 2010).

Accountability is about how best to marshal human resources so as to ensure competency in performance and receptiveness in execution. It depends upon three key components:

1 *Communication* – of goals, of activities, of problems, of expectations, and between staff, managers and subordinates.
2 *Information* – about strategic concepts, about good practices, about case examples.
3 *Conflict resolution* – concerning work performance, pay and conditions, differences of opinion or perspective.

In addition to system-level processes and procedures relating to communication, information and conflict resolution, it is vital that individual workers be guided and mentored in their work. In this regard, forms of professional supervision can be useful. This might include, for example, supervision of milestones, such as preparation of an 'individual management plan' and closure of offender files, and mentoring and guidance in the day-to-day operations of offender management.

### Clinical and general supervision

Clinical supervision, another form of external support as well as scrutiny, is helpful for practitioners to be more reflective on improving the quality of their work. Best practice in this area is for organisations to offer all case management staff independent clinical supervision that is paid, set at regular intervals (with additional appointments in special circumstances) and during work hours. This precious time away from the client caseload is certainly not a case of time wasting, but of killing several birds with one stone, so to speak.

Supervision should be seen as integral to staff relations and work performance, rather than as a threat to professional autonomy or individual discretion. Working in the areas of human services requires considerable discretion. Decisions have to be made in the field on the basis of informed judgement regarding specific offenders, specific situations and specific potential outcomes. Supervision that is too close or that is based upon inflexible rules will diminish the ability of practitioners to perform their tasks. Supervision that mentors rather than directs allows for improved work performance.

The criminal justice and corrections sectors are influenced by often complicated factors and complex relationships with offenders, colleagues and managers. Supervision and accountability mechanisms can assist workers when they are placed in uncertain or difficult circumstances that may seem minor but involve relational ethics to inform decision-making (see Bergum and Dossetor 2005), as illustrated in Scenario 4.3.

There are many other issues that impact upon how well people work together and the conditions under which this occurs. The type of human resources available, capacity for professional development,

---

### Scenario 4.3

#### An offender has a death in the family and asks you for a favour

You have been working as a case manager with an offender subject to a community-based order for the past twelve months. You have developed very good rapport with the offender and he has progressed very well, having not reoffended at all during the past year. You have never had any issues with him, and he is always on time and friendly during sessions. His father has recently passed away and he has identified that he is planning to travel to be with his family and to attend his father's funeral. He has received written authorisation to travel in order to attend the funeral, and will be gone for one week.

He is very upset by the death of his father and has come to you for assistance. He advises you that he does not have any family locally, as they all either live a great distance away or are travelling with him for the funeral. He reminds you that one of the goals you and he developed in relation to reducing his risk of reoffending was to cease contact with all past criminal associates, and he has done this. However, he has not formed any new associations or significant friendships, so now he feels that he has no one he can trust for support.

He then asks you to take care of his cat while he is away, stressing that he has no other option, and without your assistance he would be forced to give the cat away, and it is his only companion in life. You don't have long to respond because he is about to go away, and you feel a little unsure of organisational policy in this regard.

#### Questions

How do you respond to this request? How are you going to balance accountability to him and accountability to your professional obligations as a case manager and your organisation?

---

processes of recruitment and retention of staff, and basic workloads all impinge upon both work and accountability processes. We also have to acknowledge the fact that this sector of work is frequently in a state of constant change, with new people and new interventions being introduced and others leaving. Yet in some ways the essential problems do not change and neither do the solutions. Knowing what your role is (role delineation), healthy boundaries (such as between yourself and your client), good writing skills, empathy and so on are fundamental to the task regardless.

## Paradoxes and controversies

Case management is widely held as an efficient means of tailoring service provision to meet the needs of the individual. However, one unforeseen side effect of the model is that it tends to turn the criminal justice worker into a broker of services. That is, some have interpreted integrated offender management, and case management as a form of practice, to mean that the primary job is to shunt the offender into services and programs that match the offender's specific needs. While the offender is viewed holistically in the sense of having complex needs warranting close assessment, the intervention result tends to be fragmented insofar as each specific identified need requires specialist support from different people working in different agencies.

The paradox is that workers who have been in the system for a long time see their best work as when they deal with the 'whole' person, and their most effective input is in the development of a therapeutic relationship. The old model of case management emphasised relationships over services, whereas the new model tends to put the emphasis on finding services rather than building core relationships. Indeed, some argue that it is the quality of the relationship between worker and offender that most counts in forging a pathway to desistance from offending. Relationships are built upon trust and time. Service provision is about coordination and responsivity to situational requirements (such as expertise in education, training and employment or drug and alcohol expertise).

One of the unintended consequences of a brokerage model of case management is that many workers now feel that they are being deskilled and their professional training devalued because they are no longer actively working holistically with that particular offender across their spectrum of needs. Workers who have been university educated in a professional area such as social work or psychology may wonder when and how they will marshal their expertise if their job is mainly interpreted as involving referrals to other agencies and services. They become a coordinator of services rather than foundational practitioner. This pressure is exacerbated by increasing bureaucratisation and administrative responsibilities placed on case managers, as raised in Chapter 3.

A second tension is the increasing bureaucratisation of community corrections, alongside the increase in professionalism, with more administrative requirements accompanied by very high caseloads. This probation officer's perspective refers to the barriers and challenges of their work: 'There is, of course, pressure to achieve targets rather than achieve quality work – but so far it has been possible to balance these uneasy bedfellows' (quoted in Annison *et al.* 2008: 264).

The increasing push towards service improvement using certain types of performance measure can, ironically, diminish the prospects of providing a good and useful service. It also changes the core attributes of the job for practitioners.

## Conclusion

This chapter has discussed various practical facets of the doing of case management within the context of the model of integrated offender management. Among the many issues and conundrums faced by practitioners are those squarely related to the fact that those with whom we work are involuntary clients. This means that, as always, there is a delicate balancing act between fulfilling rehabilitation objectives and ensuring community (and personal) safety.

One limitation that may arise from this is that a culture of compliance may override other considerations. This is especially so if governments insist upon strict regimes of control with little leeway for error. The result is a trend towards 'breaching' – that is, targeting and acting upon failures of offenders to comply with specific conditions related to their court-mandated sanction, and to their corrective services devised sentence plan. To avoid excessive breaching, it is important to develop strategies for helping offenders to comply with orders.

Simultaneously, practitioners need to be aware of the strengths, and limits, of the use of discretion, and to use their discretion creatively and professionally in case management. Practitioners also have a significant role to play as advocates for offenders, and in supporting offender participation. These latter should not be seen as 'add ons' to working with offenders. Developing offender skills and capacities will ultimately require a degree of trust, responsibility and 'letting go', albeit within a structured process. At the heart of good case management, therefore, is the development of an effective worker–offender relationship.

## Discussion questions

1 Discuss the key features of integrated offender management as a particular approach to reintegration.
2 Discuss the key skills and competencies required to be an effective case manager in the field of criminal justice and corrections.
3 Power and control are key issues for consideration when working with involuntary and vulnerable populations, for example, forensic mental health. How would you manage issues of power and control in a case management role?

## Further reading

Barry, M. (2007) 'Listening and learning: the reciprocal relationship between worker and client', *Probation Journal*, 54(4): 407–22.

Godly, S., Finch, M., Dougan, L., McDonnell, M., McDermeit, M. and Carey, A. (2000) 'Case management for dually diagnosed individuals involved in the criminal justice system', *Journal of Substance Abuse Treatment*, 18(2): 137–48.

McCormack, J. (2007) *Recovery and Strengths Based Practice*. Glasgow: Scottish Recovery Network.

Ministry of Justice (UK) (2009b) *Intensive Help for Vulnerable People: Applying Case Management Models in the Justice System Research Summary 8/09*. London: Ministry of Justice, United Kingdom.

## Key resources

Bland, R., Renouf, N. and Tullgren, A. (2009) *Social Work Practice in Mental Health*. Sydney: Allen & Unwin.

Gursansky, D., Harvey, J. and Kennedy, R. (2003) *Case Management: Policy, Practice and Professional Business*. Sydney: Allen & Unwin.

McIvor, G. and Raynor, P. (eds) (2006) *Developments in Social Work with Offenders*. London: Jessica Kingsley Publishers.

McNeill, F., Batchelor, S., Burnett, R. and Knox, J. (2005) *21st Century Social Work – Reducing Re-offending: Key Practice Skills*. Edinburgh: Scottish Executive.

O'Donohue, D. (2004) 'Using constructive challenge during intervention', in J. Maidment and R. Egan (eds) *Practice Skills in Social Work and Welfare: More Than Just Common Sense*. Sydney: Allen & Unwin.

United Nations Office on Drugs and Crime (2008b) *Handbook on Prisoner File Management*. New York: United Nations.

**Chapter 5**

# Tools and interventions

What would a successful or miraculous outcome look like?

> A client who has outgrown you, who tells you what they have
> done, why they did it … and is aware that they have thought
> through the process; who has reached the point where they
> actually want to be and who can see where they are going. It's
> not necessarily important where they are going but that they can
> see something ahead that they are aiming for. And … that they
> have ceased offending or, at least, drastically reduced offending;
> and I suppose that at some point they have confronted the
> reasons for it.
>
> (Probation officer, quoted in McNeill 2000: 390)

## Introduction

Active intervention and support requires workers in the criminal justice
and community sectors to have good understanding of and experience
in using various tools in their professional toolbox. This chapter
provides an overview of general and specialist interventions that have
a sound evidence base as well as description of the competencies
intrinsic to a skilled worker. Common tools used in criminal justice and
corrections include such things as motivational interviewing, cognitive
behavioural therapy, risk assessment, and anger management. In our
intervention framework, the focus of these tools is strengths-based
rehabilitation and person-centred practice to promote desistance.

## Differences between treatment and rehabilitation

A distinction can be made between treatment and rehabilitation because both entail different models. An example from the alcohol and other drugs sector highlights this difference. The word 'treatment' in this sector has connotations of relating to physical addiction, medical intervention, primary health care and pharmacotherapy. A clinical perspective of rehabilitation focuses on changing the specific behaviour – substance misuse – but may not take into account contributing factors because these are not targeted specifically by chosen modes of treatment. The client adopts a relatively passive role as recipient of treatment, relying on the clinical expertise and judgement of the professionals administering or facilitating the treatment.

The term 'rehabilitation' refers to therapeutic interventions and holistic health and social care – to restoring the person as a whole. Therefore, a residential rehabilitation centre may facilitate treatment for the biological bases of the addiction and substance misuse problems, and also be instrumental in rehabilitating a person to ensure that they are able to recover both physically from their drug problem and also psychologically and socially, and achieve overall well-being.

### Restoration and rehabilitation

Restorative justice refers to an emphasis on dealing with offenders by repairing harm, and in so doing involving victims and communities as well as offenders in the reparation process. Restorative justice thus emphasises reintegrative and developmental principles and offers the hope that opportunities will be enhanced for victims, offenders and their immediate communities, with the direct participation of all concerned in this process.

Of particular interest here, with respect to what can be learned from restorative justice in regards to our example of drug rehabilitation, is the emphasis on active agency. This refers to the idea that people are to be held directly accountable in some way, and that they are meant to do things, themselves, rather than simply be passive actors in the criminal justice (or drug rehabilitation) system.

Restorative justice is complementary to the rehabilitation model, especially because it encourages active client engagement and competency development. This does not negate the use of individual treatment; instead it demonstrates how individual treatment can take place in tandem to complement broader competency development practices. The differences between individual treatment and restorative competency development are demonstrated in Table 5.1.

One relevant argument of proponents of restorative justice is that 'through understanding the human impact of their behaviour, accepting responsibility, expressing remorse, taking action to repair damage, and developing their own capacities, offenders become fully integrated, respected members of the community' (Bilchick 1998: 5). It is an approach that treats all people with dignity and worth, and this is balanced with the obligation of the offender to put things right (Bilchick 1998).

**Table 5.1** Differences between individual treatment and competency development practices

| Individual treatment | Competency development |
| --- | --- |
| Group and family counselling | Peer counselling, leadership development, service projects, and family living skills |
| Drug therapy and drug education | Youth as drug educators and drug researchers |
| Remedial education | Cross-age tutoring (juvenile offenders teach younger children) and educational action teams |
| Job readiness and job counselling | Work experience, service crews, employment, job preparation, and career exploration |
| Recreational activities | Youth as recreation aids and recreation planners |
| Outdoor challenge programs | Conservation projects, community development projects, recycling and community beautification projects |
| Cultural sensitivity training | Youth-developed cultural education projects |
| Youth and family mediation | Conflict resolution training and youth as school conflict mediators |
| Mentoring and 'big brother' programs | Work with adult mentors on community projects and intergenerational projects with the elderly |

*Source*: Bilchick (1998; adapted from Bazemore and Cruise 1995).

It can be argued that residential rehabilitation, likewise, provides a positive intervention point and opportunity for working on things such as capacity building and integration. Residential rehabilitation centres involved in court-mandated diversion of drug offenders are presented with the opportunity to consider their role in being a community of support that could promote the above goals and tasks. In a restorative justice context, competency is defined as 'the capacity to do something well that others value' (Bilchick 1998: 19). Restoration is a communal exercise, one that encapsulates principles and processes relevant to drug rehabilitation. It also represents a move towards more in-depth values-based practice.

Characteristics of restorative competency development include:

- Strategies build on the strengths of offenders, families and communities.

- Clients are given a role in work, family and community that instils a sense of belonging, usefulness and control. Clients have active roles that allow them to practise productive behaviour.

- Cognitive learning and decision-making are integrated into active, experiential and productive pursuits.

- Treatment and services (such as counselling) are used as supports for the overall restorative process rather than in isolation.

- Clients work and interact with law-abiding people within the community.

- Delinquent and non-delinquent people are mixed whenever possible to avoid the image of programs for problematic or 'bad' people.

- Activities are designed with input from the community.

- Opportunities are provided for clients to help their peers, children and people who are disadvantaged.

- Group experiences and teamwork are emphasised frequently.

The following are roles for professionals to undertake (adapted from Bilchick 1998: 19–22):

- Assess client and community strengths, resources and interests.

- Develop community partnerships with employers, religious institutions, clubs and civic groups to provide work and service roles for clients on supervision, and recruit supervisors.

- Find creative, active roles for offenders in treatment programs as helpers to others.

- Develop projects in which clients can be trained in areas such as mediation, conflict management and drug prevention, and then educate others.

- Involve clients in program planning groups and committees with staff and other adults in the community.

These strategies are accompanied by the expectation of any or all of the following possible positive outcomes. Offenders benefit from (a) 'the increased capacity to contribute to their community', (b) increased bonding to positive role models and conventional adults, (c) improvements in self-image and public image, and (d) 'measurable increases in educational, occupational, social and decision-making abilities' (Bilchick 1998: 22). The community has an increased capacity to accept and integrate people who have previously been problematic, and increased positive involvement in the criminal justice system (Bilchick 1998). Building the competencies and capacity of offenders, as well as the community's capacity to help them, are both advantageous undertakings. Positive reinforcement and constructive development results in better outcomes than those that do not include rehabilitation, reintegration, or capacity building as part of their mandate. A real example of restorative competency development is highlighted in Innovative practice 5. This story is helpful in that it also challenges the notion that a professional toolkit consists only of interventions that are overtly therapeutic by nature.

## Approaches to working with involuntary clients

As has been mentioned previously, 'involuntary clients' is a term used to refer to people who are in some way mandated or coerced into receiving service provision. Yet in practice it can often be more complex than just mandated or voluntary. There is often a continuum between those who are completely, and often legally, mandated and those who are completely voluntary in their choice to participate in a given service or program. Offenders tend to sit on the continuum closer to the first position. For example, a court may explicitly order that a person does something as a part of their bail requirements, or a parole board may mandate something as a condition of release. A medium level of coercion is the choice to participate in a therapeutic

### Innovative practice 5

### Good news stories: prison radio and in-house media training

Electric Radio Brixton is an award-winning 24-hour radio station fully operated in-house at Brixton Prison, by prisoners for prisoners. And by 'award-winning', this is not therapeutic tokenism for good deeds, but taking out two formal accolades in the competitive Sony national radio awards in the UK. Supported by the Prison Radio Association, an educational charity, and with the full support of the prison governor, it is heralded as having tangible results in prisoners' lives:

> If prisoners are nearing the end of their sentence, the station can prepare them for release, advising how to re-establish or maintain the relationship with the family, how to find accommodation, further training or employment, and how to address issues they may have while they're in here such as bullying or drug misuse. All of these are issues which have been identified as key to reducing re-offending. (Maguire, quoted in Douglas 2009)

In Downview Prison, female prisoners are being offered media training, including the opportunity to do a BTec in media and video production, through a project run by Media for Development. Graduates of the scheme can apply to work for the prison's broadcasting unit, which produces programs played on the in-house TV system, including an X Factor style talent contest called 'Drop It Like You're Hot' (Moulds 2008). In addition to entertainment value, the development of life skills and professionalism are clear components:

> Just the process of interviewing somebody, learning to look them in the eye, learning to defuse a tense conversation in order to get your interview and not let it degenerate into a fight; those things are not necessarily skills that everyone has picked up by this point. So it's a great way of doing it without putting them in a room and calling it anger management. They just pick up all those skills by stealth. (Nandi, operations director, quoted in Moulds 2008)

justice initiative, for example a drug court or mental health diversion measure, because the other choice is often incarceration.

Practitioners who work with this type of client develop in-depth skills and practice wisdom that stem from the unique nature of supporting this client group. The focus of the therapeutic relationship becomes motivation and communication to overcome the difficulty of working with someone who would not necessarily choose to be part of this relationship if it had not been for criminal justice sanction or coercion. Many different types of occupations are involved in working with involuntary clients, including child protection officers, domestic violence counsellors, probation or parole officers, alcohol and other drug workers, forensic mental health, and disability support workers. Table 5.2 explores the efficacy of different strategies in working with involuntary clients, including problematic or counterproductive approaches that should be avoided. This resonates with the sentiments expressed by a front-line mental health worker: 'How have different services put the policy into practice? What works best in different areas? And, importantly, what hasn't worked? I often wish we had more courage to be honest about what doesn't work, and then we could learn from that' (quoted in Hawkings and Gilburt 2004: 60).

Consulting the evidence base and research into efficacy can yield surprising results, especially in the section on 'approaches that sometimes work'. This guide to clinical practice is not intended as way of telling practitioners what to do; it is included to stimulate practitioners to examine the context within which they utilise certain interventions. When working with this specific population of clients, a one-size-fits-all raft of interventions will not yield the best possible outcomes (Rooney 2009). The contextual use of specific interventions therefore needs to be reconsidered in preparation for the influx of court mandated offenders out of the criminal justice system into health and welfare systems and the community sector, with the aim of achieving better practice and outcomes. The theme of this section is the importance of flexibility and the situational context for what works in given circumstances. The question of the effectiveness of different approaches also raises issues of accountability and competency of staff in relation to clients.

## Evidence based practice tools and interventions

The following section focuses on providing a brief outline of tools and interventions commonly used in offender rehabilitation. There

**Table 5.2**   Effectiveness of approaches to working with involuntary clients

| Approaches that work |
| --- |

- **Role clarification** – outcomes are improved for involuntary clients when workers focus on helping them understand the role of the worker and the role of the client in the direct practice process.

- **Reinforcing and modelling pro-social values** – involves the worker affirming and exemplifying 'pro-social' actions and values that are tolerant, non-criminal, and support and care for others.

- **Collaborative problem-solving** – involves working with the client's definition of the problem, developing achievable goals that are the client's but are collaboratively developed, and identifying strategies with the client to achieve those goals. CBT can help this.

- **An integrated approach** – integrates all of the above approaches to holistically promote improved personal development and outcomes.

| Approaches that sometimes work |
| --- |

- **Empathy and reflective listening** – popular counselling techniques; however, the research support for the use of empathy with involuntary clients is somewhat vague.

- **Humour** – can be an appropriate tool to use in the helping professions, and can be used to humanise situations or ease tension. However, it is imperative that humour be used in a way that is appropriate to the situation, the style of the worker, and the client's ability to see the humorous side. Misguided or fake humour may damage the worker–client relationship.

- **Optimism** – can promote hope, expectation and self-efficacy. However, in the case of involuntary clients, it must be used appropriately and not in a way that invalidates the client's emotions by always trying to make everything positive and upbeat.

- **Self-disclosure** – there are varying perspectives among workers on self-disclosure, and the extent or context in which it is appropriate or inappropriate is uncertain. Clinicians must use their judgement and have the sole motivation of the disclosure helping the client.

- **Case management** – widely used, although it has been criticised as being symptom-focused instead of person-focused, and needs to be more holistic. Consistency of approach to a client who has complex needs and multiple service case managers is another issue. However, individualised case management that is responsive and informative may be effective.

*Table 5.2 continues opposite*

*Table 5.2 continued*

---

- **Short-term versus long-term intervention** – time-limited specific interventions are more appropriate for some client groups, whereas others (e.g. drug addicts) may benefit from longer-term intensive and holistic interventions.

---

Approaches that don't work

---

- Approaches that **blame, punish or judge** clients with the hope of change.

- Interventions that **just focus on insight** and the relationship, without including pro-social or problem-solving dimensions.

- Interventions that are **not person-centred** but instead focus on worker goals for the client.

- **Pessimism** about the client's capacity for change and a lack of encouragement for positive behaviours.

- Situations where there is **uncertainty about roles** with the client or the worker, or the purpose of the intervention.

- Where there is a **lack of clarity** about what is negotiable and what is not negotiable with involuntary clients.

- **Poor modelling by the worker** especially with behaviours such as lateness, unreliability and lack of follow-up.

---

*Source*: Trotter (2006: 21–7, 31–40, 53–4).

is only room for description to take the form of an overview or a scoping exercise, rather than a historical presentation of the origins and theory of each approach or any in-depth analysis. Front-line workers may be familiar with many of these psychosocial techniques, as they are the mainstay of work at the coalface. Students or people wanting to start work in the field may be less familiar, particularly around practice considerations. As with all therapeutic interventions, use of different tools needs to be commensurate with personal competencies, qualifications, experience and training. Some people find one intervention will really 'click' with their personal world view and approach to their work. But it is more common for practitioners to use multiple and different interventions at different stages in working with an individual offender.

*A proviso: tailoring and matching information to understanding*

Before an exploration of the common tools that make up a worker's practice 'toolkit', it is important to start with a proviso. Any interventions need to take into account the cognitive capacity and learning styles of the individual offender, and may need to be tailored with low literacy needs in mind. Table 5.3 contains sobering data around the reality of literacy levels among prisoners, something that presents a challenge to human services sectors using increasingly sophisticated and advanced therapeutic techniques.

**Table 5.3** Percentages of 'no educational qualification' among prisoners by gender and country

| Type of data | England and Wales | United States | New Zealand |
|---|---|---|---|
| No educational qualification | 46% males 45% females | 40% males 42% females | 52% males 46% females |

*Sources*: Harlow (2003: 1); Ministry of Health (NZ) (2006: 5); Stewart (2008: 10).

The flexible use of pictures, PowerPoint presentations, multimedia (including DVDs, CD-ROMs and audio CDs), and verbal overviews of client handouts and worksheets may assist in overcoming literacy difficulties in prisons and community settings. However, for offender populations that may have particularly high levels of education and literacy, for example white collar offenders and sex offenders, it may be appropriate to keep them stimulated with interventions targeted at fairly high levels of cognitive functioning and communication skills. This reinforces the point made earlier about flexibility and avoiding universal approaches for the masses.

## Motivational interviewing and the transtheoretical model – stages of change

The aim of motivational interviewing is, as its name suggests, to enhance motivation to change behaviour by helping a person to resolve ambivalence (Miller 1996). Ambivalence is a critical opportunity for intervention because it is a common part of the desistance process, therefore, 'the ability to foster and sustain motivation is crucial to effective work with offenders' (Burnett and Maruna 2004, cited in McNeill 2009b: 32). Presentation of factual information in a non-judgemental way by the practitioner is followed by asking the client for their views, and reflective listening helps them to identify aspects of their life or behaviour that are problematic (Hawkings and Gilburt 2004). There are five general principles of motivational interviewing (Hawkings and Gilburt 2004: 46):

1 *Express empathy* – acceptance facilitates change; skilful reflective listening is essential; and ambivalence is normal.

2 *Develop discrepancy* – a discrepancy between present behaviour and important goals will motivate change, and awareness of consequences is important. The client should present the arguments for change.

3 *Avoid arguments* – arguments are counterproductive and defending breeds defensiveness. Resistance is a signal to change strategies and take a different angle or approach. Labelling and judgemental phrases are not appropriate.

4 *Roll with resistance* – momentum can be used to good advantage, perceptions can be shifted. New perspectives are invited but not imposed because the client is a valuable resource in finding solutions to problems.

5 *Support self-efficacy* – belief in the possibility of change is an important motivator, and the client is responsible for choosing and carrying out personal change. There is hope in the range of alternative approaches available.

The 'transtheoretical model', otherwise known as 'stages of change', which was originally developed by Prochaska and DiClemente, is adopted as foundational to understanding how behaviour change takes place. This model contains six stages of change, which are often depicted in a cyclic fashion with arrows illustrating that rehabilitation is non-linear and the order of transition (and potential for recidivism) is unique to each individual. Walters and colleagues (2007) accompany each of the possible stages with statements or thoughts that are common for that stage:

- Precontemplation – denying or avoiding: 'nothing to change'.
- Contemplation – thinking: 'I am considering change'.

- Preparation – planning: 'I am figuring out how to change'.
- Action – doing: 'I'm working on reaching my goals'.
- Maintenance – continuing: 'I've made my changes, now I have to keep it up'.
- Relapse – returning to the problem: 'I've slipped up. Now all is lost.'

Both the transtheoretical model and motivational interviewing can be used widely to address chronic recidivist behaviour and lack of insight, for example, assisting a person to change from a past of gambling addiction, substance addiction, or recurrent petty crime such as driving without a licence or impulsiveness involved with regular shoplifting.

## Evidence and efficacy

There is significant evidence to support the efficacy of using motivational interviewing with offenders (McMurran 2004; Cherry 2005; McNeill *et al*. 2005; Walters *et al*. 2007). The treatment effect works for both incarcerated offenders and those on probation or parole (Harper and Hardy 2000; Clark 2005), and it is also widely used in non-government community sector organisational settings. Research suggests promising evidence that it is suitable for increasing the motivation and receptiveness to treatment of particular offender groups, for example, violent and domestically violent offenders (Kistenmacher and Weiss 2008; Musser *et al*. 2008). Interestingly, despite the fact that motivational interviewing requires a certain level of insight and the cognitive ability to perceive potential for change, it has been advocated as quite effective and appropriate for use with prisoners with learning disabilities who are alcohol dependent (Mendel and Hipkins 2002).

## Practice considerations

Like most interventions, using specialist motivational techniques requires training. That notwithstanding, there are parts of a motivational conversation that exemplify good interviewing techniques and reflective listening skills in general. The emphasis of a conversation is working with a client's comments and concern about their offending behaviour and any interest in desistance or living differently. Some practical questions are listed in Box 5.1.

Following on from this, Table 5.4 is a practical illustration of how some statements and forms of questioning are more beneficial and professional than others because they will have a positive influence

Box 5.1

*Useful questions and statements to use in assessment and motivational interviewing*

Here are some things that we need to talk about (provide a short list). Which of these would you like to talk about first?

Who (or what) will help you?

How can you make that happen?

What concerns do you (or your partner) have?

When would be a good time to start?

How has ... caused trouble for you?

If you look forward to, say, a year from now, how would you want your life to be different?

What are some good things about ...? What are some not-so-good things about ...?

What worked for you in the past?

How would things be better for you if you made that change?

I think that will work for you.

What do you think will happen if you don't ...?

Thanks for your honesty.

Thanks for talking with me.

So the thing that most concerns you is ...

*Source*: Walters *et al.* (2007: 48–9).

on the chance that the person being interviewed will communicate more productively about change (Walters *et al.* 2007).

In summary, the key role for practitioners who are motivating offenders to change is to help them to identify obstacles or barriers to change and to develop the confidence and capacity to take the necessary steps to overcome them, where they can (McNeill 2009b). Motivation for change is an important start in developing human capital, a key ingredient necessary to work towards living a good life (McNeill and Whyte 2007).

**Table 5.4** What to say and what not to say in communicating with offenders

| Trap | What *not* to say | What *to* say |
| --- | --- | --- |
| Playing the expert | You don't have a job because you're not putting in enough applications. | What ideas do you have as to how you might get a job? |
| Arguing the positive side | You need to stop making excuses and find a job. | How would things be better for you if you found a job? |
| Giving unsolicited advice | You need to get up first thing in the morning, get a cup of coffee, and go in and fill out that application. | If you decided you wanted to put in a job application, how would you go about that? |
| Premature focus on change | We've been talking a lot about how important it is to get a job, and this week I'd like you to submit five job applications. | Ultimately, you're the one who has to decide whether you want to put in the hard work to finding a job. What do you think is a reasonable number of applications to put in this week? |
| Asking backward-focused questions | Why did you go to that party when you knew it would get you in trouble? | It sounds like that situation really got you in trouble. |
| | Why haven't you been able to get a job? | What can you do this week to move this forward? |

*Source*: Walters *et al.* (2007: 68).

## Cognitive behavioural therapy (CBT) and rational emotive behaviour therapy (REBT)

Cognitive behavioural therapy (commonly referred to as CBT) is one of the most effective and widely used psychosocial interventions in the western world. The basic foundation of the model is the premise that problematic behaviour and stressful states such as anxiety, depression and anger are often maintained or exacerbated by biased and irrational thinking (Leahy 2003). The use of CBT as an intervention involves teaching a person self-management strategies and tools like cognitive restructuring, doing a cost-benefit analysis, problem-solving, and challenging irrational beliefs. CBT-based skills training has been advocated as particularly effective in supporting the reintegration of offenders (Porporino *et al.* 1991).

Even though there are significant similarities and a high level of complementarity, the distinction must be made between CBT and rational emotive behaviour therapy (commonly referred to as REBT). REBT was developed by an American psychologist, Albert Ellis, in the 1950s. The focus of these therapeutic interventions is around supporting individuals to experience happiness when they set up and achieve important life goals and purposes, overcoming irrational beliefs in the process.

### Evidence and efficacy

The evidence in support of cognitive behavioural therapy is strong and well established (Maletzsky and Steinhauser 2002; Cameron and Telfer 2004; Cherry 2005; Wilson *et al.* 2005). Similarly, REBT has been shown to be quite effective as well (Kopec 1995; Altrows 2002; Dryden and Neenan 2004). The intrinsic appeal and utility of these therapeutic interventions comes from the flexibility and suitability across genders, offence types and correctional and community settings. The self-management tools that are taught to a person in a prison program are based on the same principles and tools that are used in therapeutic support in the community. CBT and REBT are particularly valuable in cases where a person may have been placed on medication as a way to help them cope, for example, benzodiazepines and other sedatives. Medication maintains the *status quo*. Offering a psychosocial intervention alongside medication or as an alternative is advantageous because it empowers the individual with the skills to start to face the underlying issues of why they can't sleep or why they are emotional or have trouble concentrating. This is instrumental in restoring a sense of control and resilience in lives that may have been out of control or had it taken away from them.

### Practice considerations

Both therapeutic interventions require a person to have a reasonable level of cognitive functioning and the ability to learn and retain information. While there may be some efficacy for tailored or modified versions of CBT and REBT to be used with offenders with low literacy levels or learning difficulties, using it with offenders with severe intellectual disabilities or pervasive acquired brain injuries is problematic.

A premier example of both CBT and REBT in practice is the emergence of the SMART Recovery model in community and correctional settings. Originating from the United States, SMART Recovery is an international non-profit organisation that offers free evidence-based mutual support groups for people wanting to deal with and recover from addictive behaviour. SMART is an acronym for Self Management And Recovery Training, and involves open, anonymous and voluntary participation in group discussions with peers with the goal of teaching practical skills for a healthy lifestyle (SMART Recovery Australia 2009). It is now offered in various countries, including Canada, England, Scotland, Australia, New Zealand, India and Iran.

The SMART model combines four key therapeutic approaches, which are quite complementary: rational emotive behaviour therapy, cognitive behavioural therapy, the social learning approach, and the transtheoretical model (stages of change). The innovative aspect of the SMART Recovery movement is that it utilises these four rehabilitation tools in a way that is accessible to those with addictive behaviour; it is focused around peer support, with facilitators there to complement or guide the flow of the group. In essence, it is not practitioner directed but peer directed. Yet it represents a distinctive move away from traditional self-help movements such as twelve-step programs and Alcoholics Anonymous, because the model advocates strict avoidance of any labelling of self or others as an 'alcoholic' or 'addict', there are no sponsors, or overt spiritual content, and participants are encouraged to attend for as long as they need – usually months or years, but not a lifetime.

The two major SMART Recovery programs in use in correctional facilities are 'Inside Out' in the United States and 'Getting SMART' in Australia. These variations of the SMART model have been designed to address identified criminogenic needs, including substance misuse, acting as an intervention to reduce recidivism (Henry-Edwards 2009). The Getting SMART materials were developed in close consultation with the target group, including a substantial amount of artwork by offenders and a low-literacy friendly approach to psychological recovery techniques. The most promising aspect of both Getting SMART and Inside Out is that the programs emphasise throughcare as paramount, encouraging ongoing participation post-release in SMART groups in the community.

In summary, the SMART Recovery movement dovetails well with the Good Lives Model and social recognition approach because the content and method offers participants the various therapeutic and practical tools necessary to support the building of different forms of capital and primary human goods in their life to work towards recovery and desistance.

## Anger management

Anger management is a common component of offender rehabilitation. There are a diversity of programs, from focused individual interventions addressing specific offending behaviour or personal characteristics and beliefs, through to general group programs offered to address common causes or roots of anger and aggression. Most anger management therapies are influenced by, if not entirely based on, principles of cognitive behavioural therapy and the stages of change model.

There are four main categories of intervention that are used alongside each other to identify and address the underlying issues of anger (Reilly and Shopshire 2002: 1):

1 *Relaxation* interventions which target emotional and physiological components of anger and any associated anxiety.
2 *Cognitive* interventions which target cognitive processes such as hostile appraisals and attributions, irrational beliefs, and inflammatory thinking.
3 *Communication skills* interventions which target deficits in assertiveness and conflict resolution skills.
4 *Combined* interventions which integrate two or more cognitive behavioural therapy interventions and target multiple response domains.

### Evidence and efficacy

In general, research has shown that anger management interventions have moderate to strong efficacy (Del Vecchio and O'Leary 2004). One study found that CBT-based anger management interventions were 76 per cent more effective, compared to those who received nothing, when used with people with complex needs, like mental health and substance dependency (Reilly and Shopshire 2002). However, there are some researchers who have highlighted concerns about limited

## Scenario 5.1

### Boundaries and issues in running an intensive group program with offenders in the community

You are working in a community sector organisation running a group-based intervention program with a group of eight offenders. Attendance of the program is fed back to the relevant probation officers case managing these offenders. You conduct the pre-program interviews and there are no identified responsivity issues; some of the more introverted guys are a little reluctant but all the offenders agree to give it a go and choose to participate. The program is intensive and runs for three hours, three days per week. Group participation involves doing activities together, learning and using cognitive skills, and the expectation that participants will open up about themselves and look at their reasons for offending; group solidarity and rapport are important in this context. As part of the group rules, the participants are advised that they will be allowed two unauthorised absences, and if there is a third they will be removed from the program. Absences can be authorised for medical purposes if they provide a medical certificate, or for court appearances.

It is week four, and by now all of the offenders know each other well and are comfortable in the group environment. There have been occasional absences from various members of the group, but no one has had any more than two. One of the participants, Greg, then misses three sessions in a row, which is the agreed number of absences before a person will be told to leave. The rest of the group identify this and give you an ultimatum that they will all stop attending if you allow Greg back, as he has breached the group rules, which they don't think is fair.

The following week, Greg contacts you prior to the group and informs you that he did not attend as he has been having major problems sleeping and could not get out of bed in the morning. He says he is willing to see his GP about it, but doesn't have a medical certificate yet. Greg begs to be allowed to stay on the program, stating that he has 'been getting a lot out of it' and really wants to finish it. If you choose to remove Greg from the program, this will require reporting the fact back to his probation officer.

*Questions:*
What do you say to Greg? What do you say to the rest of the group?

efficacy of anger management interventions in the rehabilitation of serious violent offenders (Howells *et al.* 2005), bringing to the forefront the reality that it is not a panacea for aggression but only works for those who want to change.

*Practice considerations*

Some caution has been urged in relation to blasé one-size-fits-all approaches to anger management with offenders, as some courts and correctional facilities make it a coerced component of incarceration as a precursor to release or a mandatory part of bail or probation. Williamson and colleagues (2003) investigated the efficacy of screening offenders for their motivation and readiness to change to improve responsivity and readiness for treatment. Their results showed that using evidence-based tools such as screening questionnaires to select participants for anger management interventions holds promise in optimising treatment outcomes. Even building in anger management interventions into a broader form of service delivery, like counselling or group psycho-education, can be helpful if issues like impulse control or interpersonal boundaries – common problem areas for offenders – are addressed. Anger management can be used within the parameters of any of the different rehabilitation models outlined in Chapter 2; however, it fits particularly well with the risk-need-responsivity model in helping offenders to address the problems and risks that inhibit their progress towards desistance, while being mindful of any responsivity issues and personal needs.

## Psycho-education

Much like the name suggests, psycho-education involves the presentation of information and awareness-raising activities around particular topics to enhance personal knowledge, insight and skills. It can be an effective brief intervention offered to individual clients, or it can be offered as a short or medium-length group intervention. Psycho-education in the criminal justice system is usually targeted at addressing criminogenic need and identifying problematic behaviour and unhelpful thinking, for example, involving domestic violence or sex offending. It may be used to 'remedy offender's delays in moral judgment, maturity, social cognitive distortions, and social skills deficiencies', reducing recidivism and resulting in few serious incidents or rule violations (Liau *et al.* 2004: 543). Alternatively, psycho-education can be used to support and empower people who have themselves been subject to difficult experiences (such as victims of crime) or live with complex needs, for example, trauma or anxiety and depression. A practical example might be a group intervention that presents information about living with a mental illness, with participants experiencing a sense of relief when they find out that other people are going through the same thing. Teaching self- management techniques is valuable, for example, empowering a person with strategies to take control of a panic attack instead of feeling like they are going to die.

## Efficacy and evidence

Psycho-education is likely to work with all offender groups, male and female, young and old. The only exception would be those with very low IQ or cognitive capacity, including a serious inability to concentrate or retain information. There is evidence to suggest that it is appropriate when tailored to specific offenders groups that are particularly challenging or specialist to work with, including sex offenders (Stump *et al.* 1999), offenders with personality disorders (Hubband *et al.* 2007; McMurran and Wilmington 2007), offenders with schizophrenia (Aho-Mustonen *et al.* 2008), and offenders with HIV/AIDS (Pomeroy *et al.* 2000).

## Practice considerations

It is imperative that the delivery of information is appropriate and tailored to the literacy levels and communication styles of those receiving the psycho-education. A second area for cautious consideration is the avoidance of topics that are likely to result in unhelpful impulses or cravings to return to criminal behaviour. If information is not matched to the needs and motivations of a person who is substance dependent, it may lead to cravings to use. Information presented to a group intervention with sex offenders needs to comprise only content that is beneficial for their rehabilitation, and must avoid things that will contribute to impulses to reoffend or unhelpful sexual fantasy or dwelling on the problem, rather than changing to pro-social thinking. A final consideration is that the length and intensity of psycho-education must be appropriate, and sensitive monitoring of a participant's ability to concentrate needs to be matched with flexibility to cope with attention spans and disruption. Some medications and pharmacotherapy treatments may result in a tendency for a person to fall asleep in group or be groggy and non-responsive. Group facilitators will need to work with people who appear non-compliant to assess if it is an issue of responsivity or other influencing factors.

## Assertive community outreach and throughcare

Assertive community outreach is a service approach originating from the mental health sector in the 1970s. Following deinstitutionalisation, it was used to support people living with serious mental illness to continue to live in the community. However, there is increasing recognition of the need for offenders with complex needs and those who continue to reoffend and become institutionalised to receive intensive rehabilitation and practical life skills training upon release into the community.

Assertive community outreach combines rehabilitation with support services using a multidisciplinary team, usually without time limitations on the length of service provision. The following are examples of the types of services offered by assertive community outreach case workers (adapted from Phillips *et al.* 2001: 772):

- *Daily living skills* – grocery shopping, cooking, catching public transport, buying clothes, laundry, filling out forms, booking appointments, navigating the public service system of entitlements, pensions or benefits, maintaining hobbies and interests.

- *Family relationships* – crisis management, counselling and psycho-education with family members to raise awareness of the issues at hand, coordination with family services.

- *Employment and work* – help to find volunteer and vocational opportunities; skills for job interviews, provide liaison with and educate employers, serve as a job coach.

- *Health promotion and medication support* – provide preventative health education, help with ordering or collecting medications from pharmacy, monitoring medication compliance.

- *Housing assistance* – find suitable shelter or accommodation, help to improve housekeeping skills.

- *Financial management* – budgeting, helping keep on top of bills, increase independence in money management.

- *Counselling* – Use a problem-oriented approach, ensure that goals are addressed using a team approach, problem-solving, goal-setting, communication skills development.

### Evidence and efficacy

Assertive community treatment is thought to be more cost-effective than incarceration or inpatient treatment (Phillips *et al.* 2001). However, the evidence for use with forensic populations still needs ongoing improvement and investigation (Morrissey *et al.* 2007).

### Practice considerations

It should be noted that assertive community outreach often involves a team approach, where a person may not always just interact with the one worker. This is helpful for a number of reasons, and avoids issues of client dependency or enmeshment and worker burn-out. The assertive community outreach approach has more synergy with the principles and approach of the good lives and social recognition models.

## Other psychosocial interventions

There are many other psychosocial interventions that are used in offender rehabilitation; this is by no means a comprehensive review of a practitioner's 'toolkit'. Other eminent interventions worthy of mention, but without the room to explore in detail here, are:

- *Life skills, communication and coping skills training* – providing offenders with specific training and social skills development to enhance their ability to respond to and cope with life events and social relationships (see Robinson 1995; Sharma *et al.* 2008).

- *Parenting programs and family intervention* – providing offenders with the skills and strategies necessary to improve parenting practices and family relationships, as well as working towards regaining access or custody where necessary (see Harris and Pettway 2007; Sandifer 2008).

- *Dialectical behaviour therapy* – uses a combination of skills training, problem-solving, mindfulness, relaxation and empowerment to reduce self-destructive, impulsive and aggressive behaviours (see

Trupin *et al.* 2002; see also Berzins and Trestman 2004; Rosenfeld *et al.* 2007).

- *Harm minimisation and relapse prevention* – offering harm reduction information and practical support and resources to ensure that offenders who engage in risky behaviours are able to mitigate some risk until they are able to reach a place where they no longer engage in these behaviours. Relapse prevention involves specific planning to avoid triggers and cope with impulses and cravings (see Parks 2007; Bewley-Taylor *et al.* 2009).

- *Art therapy and creative art programs* – offering offenders the opportunity for therapeutic creative expression and building personal artistic and craft-making skills as a pro-social behaviour (see Gussak 2007; Johnson 2007, 2008).

- *Animal care and training programs in prison* – providing prisoners with the opportunity to be a trainer or carer for animals, usually in the form of pet therapy, training assistance or guide dogs, caring for injured wild animals, or working with livestock on prison farms (see Correctional Service of Canada 1998; Strimple 2003; Furst 2006; Ormerod 2008).

- *Environmental conservation and gardening projects* – providing offenders in prison and the community with the opportunity to develop horticultural skills, to spend time outdoors in a vocationally oriented activity, to work alongside volunteers and community members (social inclusion and pro-social modelling) and contribute to the community in a restorative capacity through working on environmental and recycling projects (see Jiler 2006, 2009; Arun 2007; Randerson 2008; Ahmad 2009; Carter and Pycroft 2010).

While many different types of specific interventions can be identified it is important to acknowledge that their effectiveness not only depends upon how these are used and with whom, but when and under what circumstances. Case study 5.1 illustrates why the question of timing is important in determining what is provided to an offender.

As discussed in the previous chapter, the backbone of case management is screening and assessment. Here there are a number of potential contributions to a practitioner's toolkit, although there are important *caveats* on what is most suitable or appropriate to include.

### Case study 5.1

### Reimagining intervention: there when you need them most – first night in custody services, United Kingdom

Intrinsic to tertiary education and professional culture in the human services is a tendency to accumulate increasingly sophisticated forms of intervention and service delivery frameworks. From the first year of study, budding social workers and psychologists are imbued with the expectation that working with offenders is this nebulous world of practice, where precise tools are used to intervene in often messy life histories and for diffuse purposes. In other words, everything has increasingly individualised context, texture and practice. Without arguing to the contrary, it may be useful here to position the value of conceptual frameworks and intensive psychosocial therapies in the context of the bigger picture, balanced by the recognition that, for offenders, they mean little at critical transition points or in a moment of crisis. Who cares about cognitive behavioural therapy or integrated offender management when you are worried about surviving your first night in prison, stressed about what's going down in your unit right now, or thinking of killing yourself?

Hence the need for 'reimagining intervention'. Given the complexity of the professional realm described above, there are times when a reality check of getting back to basics is needed. A case in point is the First Night in Custody Services offered by the Prison Advice & Care Trust (PACT) in the United Kingdom. The brief interventions used by this service represent a 'rubber hits the road' approach that is incredibly practical and vital to the psychological and emotional well-being of a newly incarcerated offender who is anxious and trapped. The aims of the service are as follows (see Jacobson and Edgar 2007:1):

- To reduce the likelihood of prisoners attempting suicide or harming themselves in their first 72 hours of custody.
- To reduce the anxiety faced by prisoners to enable them to cope better with the emotional impact of imprisonment.
- To reduce the anxiety faced by prisoners' families and loved ones.
- To support the maintenance of contact and visits between prisoners and families.
- To ensure that information and support available to new prisoners is provided.

The activities of a PACT worker in this service are to: identify the prisoners' needs; ask what worries them most; refer them to appropriate services; liaise with families; and follow up individuals who need longer term support (Jacobson & Edgar 2007). In summary, this case study demonstrates interventions that are simple and yet vital.

## Common screening and assessment tools

Different jurisdictions require proficiency in different types of tools; however, a common focus across most modes of screening and criminogenic assessment is on identification and management of risk. The following represents a general list of the screening and assessment tools currently in use in criminal justice systems and community agencies around the world; it is important to acknowledge, however, that this list is by no means comprehensive.

1 *General criminogenic screening tools and risk assessment*
- Criminal Sentiments Scale – Modified (CSS-M)
- Correctional Treatment Resistance Scale
- Level of Service/Case Management Inventory (LS/CMI)
- Offender Group Reconviction Score (OGRS)
- Pride in Delinquency Scale (PID)
- Risk of Reconviction and Re-Imprisonment (RoC*Rol)
- Statistical Information on Recidivism Scale (SIR)
- University of Rhode Island Change Assessment Scale (URICA)

2 *Arson*
- Fire Assessment Interview
- Fire Interest Rating Scale
- Fire Attitude Scale
- Fire Setting Risk Inventory

3 *Addiction and alcohol and other drugs misuse*
- Addiction Severity Index (ASI)
- Alcohol Use Disorders Identification Test (AUDIT)
- Drug Abuse Screening Tool (DAST)
- PsyCheck

4 *Mental health*
- Co-Occurring Disorders Screening Instrument for Mental Disorders (CODSI-MD)
- DASS21
- Diagnostic and Statistical Manual IV (DSM-IV)
- Edinburgh Postnatal Depression Scale
- Jail Screening Assessment Tool (JSAT)
- K10
- Kohlberg's Standard Moral Judgment Interview
- Major Depression Inventory
- Post Traumatic Stress Disorder Checklist

5 *Sex Offenders*
- Abel Assessment for Sexual Interest (AASI)
- Hare Psychopathy Checklist – Revised (HPC)
- Minnesota Sex Offender Screening Tool – Revised (MnSOST-R)
- Rapid Risk Assessment for Sexual Offender Recidivism (RRASOR)
- Risk of Sexual Violence Protocol (RSVP)
- Sex Offender Risk Appraisal Guide (SORAG)
- Sexual Violence Risk 20 (SVR-20)
- Structured Anchored Clinical Judgment (SACJ)

6 *Violence*
- Family Violence Risk Factor Checklist
- Historical Clinical and Risk Management Scheme – 20 (HCR-20)
- Ontario Domestic Assault Risk Assessment (ODARA)
- PCL-R-2
- Spousal Assault Risk Assessment Guide (SARA)
- Violence Prediction Scheme (VPS)
- Violent Risk Appraisal Guide (VRAG)

Some of these tools are available freely in the public domain, found simply by Googling them. Others are very exclusive and very expensive, representing a booming para-psychological industry and the increasing commercialisation of professional therapeutic resources. Entrepreneurial companies and savvy consultants continue to develop new training packages in the hope, and likelihood, of extensive buy-in from large criminal justice agencies who are prone to handing over lump sums for off-the-shelf standardised tools, if only for the ability to roll them out *en masse*. Entire cohorts of prison officers or case managers are dispatched to attend a few days of rapid-fire group training (consultants' time is expensive) in tools and interventions that they will be required to use daily for years, or at least until the next new tool is rolled out.

This cynicism does not stem from the fact that there is money to be made, but more so that the process allows and even encourages those without well-developed competencies to fly under the radar in the one-off group training and then be approved to use a tool – skilfully or otherwise – to make decisions and judgements that impact the life of the offender being assessed. The best training packages incorporate 'follow-up' days and opportunities for ongoing supervision, tailoring and troubleshooting. A second critical reflection on the use of screening and assessment tools is that the issues, qualities or risks that are being measured and the way in which this scrutiny and measurement is undertaken often indirectly reflects broader correctional policy (and dominant rehabilitation paradigm) for an institution or a jurisdiction.

Both of these issues point to the need for increased reflexivity around the choice and utility of different tools and interventions; the most popular tools are not necessarily the best resources – something that needs to be acknowledged in the midst of increasing quality assurance agendas driving departments of justice and public service around the world. Asking the front-line practitioners who tick boxes and assign risk ratings and classifications daily about which tools to choose would be a good starting point but (particularly when compared to cost) this is a perspective that is incorporated into governance and managerial decision-making much less often than otherwise thought. Moreover, asking offenders what they think are useful assessment methods and tools is or ought to be a vital part of determining what best works for whom (see Morash 2009).

Part of the problem lies with uncritical reliance upon tools based upon actuarialism (predictions founded upon broad population characteristics, such as drug use or age of offending). This generally involves tools that chart up specific risk and protective factors that are statistically correlated with certain types of behaviour and certain types of people. The implication is that if certain factors are added together there will be a predictable certainty that the specific causes of criminality (or pathology) will be identified. Such diagnostic tools may be useful in trying to pinpoint a person's specific needs and risks, given what we know about people with similar attributes and who are in similar circumstances. However, the individuality of each person also demands assessments that take into account specific life histories and unique biographies that constitute the make-up of that particular person and that cannot be easily measured *via* actuarial methods (see MacDonald 2006; Case and Haines 2009).

## Paradoxes and controversies

Risk and needs assessment is an essential part of developing suitable and responsive intervention strategies for individual clients. How such assessments are carried out, therefore, has major implications for how client profiles are constructed, and the choice of treatment or rehabilitation program. One issue relating to assessment is the ways in which some instruments are, in effect, based upon 'universal' categories and assumptions that may be cross-culturally insensitive. For instance, some Australian assessment tools have cited 'Aboriginality' as a 'risk factor'. This is insulting to indigenous people, and automatically increases their negative risk ranking based upon ascribed characteristics (Palmer and Collard 1993; Priday 2006).

A related issue pertains to the use of pro-forma testing instruments (that is, instruments that encompass a series of pre-tested questions, frequently accompanied with a certain range of available answers that provide a rank or categorisation of the person doing the test depending upon how they respond to these set questions). This approach is contrasted to narrative-based assessments that are more open-ended in nature and that involve offenders telling their stories in ways that feel comfortable and make sense to them. Narrative assessment and 'objective' assessment methods are complementary, and together can provide a more sophisticated picture of offenders' lives than reliance on any one particular method.

Working with offenders is about working with people who share most things in common with the rest of the population but who for a wide variety of reasons engage in deviant behaviour of some kind. Communication, assessment and intervention has to take into account the static (gender, age, cultural background) and dynamic (such as substance misuse, violent events) factors that have combined to form who the offender is, at that moment in time. Talking with and listening to what offenders have to say is important to ascertain how and why they live and act as they do, and what the possibilities are for future change. Burnett (2007) refers to this as 'relationship based practice'. McNeill and colleagues (2005) emphasise the extent to which the worker–offender relationship is paramount throughout the course of intervention:

Although we have described the ability to build and utilise relationships as a discrete skill set in its own right (including communication, counselling and interpersonal skills), in fact it underpins each of the other skills sets and each aspect of the [offender] supervision process ... Whether we look to the latest versions of the 'what works' research, to the psychotherapy literature or to the desistance research, similar messages emerge. The accumulated weight of evidence, coming from studies that start with quite different assumptions and using very different methodological approaches, drives us towards recognition that practice skills in general and relationship skills in particular are at least as critical in reducing re-offending as programme content. (McNeill *et al.* 2005: 39)

Thus the relational content of interventions and rehabilitation is paramount. Client participation and self-determination is also integral to any intervention process.

## Conclusion

This chapter has provided a survey of the methods and approaches to working with offenders that seem to work best. The basis for this assessment is twofold: first, 'what works' is based upon tried and true methods that have been evaluated and thoroughly researched. This is the essence of evidence-based intervention. Second, 'what works' is also based upon experience and empathy. That is, practitioners have developed a reservoir of knowledge over time that indicates what is successful and what is less than successful when working with clients. Treating people with respect is crucial to this.

## Discussion questions

1 Identify and discuss some minority groups or special populations from within the broader offender population that might require special consideration or tailoring of intervention. What are the types of issues that might arise during routine professional activities like screening, assessment and treatment with this group?
2 What should be considered as 'evidence' when assessing the

efficacy of an intervention or tool? Related to this, what are the strengths and challenges associated with reliance on practitioner discretion and personal discernment in everyday screening and assessment, in addition to the use of standardised interventions and instruments?

3 While recognising that offenders are far from homogenous, what are some topics and specific questions that an offender might not want to answer? How would you like to be asked these kinds of questions? Practise asking difficult questions in a constructive and sensitive manner, using different angles to suit different personality types.

## Further reading

Brayford, J., Cowe, F. and Deering, J. (eds) (2010) *What Else Works? Creative Work with Offenders*. Cullompton: Willan Publishing.

Cameron, H. and Telfer, J. (2004) 'Cognitive-behavioural group work: its application to specific offender groups', *Howard Journal of Criminal Justice*, 43(1): 47–64.

Lipsey, M. and Cullen, F. (2007) 'The effectiveness of correctional rehabilitation: a review of systematic reviews', *Annual Review of Law and Social Science*, 3: 297–320.

MacKenzie, D. (2000) 'Evidence-based corrections: identifying what works', *Crime and Delinquency*, 46(4): 457–71.

McIvor, G., Kemshall, H. and Levy, G. (2002) *Serious Violent and Sexual Offenders in Scotland: The Use of Risk Assessment Tools in Scotland*. Edinburgh: Scottish Executive.

Ward, T. and Stewart, C. (2003) 'The treatment of sex offenders: risk management and good lives', *Professional Psychology, Research and Practice*, 34(4): 353–60.

## Key resources

Fleeman, W. (2003) *Pathways to Peace: Anger Management Workbook*, 3rd edn. Alameda, CA: Hunter House Inc.

McMaster, K. (2004) 'Facilitating change through groupwork', in J. Maidment and R. Egan (eds) *Practice Skills in Social Work and Welfare: More than just Common Sense*. Sydney: Allen & Unwin.

Reilly, P. and Shopshire, M. (2002) *Anger Management for Substance Abuse and Mental Health Clients: A Cognitive Behavioural Therapy Manual*.

Rockville, MD: Centre for Substance Abuse Treatment and Mental Health Services.

Rooney, R. (ed.) (2009) *Strategies for Work with Involuntary Clients*, 2nd edn. New York: Columbia University Press.

Walters, S., Clark, M., Gingerich, R. and Meltzer, M. (2007) *Motivating Offenders to Change: A Guide for Probation and Parole*. Washington: US Department of Justice.

# Chapter 6

# The worker–offender relationship: roles and respect

To me, being treated with humanity means being provided with adequate, reasonably comfortable and clean accommodation and being acknowledged as a person with individual needs, desires, concerns, strengths and weaknesses.

(Prisoner, quoted in Liebling and Arnold 2002: 2)

## Introduction

There is much diversity within the term 'offender' including different roles and needs. Respect is a universal construct that is woven throughout all work with offenders and yet it is a term that can be understood in different ways by offenders, and can be associated with different agendas or approaches by workers. This chapter explores the diverse nature of the offender community, by examining different kinds of offences and offender characteristics that may impact upon general offender status. Communication is crucial to developing positive forms of respect, as are boundaries when it comes to worker–offender relationships at work and outside of work. Respect is also contingent upon sustaining professional integrity on the part of practitioners in dealing with a wide spectrum of offenders.

Adoption of rehabilitation as a general aim, and integrated offender management as a specific strategy, means that those who work with offenders have to orient their work around what the offender needs and desires. What works has to be constructed around what works for this or that particular client. Obviously this implies close working relationships with offenders, and with other professionals who deal with offenders.

The articulation of key values in the service delivery context is essential to implementation of strengths-based approaches. The main focus of intervention is the client and the needs and interests of the client. In Scotland, the National Care Standards for residential accommodation, for example, are based on seven key values (Rome *et al.* 2002):

- Dignity
- Privacy
- Choice
- Safety
- Realising potential
- Equality
- Diversity.

An organisation may adopt key values such as those outlined above, or may go further and add other values. Examples of these may include respect and esteem, sensitivity of care, compassion and empathy, trust, hope, accountability, positive change and empowerment, and transparent communication. Once an agency has chosen their key values, it is important that these are made public and simply explained, and are written down so that all members of the relevant community are able to view them at any time. The rationale for the existence and influence of key values is the importance of maintaining a truly client-centred service.

In a corrective services context, the question of values is always complicated by the fact that we are dealing with involuntary clients. Practitioners are bound by certain obligations related to the maintenance of security and community safety. Offenders are required to undertake certain tasks or to be placed in certain facilities as determined by court and other criminal justice authorities (such as probation and parole boards). An element of compulsion guides both worker and offender; neither is completely free to do as they wish. Yet, at the same time, treating each other with respect and in light of human rights considerations is not only a baseline of professional practice, it is also essential to good practice generally. This chapter provides a discussion of why values count in correctional work, and why respect that is mutually reinforced is the best guarantee that steps towards rehabilitation can be taken.

## Human rights and corrective services

Human rights are rights accorded to individuals by virtue of their status as humans. Human rights are not negotiable, since they are deemed to be intrinsic to the very definition of humanity itself. As a formal concept, to claim something as a right is to demand it as one's due, as something one is entitled to, rather than to request it as something one desires. The violation of a human right therefore constitutes an injury to the right-bearer. Thus a right is a claim, interest or advantage that a person possesses and that will be protected by the law. The denial of human rights can take the form of the passing and enforcing of unjust laws, or the unjust discrimination against groups or individuals.

There are different types of human rights:

- *Political* – freedom of expression, assembly, religion
- *Economic* – to own property, make contracts, to work or refuse to work
- *Legal* – to rule of law, due process, security of person
- *Egalitarian* – anti-discriminatory on basis of sex, creed, nationality, race
- *Special area*s – language, prisoners, children, indigenous people.

The content and extent of human rights has been constructed over many centuries, from the days when the nobility restricted the power of absolute monarchs to the twentieth-century concern with civil rights and matters pertaining to social inequality.

An international human rights framework relating to prisoners and prisoner rights has similarly evolved over time, affecting both adult corrections and juvenile justice. These include instruments that deal directly with punishment, and those that deal with specific population groups. Some of the principal conventions, rules and guidelines that are of relevance to corrective services include:

- Universal Declaration of Human Rights (UDHR)
- International Covenant on Civil and Political Rights (ICCPR)
- Convention for the Elimination of All Forms of Racial Discrimination (CERD)
- Convention Against Torture and Other Forms of Cruel, Inhuman or Degrading Treatment or Punishment (CAT)
- Convention for the Elimination of All Forms of Discrimination Against Women (CEDAW)

- Convention on the Rights of the Child (CROC)
- Standard Minimum Rules for the Administration of Juvenile Justice 1985 (Beijing Rules)
- Standard Minimum Rules for Non-custodial Measures 1990 (Tokyo Rules)
- Guidelines for the Prevention of Juvenile Delinquency 1990 (Riyadh Guidelines)
- Rules for the Protection of Juveniles Deprived of their Liberty 1990

Not all countries are signatories to all of these instruments (for example, the US has not signed the Convention of the Rights of the Child), and even where national governments have become signatories to the instrument this does not necessarily mean that the content of such become embedded in national or state/provincial law (this does not generally occur without special legislation in Australia, for example).

Regardless of national adherence or legislative entrenchment, many countries have utilised human rights instruments in order to develop basic standards within the corrections field. For example, according to the Revised Standards for Corrections in Australia 'people are sent to prison as punishment not for punishment. Prison systems should ensure that prisoners are not further punished for their crimes over and above the sentence imposed by the Court' (Attorney-General's Department 2004: 14). The human rights and fundamental freedoms of prisoners in this regard are clearly outlined in a number of international covenants and conventions as provided above. Human rights standards have been developed in relation to particular national and jurisdictional contexts (such as England and Wales) and across jurisdictions (like the Council of Europe). How these are translated into practice, however, is subject to ongoing contestation, as the debates over prisoner voting rights attest (for example, the European Union was to rule against the restriction of such rights within England and Wales on the basis of human rights agreements).

At the core of human rights is the notion of human dignity. A recent English report on prisons echoes the Australian Standards statement above in that it emphasises that 'the loss of liberty is the punishment not the loss of citizenship' (Commission on English Prisons Today 2009: 33). The report quotes David Faulkner of the University of Oxford Centre for Criminology: 'If offenders are to be reformed and take responsibility for themselves and their families, they should not be regarded as different from, and inferior to, other people. They should be seen as citizens, still having responsibilities and rights which the state should respect' (Commission on English Prisons Today 2009: 33). Thus, the essence of prison reform is to exhibit a respect for human worth of all those within corrective services. At a practice level, this translates into treating offenders humanely and putting rehabilitation at the centre of what it is that corrections is trying to achieve.

From the point of view of practitioner and offender relationships, a human rights approach necessarily promotes change from the traditional and paramilitary styles of containment and dealing with offenders. For a start it emphasises values of responsibility and mutual respect. These are vital to the future project of empowering offenders to make changes in their lives for the better and in pro-social ways. Such values also put to test the usual emphasis on security, containment and top-down exercises of custodial and professional power.

> One feature of a rehabilitative regime is that there should be activities for prisoners to fill their time which are socially meaningful. These activities should allow prisoners to rehabilitate themselves if they wish and are able to do so, but rehabilitation cannot be imposed from the outside. It does not follow that such activities will of themselves rehabilitate the people who take part in them. Some prisoners come to prison after such damaging childhoods and life experiences that whatever is done in prison cannot undo that damage. Most prisoners leave prison to enter an environment of such gloomy personal prospects that changing their lives is too high an expectation. Some prisoners are not convinced that they want a different way of life. (International Centre for Prison Studies 2004: 3)

In the light of these observations, the task of corrective services is to provide opportunities for change, without the expectations of change.

## Held against our will

The crucial aspect of being an offender within correctional services is that one is basically compelled to do certain things, and to be in certain places, against one's will. That is, the system as a whole is, by necessity and by definition, a coercive system of social control. This one central fact overlays everything that practitioners do, and how offenders respond to practitioners. The potentials and the dilemmas of being in corrections are intrinsically related to this fact.

As discussed elsewhere throughout this book, offenders generally come from socially disadvantaged backgrounds. They also generally have a bad or difficult relationship with authority figures such as the police, immigration officials, judges and corrections staff. The longer offenders are contained within the system, the more likely they are to reoffend. The longer they are exposed to each other, the more likely they are to assume the mores and cultural attributes of 'crim' and 'con'. Being in corrections thus carries with it significant social and cultural baggage.

On the part of correctional services staff, there are likewise cultural aspects to the job that influence how officers relate to the client population. Institutions and groups of workers may vary in whether or not they view offenders as deserving or undeserving of services. For example, having an inmate studying a university course can be galling for prison officers who have minimum high school qualifications themselves. Workers may be divided on how much emphasis to place on security considerations and how much on rehabilitation. They may also disagree on the extent to which offenders should be trusted. Bad experiences such as being confronted by rioting inmates may shape subsequent behaviour. Meanwhile, the occasional good news story of offenders moving on to more constructive lives in prison and post-release can motivate officers to persist with innovative methods of dealing with their charges. The following account from a prison officer highlights the benefits of a communicative and forthright worker–offender relationship:

> I am making huge inroads with [inmate's name] who's constantly been a belligerent and recalcitrant inmate. I think he's really doing well. I have got him doing three courses and he's enjoying them, he's turning up every time and his attitude's improved. Another one there, we recently found shivs [material fashioned into a blade] in his cell. He started off treating officers like a dog when he wants something. I sat him down and told him, 'look, you are not going to get anywhere when you talk to someone like that. I suggest you think about how you communicate and talk civilly and see what happens.' He turned around and said to me sometime later, 'it's amazing, you were right. I get twice as much now as I asked for.' So I mean, little things happen all the time. (Cianchi 2009: 43–4)

Table 6.1 provides a summary of what matters within a prison context. The positives tend to revolve around relationships and values that are universally shared (see Liebling 2004; Ward and Maruna 2007). The negatives relate to attacks on one's bodily and psychic integrity. The positives express what it is to feel human and to have human rights respected. The negatives reflect situational circumstances and are linked to events and institutional locations. The challenge, in both a prison and a community context, is to maximise the positives while minimising the negatives.

**Table 6.1**   What counts in prison

| Positives | Negatives |
| --- | --- |
| Respect | Fights |
| Humanity | Assaults |
| Trust | Arguments |
| Support | Threats of violence |
| Fairness | Isolation |
| Safety | Fear |
| Order | Rape |
| Well-being | Bullying |
| Decency | Claustrophobia |
| Meaning | |

For this to happen, it is essential that we start with a concept of the offender as a whole person. The limits of defining people in terms of a master status are discussed below. For the moment our concern is with the notion that while offenders have complex needs, they are also simultaneously many different people – they are family members (father, mother, son, daughter, brother, sister), they are workers (with specific skills and experiences), they are law-abiding as well as law-breaking (in most facets of their everyday life, such as driving a car), they are happy and angry, sad and glad (depending upon the occasion). In other words, offenders are ordinary humans who have generally been caught up in extraordinary circumstances (as children growing up in chaotic households, as drug users, as criminals).

To engage with offenders in a relationship of respect it is first necessary to respect offenders as persons. This is not always easy, given the aggression and hurt, the humiliation and bravado, that can characterise the public persona of some offenders. Prison culture can magnify the worst aspects of humanity, and the experience of containment within corrective services can be dehumanising, especially if basic rights are not respected. For a practitioner to gain an offender's respect, it is vital that they acknowledge the humanity of the offender, without compromising the fact that respect is a two-way street. Respect in either case has to be earned. It is earned in the doing of relationships, and as such cannot be assumed from appearances or from expectations:

> I had a confrontation with an inmate on the division front which was quite intimidating. And then after I had booked him, I went to see him to explain why he was booked. He tried to argue the point and I finally understood that I wasn't going to enter into the argument and I explained to him to put himself in my shoes and he turned around and said 'I got it. I'm sorry.' If you simply book the person, you are shirking your responsibility. Perhaps some officers would let their nerves or fear get in the way, but you have got to follow it to the final point and you have got to show the inmate that you are not backing away from the challenge. (Prison officer, quoted in Cianchi 2009: 43)

What 'respect' means, however, will partly depend upon how it is culturally and socially construed by different groups. Acknowledgement of social and individual difference is crucial in this regard. Offenders vary greatly in terms of gender, social and cultural background, religion, language, age, country of origin, indigenous or non-indigenous status, prior imprisonment and type of offence. Table 6.2 provides a snapshot of criminal offences types across Australian states and territories. The reasons why offenders are in prison impacts upon who is likely to be respected/feared (such as those who are part of violent and criminal subcultures) and who is actively disrespected/despised (such as those who sexually abuse children).

Who and what is respected is not static. For example, Table 6.3 outlines the religious background of offenders and demonstrates that this is changing over time (see also Scenario 6.1). In a prison context, the weight of numbers does count insofar as the more there are of any particular population group, the greater chance that 'respect' takes on a communal flavour. This works both ways – in terms of how people feel about themselves and the power they might claim as self-identified members of a group, and how prison staff perceive the group and its needs as a whole.

**Table 6.2**  Criminal offence type, Australia

| Offence type | National |
|---|---|
| Homicide and related offences | 2,220 |
| Acts intended to cause injury | 3,357 |
| Sexual assault and related offences | 2,880 |
| Robbery, extortion and related offences | 1,988 |
| Unlawful entry with intent | 2,404 |
| Illicit drug offences | 2,076 |

*Source*: Australian Bureau of Statistics (2008).

**Table 6.3**  Prison populations in England and Wales by religion or world-view in 1998 and in 2008

| Type of data | 1998 | 2008 |
|---|---|---|
| **All Christian** | 40,609 | 41,839 |
| Anglican | 27,299 | 23,039 |
| Free Church | 1,337 | 1,213 |
| Roman Catholic | 11,172 | 14,296 |
| Other Christian | 801 | 3,291 |
| **Buddhist** | 324 | 1,737 |
| **Hindu** | 304 | 434 |
| **Jewish** | 214 | 220 |
| **Muslim** | 4,188 | 9,795 |
| **Sikh** | 491 | 648 |
| **Other religious groups** | 95 | 448 |
| **No religion** | 18,072 | 27,710 |

*Source*: Adapted from Ministry of Justice (2009a: 124).

The practitioner has to be aware of how specific differences, specific attributes and specific 'ways of being' are constitutive elements in how people behave towards others. Respecting where people are coming from does not mean that we accept everything about that person's beliefs, attitudes and behaviours. It does, however, require sensitivity to social context, and an ability to listen to what matters for other people besides ourselves. Respect, therefore, starts with listening. It also impacts upon the processes of asking.

Scenario 6.2 presents material relating to communication strategies. If diversity is about similarities and differences between people,

## Scenario 6.1

### Working with religious diversity in a prison environment

People look at the world differently depending upon the personal biographies, their engagement in criminal and anti-social activity, their religious outlook and the idiosyncratic ways in which each of us tries to make sense of the world around us. The fact that offenders are not in corrective services for the same offence, and that the composition of the offender population is changing when it comes to religion and world-view (see Table 6.3), means that working with respect cannot take the form of treating everyone exactly the same way.

*Questions*

1 How can we approach diversity in a correctional environment?

2 Consider the examples listed below. What are some of the benefits, as well as operational challenges, that might arise from having a prison population with religious diversity?

• Some pagan and new age religions may involve the ritualistic use of items such as oils, substances, needles, crystals, and practices that focus on and worship the natural world outdoors at times relating to the lunar calendar.

• The Australian Aboriginal people have a strong emphasis on walking the land, returning to country, 'songlines' and traditional rituals based on things like gender, initiation or community cohesion.

• The Islamic religion has various times throughout the day involving prayer rituals facing Mecca. Yet there are people from certain countries or sections within Islam that do not formally recognise or associate with other sections and may refuse to undertake prayers with them.

• Some women from the Muslim faith, and some groups such as Exclusive Brethren and the Mormons, may have a desire to wear traditional head coverings or special items of clothing. Some religions may not encourage women to publicly display areas of their body such as their hair, ankles or the back of their neck. Yet prison routinely involves strip searches, or there may be concerns about use for the trafficking of contraband.

*continued*

- Various religions believe in having the concept of a day of complete rest, some call it the Sabbath and others simply adhere to it as a holy day. These occur on different days for different religions.

- Some important elements of mainstream Christianity are Communion (possibly including sacramental wine), baptism and the opportunity for attending and participating in a faith community.

- Some religions have very strict practices around food preparation and what can and cannot be eaten.

- Prison healthcare staff may have different perceptions on health and illness from an individual who may believe in prayer, miracles or divine intervention, or alternative medicine practices and recognised religious 'doctors' or healers. Also, some religions have very specific understandings and rituals surrounding death and the afterlife which need to be taken into account when an offender's family member or friend passes away, or the offender dies.

- What about festivals or special holy days or seasons that are quite spiritually significant for some inmates? For example, Ramadan or Lent.

and if respect is founded upon an appreciation and acceptance of diversity, then finding out where individuals are coming from is vital to working with offenders.

We need to continually remind ourselves about the realities of living and working in the prison. Prisoners live in the prison. Workers work in the prison. Improving the overall living and working environment is crucial to the success or otherwise of strategies such as integrated offender management. So too it needs to be remembered that the prison, as a home, is also a place where 'bad moods' (that we all get into) can happen, and ordinary 'ups and downs' may be exaggerated or penalised due to the artificial environment. How we deal with these issues likewise is part of the respect building and communication process.

## The problem of master status

Working with respect demands that practitioners explore values, beliefs and ethics on an ongoing basis. As emphasised above, this

## Scenario 6.2

### Communication activity: asking open-ended questions

Front-line workers are the most likely to pick up on issues in the client's life and to be told important pieces of information. It is important to communicate well and practise asking the right types of questions to gain the best information. For each not-so-helpful question or statement listed in the table, think of a better, more helpful question or statement that could be used instead.

| Not-so-helpful questions and statements | More helpful question or statement |
|---|---|
| You're up and down all over the place. You've been having some emotional problems, haven't you? | |
| You say that you don't like hearing voices. Why can't you just make them stop and go away? | |
| If you use again, you'll break your order and go to jail, is that what you want? | |
| You need to stop making excuses and just get straight and sober. | |
| Why did you go to that party when you knew it was going to get you in trouble? | |
| What are you getting upset for? Don't be stupid, you'll get over this, it will all go away. | |

Many not-so-good questions are suggestions or accusations in disguise. Without trying, questions asked in a closed manner can limit or close off opportunities for a client to talk with you about things that are important. Avoid closed questions that require a yes/no answer or an automatic limited answer.

Useful open-ended questions and statements include the following:

*continued*

- Tell me about …
- Why do you think that is the case?
- What was happening around you when …?
- What concerns do you (your wife, girlfriend, family) have?
- How has … affected you? How does that make you feel?
- What are some good things about …? What are some not so good things about ….?
- How would you like things to be like when you finish the Program? Where do you want to be?
- How are you going to do that?
- How would things be better if you made that positive change?
- What happened, do you think, to trigger that relapse?
- What has worked well for you in the past? Does it work well for you now?

As with all of us, offenders do not like to be talked *at*. Talking *with* people is the first step in being able to communicate with them.

means listening to what other people have to say, and respecting what is being said (even if one disagrees with the content of what is being said). Appreciative enquiry is precisely based upon such notions (Liebling *et al*. 1999).

It is also important to distinguish behaviours and persons. The insights of republican criminology are quite useful in this regard. The republican response to crime bases itself on the concept of reintegrative shaming (see Braithwaite 1989). This involves a process in which the offender is shamed for the action, but is not 'cast out' as a person. It describes a process whereby the offender is publicly rebuked for the harm caused, but is then forgiven and reintegrated into the mainstream of society.

When an individual is labelled 'bad', that label can stigmatise the individual. There is a need, therefore, to distinguish between stigmatisation, which increases the risks of reoffending by the shamed actor, and reintegrative shaming. In terms of the preferred second approach, disapproval is extended while a relationship of respect is sustained with the offender. Stigmatisation is disrespectful – it is seen as a humiliating form of shaming, where the offender is branded an evil person and is cast out permanently. Reintegrative shaming, by contrast, seeks to shame the evil deed but sees the offender in a respectable light. The shaming is finite, and the offender is given the opportunity to re-enter society by way of recognising the wrongdoing, apologising and being repentant.

A persistent problem within the field of corrections, however, is that too often offenders and practitioners are labelled in ways that generate and maintain a sort of 'master status'. These can work against building respectful and productive relationships. Offenders are constantly reminded of the stigma attached to their master status, long after they have been released, and it can be internalised to become a form of self stigma as well as act as an ongoing barrier that seemingly overrides the contribution of other skills and strengths to personal identity. This is well illustrated by the narrative of a female prisoner in Minnesota, aged 39, who is seeking to gain employment post-release:

> It doesn't matter what your felony conviction is, it's still there. I have to realize that I am more than what is written on and in paper about me. I am more than a felon. I am educated, I am intelligent, I'm hard working, I'm a good mother, I'm dependable, all of those things. I don't have to worry about parole telling me I'm a felon because there's gonna be a ton of other people that are going to say 'You're a felon' … And without that, if you can't stand up for yourself and say, 'I understand you're concerned about hiring me as a felon', it doesn't matter that I'm college educated, graduated valedictorian of my class. None of those things matter because 'felon' is what matters. (Uggen *et al*. 2004: 270)

This prisoner demonstrates a strong awareness of other labels that can and should override the 'master status' of felon, and yet she is pragmatic in describing how other people's perception of her identity is paramount to her opportunities and what she is able to become. Consider the following typical cases in which certain presumptions and assumptions impact upon how certain people are viewed within the corrective services arena.

### Women and girls – master status of 'abused'

The majority of women and girls who end up under the purview of the criminal justice system have at some time experienced physical abuse, sexual assault and neglect as children. Especially for young female offenders, this can manifest itself in system-generated concerns about their abuse. However, where these concerns come to dominate worker interventions, they can ultimately be counterproductive. This is so insofar as practitioner work continually reinforces the 'victim' status of the young female offender, as well as only focusing on one aspect of her life. The result can be too much focus on the abuse, rather than on the whole person, thus alienating individuals who want to enjoy other dimensions of their lives (see Baines and Alder 1996). This is highlighted in the following comment from a 27-year-old female offender when she was asked about what type of support would aid desistance:

> Give [offenders] support that suits that individual because everybody – there's that many different people out there that need that many different types of support. But people assume, like, because like you've been sexually abused, they think you just need counselling for abuse, but there's a lot more to it. (Barry 2007: 417)

### Sex offenders – master status of 'abuser' or 'pervert'

The intransigent nature of sex offending on the part of some individuals convicted of sex offences is well known. However, not all sex offending is committed by this type of sex offender (Chapman 2003). Moreover, some sex offenders can genuinely be assisted by their participation in sex offender programs. The content of such programs, however, can skew identity in certain directions. As one recent Canadian study has argued, too much focus on difference and the 'othering' of sex offenders as distinctive (in the course of therapy) can create pressures to snap, rather than to develop the offender as a human being and citizen (see Lacombe 2008). Relying on and reinforcing a particular master status can, again, be counterproductive, especially if the reintegrative goal is for identity and behavioural change.

### Prison officers – master status as 'screw'

The traditions of prison work combined with, in many cases, the crossover in occupations between military and police personnel with prison staff, can reinforce the paramilitary aspects of prison officer work. Where uniforms and weapons are prevalent, and where prison regimes correspond to military-style camps with rigorous rules and rigid hierarchical command structures, the role of the prison officer is thereby narrowed. Too much focus on a containment role and security issues not only reinforces the distance between staff and inmates, it actively undermines the promise of integrated offender management and case management systems.

### Professional staff – master status as 'professionals'

Who does what in a corrective services context is partly shaped by clear occupational distinctions, involving, for example, social work, psychology, criminology, penology and prison officers. The hallmark of professionalism is in fact boundary maintenance that is premised upon specialist knowledge, specialist credentials and official accreditation for undertaking specific occupational tasks. However, taking professionalism to its extreme can impede the necessary processes of collaboration required under contemporary policies and intervention models. Too much focus on role definition and specific occupational tasks thus can reinforce the distance between different groups of workers with offenders, and thereby undermine the prospects of an integrated intervention strategy. Ongoing emphasis on professionalisation of the workforce can also result in the homogenisation of the workforce, for example, resulting in only those from the middle and upper classes working as skilled clinicians, because they are the ones who can afford the years of study at university to attain clinical psychology or psychiatry credentials. Another area is dress and appearance. People who work with offenders need to dress in a way that considers their own identity, and also the appropriateness of the context in which they work and who they see every day. In some cases, dressing down (casual clothes) is a sign of respect and insight into relational dynamics, as it is more appropriate than a suit.

Going beyond the notion of 'master status' is achieved by thinking about people as whole persons, rather than simply referring to and dealing with them in a one-sided fashion. Perhaps one way to appreciate this is to consider offenders as people who love others and who have their own loved ones. We need to humanise the deviant in order to deal with the deviancy.

## Working with respect

In working with involuntary clients, most of whom have experienced considerable social disadvantage, it is clear that literacy skills and vocational experiences may be limited on the part of the offender.

The need for quality education and vocational training in prisons and community-based programs is manifest, and the information presented in Table 6.4 illustrates this. Any interventions must be appropriate and targeted to the learning abilities of the offender. Psycho-education about the issues that they are working through is important, and vocational education and training is vital to their reintegration.

Yet, working through issues of literacy and vocational development has to be undertaken sensitively and carefully. For instance, programs in prison that target fathers can combine social objectives in a genuinely enjoyable and non-patronising way (Meek 2007). Such is the case, for example, in the snapshot of prisoner rehabilitation in Innovative practice 7 in the next chapter.

Working with respect means doing something with a purpose. It means taking the time to build relationships between practitioner and offender. A respectful relationship is one that is characterised by rapport, trust and confidentiality. How practitioners relate to one another is also an important aspect of offender–practitioner relationships. It is important that practitioners develop relationships with colleagues (rapport, trust, confidentiality) that publicly demonstrate what a respectful relationship looks like and involves. Saying things out loud that undermine, and being disrespectful behind another's back are unlikely to be hidden in contexts where ears and eyes are everywhere.

This last observation brings us back to consider the nature of the 'respect' that we are talking about. Namely, the context for trying to develop relations of respect is one based upon involuntariness. People are forced into relationships with each other. While from a therapeutic perspective this may be seen as a good thing, insofar as it provides leverage for professionals to work with individuals who otherwise would avoid such assistance (Denckla 1999–2000), it immediately creates tensions and divisions among those forced into the situation. Research has demonstrated, however, that although all involuntary clients are in effect coerced, it is the perception of coercion more than the actual coercion that has a detrimental effect on coerced treatment outcomes (Day *et al.* 2004). To put it differently, there are ways of working with offenders that reduce the perceptions of coercion, and thereby increase the likelihood of offender motivation to work with practitioners in a more productive way. Yet, the overall environment can nonetheless stifle the development of such relationships or skew them in certain directions.

**Table 6.4** Prisoner engagement in education and training rates by Australian state and territory, 2007–08

| Type of data | NSW | VIC | SA | WA | QLD | NT | ACT | TAS | National |
|---|---|---|---|---|---|---|---|---|---|
| Pre-Certificate Level 1 course | 1.7% | 3.9% | 3.3% | 0 | 9.6% | 0 | N/A | 0 | 2.9% |
| Secondary school | 15.8% | 0.5% | 1.8% | 0.1% | 2.3% | 1.2% | N/A | 27.2% | 6.7% |
| Vocational education and training | 24.9% | 29% | 41.1% | 35.6% | 16.4% | 24.1% | N/A | 37.6% | 24.3% |
| Higher education | 1.1% | 2.4% | 4.3% | 1.2% | 3.1% | 1.1% | N/A | 2.4% | 1.1% |
| **Total** | **32.3%** | **32.5%** | **47.2%** | **36.2%** | **29%** | **26.4%** | **N/A** | **50.5%** | **30.2%** |

*Note:* Individuals may be counted more than once in this table.
*Source:* Australian Commonwealth Government Productivity Commission (2009).

### Innovative practice 6

#### Prisoner rehabilitation, Italian style

Located in what is arguably the fashion capital of the world, Milan's San Vittore Prison is home to a very innovative approach to prisoner rehabilitation. In 2008, the sophisticated handiwork of female inmates, including wedding dresses, were showcased on the catwalk alongside creations by big Italian names and labels like Giorgio Armani and Prada (Reuters 2008). Celebrities and correctional officers inspected the glamorous display of tailoring skills represented in the *haute couture* strutting the catwalk. Run by Cooperative Alice, for 18 years the project has offered opportunities for female prisoners to make costumes for theatre and television, as well as launch their own womenswear lines including 'Jail Cats' and 'Sartoria San Vittore' (Reuters 2008). Alice's headquarters in Milan are staffed by prisoners on day release and ex-prisoners who opted to continue. Some ex-prisoners have secured employment elsewhere in the fashion industry, with one starting her own tailoring business and hiring former offenders. So, 'does redemption through fashion actually work? It seems so ... of the 100 plus women who have joined since Alice was founded, only one has gone back inside' (Hooper 2007).

Another inherently Italian creative collaboration is under way in Velletri Prison. Within the whitewashed prison walls, inmates are being trained as vintners, producing two varieties of wine: *Fuggiasco* (Italian for 'fugitive') and *Seven Turns of the Key* (an Italian expression about the depressing finality of imprisonment), resulting in the production of 45,000 bottles of wine a year (Williams 2005). Rodolfo Craia teaches inmates the craft of winemaking, imparting knowledge and skills and building a sense of culture and community. As he explains: 'The primary goal is to train inmates to do useful things. We also want to be part of the fabric of this country, so naturally, some things are very Italian' (quoted in Williams 2005).

Key issues here include those of safety and security, and how best to deal with collusion and manipulation within a corrective services setting. These issues are partly driven by the overarching regulator framework of corrections itself. That is, offenders have been sentenced, against their will, to some form of sanction. This may involve different obligations. The net result is deprivation of the liberty to do what one might wish to do if in otherwise free circumstances.

The rules of the system and the practices of particular practitioners can reinforce the lack of trust in offenders, and foster a culture of 'getting away with it' among offenders as they negotiate their time within corrections. Zealous use of breaching powers firmly establishes the 'us' and 'them' distance between practitioner and offender. Being told what to do, when to do it, with whom and how, are likewise empirical signs that there are major differences in power between the key stakeholders. In this environment, building respect and trust can be very difficult. It is compounded by advancements generally within corrective services: 'Given the increasing arsenal of surveillance tools available to parole agencies – urine screening, electronic monitoring, integrated data systems, global positioning technology, and the like – the ability to detect even minor violations is substantial' (Burke 2001: 14). How corrective service practitioners utilise these powers has huge implications for their relationship with offenders.

Whether forced or not, the fact that practitioner and offender spend a considerable amount of time together is bound to have an impact. In some cases, the length of association itself, much less the quality of the association, will create a certain bonding between worker and client. This can lead to potentially uncomfortable situations, as discussed in Scenario 6.3.


## Paradoxes and controversies

It is difficult but essential to define what is meant by the notion of 'respect'. Respect means different things to different people, so clarity is important. From a practitioner perspective respect should be linked to a human rights conception, the idea that human dignity is important and should be acknowledged at all times. For some prisoners, respect is forged in the crucible of violence and stand-over tactics. This is not the kind of respect that we can ignore; but it certainly is not the kind we want to encourage or emulate either.

Respect has other dimensions as well. It incorporates respect for oneself, as well as one's co-workers. There is much truth in the saying, 'Do unto others as you would have them do to you', or other versions of the Golden Rule. But the rule has to be applied consistently across a myriad of relationships, and it has to be demonstrated constantly in daily practice. This can be difficult, as petty jealousies and disputes, stereotypes and apprehensions cause us to act 'hard' or betray a trust. All of this is bound up in social processes that are ongoing – respect

## Scenario 6.3

### Boundaries outside the workplace

You have been working with an offender for the past six months and have developed a high level of rapport with that person. They do not have any identified issues with alcohol or drugs and they have demonstrated considerable stability in their life since they first began working with you. They now have full-time employment, stable accommodation and there are no signs that they are likely to reoffend.

It is Friday night and you have arranged to meet your friends at the local bar after work for a drink. You arrive early and no one is there yet. You sit down at the bar and order a drink while you wait for your friends. You then see the offender sitting on their own on the other side of the bar and you smile politely to them. The offender then proceeds to buy two drinks (one the same as the drink you have just purchased) and comes over to you offering you one of the drinks.

Question: What do you do in this situation?

You explain to the offender that you have just bought a drink for yourself and you are only planning to have one while you wait for your friends who are due to arrive any minute. The offender is insistent that you accept the drink, sits down next to you, and begins to talk to you about their week at work.

Question: What do you do in this situation?

is never finite; it continues as long as the relationships that sustain it continue.

Being professional is about knowing the boundaries of sensible behaviour and making sure that everyone knows where the boundaries lie. Gaining respect may *segue* into relationships that are less than healthy. For example, co-dependency and enmeshment are not good practice, even if they make you feel good. Getting too close to the client, and forming a mutually reinforcing dependency with them, goes against the ideas of self-empowerment and self-determination. Working with respect is not about this kind of personal (lack of) control. Role delineation is one way in which to keep things honest and upfront.

## Conclusion

This chapter has explored some of the ways in which human rights considerations can be put into a practitioner context. This is basically informed at a philosophical level by the notion of human dignity and worth. It is transmitted at a practical level in systems of governance and ways of working that allow for active offender participation in the rehabilitation process. Not everyone wants to change. Not everyone can change. This applies to workers as much as it does to offenders. But in either case it is absolutely essential that options for change be provided, that a culture of change be fostered, and that personal responsibility for change be emphasised. These, too, are among the manifold signs of respect.

## Discussion questions

1 Prisoners are separated from loved ones, and they are often parents. Being in prison is an emotional experience. What are the implications of this for working with offenders?
2 How does the notion of 'master status' influence how workers work with certain offenders, and how offenders relate to certain correctional staff?
3 Respect is not only bestowed but is something that is earned. What does this mean when it comes to working with offenders in the community?

## Further reading

Austin, W. (2001) 'Relational ethics in forensic psychiatric settings', *Journal of Psychosocial Nursing and Mental Health Services*, 39(9): 12–17.

Bonta, J., Rugge, T., Scott, T., Bourgon, G. and Yessine, A. (2008) 'Exploring the black box of community supervision', *Journal of Offender Rehabilitation*, 47(3): 248–70.

Butler, M. (2008) 'What are you looking at? Prisoner confrontations and the search for respect', *British Journal of Criminology*, 48(6): 856–73.

Trotter, C. (2006) *Working with Involuntary Clients: A Guide to Practice*. Sydney: Allen and Unwin.

Ward, T. and Birgden, A. (2007) 'Human rights and correctional clinical practice', *Aggression and Violent Behaviour*, 12(6): 628–43.

## Key resources

Bergum, V. and Dossetor, J. (2005) *Relational Ethics: The Full Meaning of Respect*. Maryland: University Publishing Group.

Cherry, S. (2005) *Transforming Behaviour: Pro-Social Modelling in Practice*. Cullompton: Willan Publishing.

Commonwealth of Australia (2009) *Father Inclusive Practice Guide: A Tool to Support the Inclusion of Fathers in a Holistic Approach to Service Delivery*. Canberra: Australian Government Department of Families, Housing, Community Services and Indigenous Affairs.

Pryor, S. (2001) *The Responsible Prisoner: An Exploration of the Extent to which Prison Removes Responsibility Unnecessarily and an Invitation to Change*. London: Her Majesty's Inspectorate of Prisons.

United Nations (2005) *Human Rights and Prisons: Manual on Human Rights Training for Prison Officials*. New York: Office of the United Nations High Commissioner for Human Rights.

## Chapter 7

# Working with complex needs and special populations

Each day, a disturbingly large number of people with mental illness cycle through the criminal justice system across the nation. Before arriving in the criminal justice system, these individuals have frequently fallen through the 'safety net' of families, hospitals and community based treatment providers ... The results are painfully clear: many defendants with mental illness churn through the criminal justice system again and again, going through a 'revolving door' from street to court to cell and back again without ever receiving the support and structure they need. It is fair to say that no one wins when this happens – not defendants, not police, not courts, not victims, and not communities.

(Court planners, quoted in Denckla and Berman 2001: 1, 4)

If nothing meaningful is done to arrest this tide of ragged, angry, embittered, and isolated humanity the workload will simply multiply – a simple cost benefit analysis would show the abject futility of this. It is also wasting humanity.

(Magistrate, quoted in Auty 2006)

## Introduction

This chapter explores what is involved in responding to offenders holistically. The whole person comprises many individual facets, and these need to be addressed in the context of the whole person. For generalist workers, such as probation officers or prison officers, the chapter is intended to provide an opportunity to learn more about the specific issues they will encounter in the course of their work, as well as become familiar with the language and specific interventions and approaches adopted by colleagues in multidisciplinary teams that may be specifically working with the special populations and individuals' needs outlined here. Our concern is with the practical but not the clinical aspects of working with offenders. Accordingly, tables and statistics are used to inform practitioners about the scale and nature of different issues, and the strategies outlined are provided as the groundwork for practical responses in relation to these.

The diverse needs of various vulnerable populations in the criminal justice system are presented in this chapter, including observations about the added layer of complexity of responding to these issues in a correctional environment. The health and well-being of offender populations is examined, with particular attention to issues such as mental illness, substance misuse and physical health problems. Special populations include groups such as women, indigenous people, sex offenders, young people, culturally and linguistically diverse groups, and foreign prisoners.

Throughout this book we have stressed the fact that offenders have complex needs. Most offenders who end up in the criminal justice system come from severely disadvantaged backgrounds. As this chapter demonstrates, most, as well, have a wide range of serious health and well-being problems. To work well in working with offenders we need to develop generalist skills, as explored in Chapter 6. We also need to develop the capacity to respond to the multidimensional nature of individuals, as outlined in this chapter.

## Complex needs, principles of recovery and strengths-based rehabilitation

The rehabilitation models and strategies described in Chapter 2 emphasise the individuality of each offender, their commonalities with other offenders, and the importance of clear assessment of dynamic risk factors and positive strengths in determining an appropriate intervention. A strengths-based rehabilitation strategy provides a kind of antidote to the 'othering' and social exclusion frequently experienced by vulnerable population groups. An approach that fosters inclusion and participation, and that offers the benefits of hope and resilience, will at the very least assist in the desistance process.

When it comes to dealing with complex needs, a paradigm that is increasingly influential, particularly in the mental health and alcohol and other drugs sectors, is the Recovery model. This paradigm represents movement away from focusing on problems (pathology, illness, deficit or symptoms) towards health, building on strengths and achieving well-being. Recovery is about building a meaningful and satisfying lifestyle, as defined by the person themselves, whether or not there are symptoms or reminders of the problems they are recovering from (Shepherd *et al.* 2008: 2). Self-management and hope are foundational to strengths-based rehabilitation, but are best complemented by social support, compassion and empathy, empowerment, opportunities and resources. The aim of strengths-based rehabilitation, as with most offender rehabilitation more widely, is supporting a person to discover a new sense of identity, drawing on positive personal capacity, external influences, and pro-social values. As such it shares much in common with the Good Lives Model of offender rehabilitation.

Social inclusion is paramount in terms of strengths-based rehabilitation and offender reintegration. Communities and social networks need to learn how to live with and include members who have complex needs. The development of social capital involves identifying and tapping into the resources, people, networks and opportunities available to support a person in their recovery and reintegration. Examples of sources of social inclusion and social capital could include: a helpful and supportive partner, getting a new house to rent or a new job, finding a great GP/doctor, pets, getting involved in a church community, or attending a peer support group or common interest group (hobbies, for example). Expenditure of capital is also important, as acknowledged in the 'social recognition' approach (Chapter 2). The example provided in Innovative practice 7 shows how complex needs can be addressed in a specific program in a way that brings skills, and joy, to the participants. Treating people and issues holistically in such ways also reinforces respect and the building of trust between various actors within correctional settings.

### Clusters of need

Practitioners working in criminal justice and corrections are, by the nature of their work, supporting people with complex needs, and in so doing will need to draw upon a wide spectrum of expertise. We cannot do everything, and we cannot do everything by ourselves.

### Innovative practice 7

#### Daddy's bedtime stories: the power of reading beyond the lines

StoryBook Dads is an initiative enabling fathers in prison to record bedtime stories to give to their children to play at home. Six community members work on the project in Dartmoor Prison, England, alongside prisoners who are learning editing skills and technical knowledge through the production of DVDs and audio CDs (Kemp 2008). Dominic, a prisoner who volunteers to help run the project, comments: 'Back on the wings, it's all the typical macho, hard man stuff you probably expect prison to be. But in the editing suite, you see a more human side. When they're talking about their kids or flicking through the storybooks or choosing which puppet they'll do a DVD with, you see some blokes soften up' (quoted in Kemp 2008).

In a similar initiative called Reading Together in the Tasmanian Prison Service in Australia, prisoners record stories onto CD, with the support of literacy and numeracy tutors, and send the CD along with the book to their children. The tutors work with fathers to plan how the story can be animated in a way that is age appropriate, with theatrical elements like animal noises added where relevant. One prisoner talks of the positive personal impact: 'I am going to be in here a long time, and the stories I will be reading will get harder. I have enrolled in literacy courses so I can read harder books as my kids get older.' Another commented: 'My daughter is so much more settled now that she can hear my voice' (quoted in Duncan 2009: 4).

Positive outcomes of both projects include improved prisoner literacy rates and self-esteem, and stronger communication skills; involvement in children's education and learning; ongoing development of positive family ties; and constructive use of time while inside. This is summed up by Troy, a prisoner and father of five:

> It's a good way to communicate and I suppose it's educational, too, for me and the kids. I'm not the best reader and the first book was a bit awkward; sort of having someone around, it was a bit embarrassing. But maybe I've become a bit more open in reading and less judgmental. If I do make mistakes, like reading and that, no one's perfect. I just want the best for my boys ... It's just opened a door that was closed for a long time and it makes me realise that there is nothing wrong with being affectionate towards your kids. (quoted in O'Dwyer 2010: 30)

This is illustrated in Figure 7.1, showing a series of clusters of need pertaining to offenders.

One result of assessment processes, as described in Chapters 2 and 6, is that we should gain a fairly good idea about the dynamic risk factors and individual character profile of the offender. Let us consider, for example, the health and well-being of offender populations. People with offending histories may also live with one or more health issue, exemplified by the following list of common health problems:

- Mental illness, forensic mental health, and trauma
- Intellectual disabilities and acquired brain injuries
- Physical disabilities and health problems (such as diabetes)
- Substance misuse and addiction (including cigarettes)
- Lack of nourishment and lack of physical health and fitness
- Poor dental hygiene
- Sexual health and victims of sexual abuse
- Blood-borne viruses: Hepatitis C and HIV AIDS
- Co-morbidity: mental illness, alcohol and other drug misuse, other problems

Following on from the notion of 'clusters of need', Table 7.1 illustrates how US prisoners with current medical problems, impairments

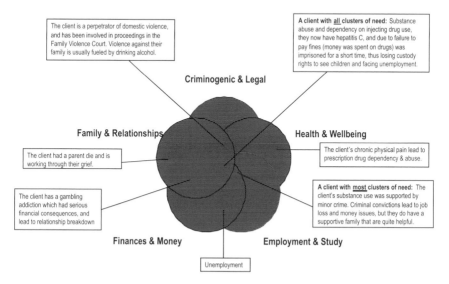

**Figure 7.1**  Clusters of need and clusters of expertise

or injuries are significantly more likely to also have experienced homelessness, unemployment and substance use.

The category of 'impairment' can be briefly highlighted here as it raises the ethical and operational mandate to adequately support the needs of prisoners with impairments, including physical disabilities:

> The difficulties that people with disabilities face are magnified in prisons, given the nature of the closed and restricted environment and violence resulting from overcrowding, lack of proper prisoner differentiation and supervision, among others. Prison overcrowding accelerates the disabling process with the neglect, psychological stress and lack of adequate medical care characteristic of overcrowded prisons. (UNODC 2009: 43)

Special practice considerations when working with prisoners with disabilities include: classification and accommodation; prison architecture and access issues; supervision, violence prevention and monitoring vulnerability; staff attitudes and training around

**Table 7.1** Health-related conditions reported by prison inmates by background characteristics in state prisons in the United States, 2004

| Type of data | Have current medical problem | Have any impairment | Injured since admission to prison |
|---|---|---|---|
| Homeless in year before arrest? | | | |
| Yes | 51.2% | 48.9% | 35.1% |
| No | 43.0% | 34.8% | 32.3% |
| Employed in month before offence? | | | |
| Yes | 43.8% | 34.9% | 32.7% |
| No | 43.8% | 39.2% | 31.9% |
| Used drugs in month before arrest? | | | |
| Yes | 42.9% | 37.2% | 34.3% |
| No | 45.2% | 34.8% | 30.7% |

*Note*: 'Impairment' includes the following areas: learning, speech, hearing, vision, mobility and mental difficulties.
*Source*: Adapted from Maruschak (2008).

disability; and the need for partnership and collaboration with external service providers specifically catering for the needs of people with disabilities.

Incarceration provides a critical intervention point for health promotion with demographics (particularly young men) that are traditionally reticent to see doctors for personal health problems and, similarly, health professionals in the broader community are often wary of them (especially if they have been 'burned' by doctor shopping or pressure to prescribe certain drugs). Comments by a nineteen-year-old prisoner illustrate the opportunity inherent in a captive audience: 'It's time to get healthy ... get back to normal. It's just a thing with prisoners – come in jail and get yourself sorted. I had better things to do when I was out, but in here you've got all the time in the world, so you might as well get everything done' (quoted in Condon *et al.* 2007: 221).

What the data in Table 7.1 also reinforces is the importance of issues of duty of care and the need for collaboration because no one worker can address an individual's needs adequately alone, as well as balance a (usually high) caseload and other job requirements and tasks. Collaboration across multidisciplinary teams and systems is essential; this is covered in Chapter 9. In terms of a more structural or 'big picture' level, work is being spearheaded by the World Health Organisation to move towards a notion of 'health promoting prisons' as a critical intervention point for improving the health outcomes of offenders (see Moller *et al.* 2007).

Interestingly, we have noted an apparent split in existing literature, particularly in relation to the health and well-being of offenders. On the one end of the spectrum there is a proliferation of highly specialised (usually quite medical or clinical) articles that incisively outline one specific subset of problems, and those are analysed in detail. At the other end of the spectrum is a fair proportion of literature and broad guides from generalist practitioners (probation officers, social workers) on the practical mechanics of working with offenders. The problematic part about this end is that the application of principles and practices leans towards one-size-fits-all interpretation and intervention. The rest of this chapter therefore attempts to bridge this gap somewhat by providing detailed summaries of some of the issues and circumstances that together make up what we describe as the complex needs of offenders. At the very least, it is essential that practitioners across the board have some idea of the real and potential difficulties experienced by the clients with whom they may have to work.

## Psychiatric disorders, personality disorders, and intellectual disabilities – similarities and differences

Mental illness and psychiatric disorders are a major and increasing concern in the criminal justice system, from entry into the courts through to incarceration and reintegration back into the community.

The process of deinstitutionalisation is one of the most significant occurrences in the history of mental health policy and practice. The decision and process of closing down asylums for people with a mental illness occurred from the late 1950s onwards; this was a positive breakthrough made possible with the promise of care and support in the community. However, the transition towards community support has not been a smooth one. Some commentators hold the view that one institution (the asylum) has been swapped with another (prisons), with the increasing criminalisation and incarceration of the mentally ill in Australia and other countries such as the US and UK (see Table 7.2) (Meadows *et al.* 2007).

When associated with inconsistent and lacking community support, deinstitutionalisation has been linked to the exacerbation of what was an already well-established 'revolving door' phenomenon (Graham 2007). Popovic describes the traditional court process in relation to mentally ill offenders as a case of 'sentencing the unsentenceable' with 'meaningless sentences' (2006: 1). Judicial officers, lawyers and other practitioners in the court are aware of these problems, including the costs and complications associated with cyclic and counterproductive measures. Heightened awareness in the judiciary and legal circles is

**Table 7.2** Comparative rates of mental illness and substance misuse in prisoner populations and the general community in England and Wales

| Type of data | Prevalence among prisoners | Prevalence in the general population |
| --- | --- | --- |
| Psychosis | 8% | 0.5% |
| Personality disorder | 66% | 5.3% |
| Depression or anxiety | 45% | 13.8% |
| Drug dependency | 45% | 5.2% |
| Alcohol dependency | 30% | 11.5% |

*Note*: This data refers to people aged 16–64 years.
*Source*: Singleton *et al.* (1998, 2000), cited in Sainsbury Centre for Mental Health (2009: 2).

contributing to the emerging trend of therapeutic jurisprudence, as discussed in Chapter 2, as a more humane way of dealing with this vulnerable population.

### Supervision strategies for offenders with a mental illness in the community

The following checklist of guidance strategies (from Federal Judicial Center 2003: 25–6) is fairly basic, and may be taken as a given for more seasoned practitioners, but it is useful nonetheless.

- Schedule the initial contact with a person with a mental disorder in the office because the individual may view home visits as threatening.

- Review all psychiatric and medical documentation.

- Assess the degree of general danger and third-party risk that the individual poses to himself or herself or to others. Note any history of dangerous behaviour. Review the supervision plan with your supervisor and alert the supervisor to any special issues associated with the case.

- Identify any areas in which the person may need assistance (obtaining medical assistance, disability income, housing, or vocational training).

- Have the individual sign release of confidential information forms.

- Work with the mental health treatment provider to monitor the individual's compliance with the medication regime and to assess his/her therapeutic progress. Familiarise yourself with the individual's psychotropic medication so that you can talk with him or her about the medication regime and encourage him or her to take the medication as prescribed.

- Be alert to drug and alcohol abuse relapses associated with co-occurring cases.

- Coordinate treatment services. Share information with the providers as needed and in accordance with confidentiality regulations and statutes.

- Schedule contacts with the individual based on the severity of the mental disorder, the state of his or her physical health, and occupational and social circumstances.

- Clearly establish and explain the limits of acceptable and unacceptable behaviour. Explain the consequences of non-compliance with the conditions of supervision.

- Identify the individual's support system (family, friends, employers, and others) and make frequent contact with these individuals. Note that officers should not disclose any more pre-trial, pre-sentence, or supervision information than necessary to obtain requested information from collateral contacts.

- Prepare crisis intervention plans for handling suicide threats or attempts, psychotic episodes, assault threats, and other crises that may arise as a result of the individual's mental disorder. Officers may want to consult with local crisis screening centres or crisis intervention teams in preparing these plans.

Table 7.3 builds upon the supervision strategies by providing some considerations unique to specific mental health disorders. A preface to Table 7.3 is the explicit assumption that not all people with a specific mental health disorder experience the same set of symptoms or should be watched for exactly the same risks or concerns. It is possible for people with the most severe disorders and life circumstances to avoid relapse and recidivism, to maintain hope and resilience, and to work towards recovery and self-fulfilment. That notwithstanding, these concerns are provided as a general guidance for community corrections officers in the United States.

In the light of the offender supervision considerations outlined in Table 7.3, and to basically reiterate a point we made in Chapter 5, practitioners should be flexible and responsible in offering interventions and professional guidance in keeping with their personal qualifications, training and experience.

### Practical strategies for people who have panic attacks

Panic attacks are a very scary and overwhelming experience that can occur at random in response to various situations, and are commonly reported among client groups of a variety of services, ranging from people anxious about returning to work through to those who are incarcerated or preparing for release. A person having a panic attack may feel like they are very sick or going to die. For medium to long-term management of/coping with panic attacks, clients may benefit from these tips from Teevan and Gorman (2008: 8–11), which are directly intended for clients themselves:

Table 7.3  Supervision considerations for offenders with severe mental illness

| Bipolar disorders | During a manic episode, poor judgement, hyperactivity and other symptoms of the disorder may lead an individual into activities such as reckless driving, foolish business ventures, spending sprees or crime. When an individual is experiencing a major depressed state, monitor him or her for suicidal thoughts, self-harm, or potential for harm to others. Although elevated mood is the primary symptom of a manic episode, in instances where the individual is hindered or frustrated, the mood disturbance may be characterised by complaints, irritability, hostile comments or angry tirades. |
|---|---|
| Schizophrenia | People with schizophrenia are often impaired in several areas of routine daily functioning, such as work, social relations and ability to care for self. Placement in a supported or group house or structured day treatment program may be necessary to ensure that the person is properly fed and clothed, and to protect the individual from the consequences of poor judgement, impaired thinking or actions based on hallucinations or delusions. Patients with schizophrenia have a higher rate of suicide than the general population. Non-compliance with the medication regime as a result of the medication's side effects is a common supervision problem. Research indicates that violence is no more common in patients with schizophrenia than in the general population. |
| Paraphilias (sexual dysfunction disorders) | Many individuals with paraphilias do not respond well to traditional psychotherapy. Whereas sex offender treatment teaches coping skills to help the individual resist acting on his or her abnormal sexual interests, it does not cure the paraphilia. Relapse prevention is a critical part of the treatment regime and generally consists of requiring the individual to attend aftercare groups. Managing risk is the primary focus of supervision and necessitates an extraordinary amount of contact with both the offender and the treatment provider. Be mindful of the need to restrict the offender's travel, as offenders with paraphilias often travel to find new victims. Suicide is a possibility for some sex offenders who experience severe depression upon entering the criminal justice system. For example, a middle-class offender who loses family, friends, job and personal reputation because of an arrest or conviction for child molestation may become suicidal. |

*Source*: Drawn from Federal Judicial Center (2003: 33–51).

Panic attacks are likely to make a person feel out of control and dependent, the victim of their bodily reactions and external circumstances. The first step on the road to recovery is recognition by the individual that you have the power to control your symptoms. Here are some practical strategies:

- *Take control* – start by really looking, in detail, at your panic attacks. When did they happen? Where were you? What were you thinking? See if you can identify particular thoughts that trigger a panic reaction.

- *Don't fight them when they happen* – a number of experts have emphasised the need to accept the panic attacks when they occur and that it may in fact be most helpful if you try and ride out the attacks to learn that no harm will come to you. This may sound strange, but fighting them only increases your level of fear and allows your panic to take on tremendous proportions. By going with the panic, you are reducing its power to terrify you.

- *Creative visualisation and affirmations* – you can use these techniques to retrain your imagination and to get yourself moving in a more positive direction. Many people who suffer panic attacks have a vivid imagination, which they use to conjure up disaster, illness and death. You can train your imagination to focus on situations that give you a sense of well-being. You can use visualisation to focus on situations that you fear. Imagine the situation and speak positively to yourself, 'I am doing well', 'this is easy'. These simple, positive present-tense affirmations are messages that you can say silently or out loud. These techniques do not provide a quick fix.

- *Assertiveness* – you may be having panic attacks because there are aspects of your life that are undermining your self-confidence. It may be useful to look at your family life, your job, and so on, and identify changes you would like to make. If you feel trapped in a situation, and find it very difficult to express your true feelings, you may find assertiveness training helpful.

- *Learn a relaxation technique* – if you habitually clench your jaw and your shoulders are tensed up, this will generate further stress. Relaxation techniques focus on easing muscle tension and slowing down your breathing. It helps your mind to relax.

- *Breathing* – hyperventilation (over-breathing) commonly leads to panic attacks. Many people get into the habit of breathing shallowly, from the upper chest, rather than more slowly from the abdomen. Put one hand on your upper chest and the other on your stomach. Notice which hand moves as you breathe. The hand on your chest should hardly move, if you are breathing correctly from your diaphragm. Practise this breathing, slowly and calmly, every day.

- *Diet* – unstable blood sugar levels can contribute to levels of panic. Eat regularly and avoid sugary foods and drinks, white flour and junk food. Caffeine, alcohol and smoking all contribute to panic attacks and are best avoided.

- *Cognitive behavioural therapy* – our thoughts have a very powerful impact on our behaviour. You may be unaware of seemingly automatic thoughts and misinterpretations that provoke attacks. The way we interpret things can cause extreme distress. But it is possible to bring about a state of well-being by changing habitual thought patterns. If we think that our racing heart is a possible heart attack we'll be very frightened, but if we think it is due to excitement or too much coffee, we'll feel very differently about it. Cognitive behavioural therapy aims to change the negative thought patterns and misinterpretations that can feed panic attacks.

Offenders who are incarcerated will have less control over their environment, as prison presents a number of constraints that impact on a person's help-seeking behaviour and ability to have privacy during a panic attack.

### Personality disorders

Personality disorders are classified differently from most mental illnesses in that the DSM-IV, the dominant classification tool for mental health disorders in the western world, states that they actually fall under the domain of 'behavioural disorders'. In practice, the links between psychiatric disorders and personality disorders are complicated, and people often have diagnoses from more than one axis (or section) of the DSM anyway. Add offending behaviour to

### Scenario 7.1

**An offender is socially isolated and experiencing emotional difficulties**

You are interviewing an offender pre-sentence in order to provide a report to the court. He discloses a life filled with trauma going back to his childhood. He states that currently he is having difficulties with his son who got in with the wrong crowd and commenced a life of petty crime, which in recent months has progressed to more serious property crime. His son lives in a caravan on his property, and recently he took the keys to the house from his son as he became aware that his son was stealing possessions from him and selling them for drug money. Since he took the keys his son has smashed windows to get into the property to steal more of the offender's possessions.

He advises that the stress of his son's behaviour has caused problems between him and his wife, and that she told him yesterday that she wanted a divorce and he needed to move out of the house by the end of the week. The offender informs you that he has no family support and no close friends, and has no accommodation prospects so is beginning to get very stressed about that as well.

When you come to question the offender about any suicidal ideation he informs you that it is something he thinks about on a daily basis. He further states that he stood on the edge of a bridge approximately three weeks ago but did not jump. He advises you that his neighbour has firearms and he has offered to lend one to the offender in the past so that he could go hunting. It appears as if things are getting progressively worse for the offender, and there is a real risk that he will commit suicide.

*Question*
Given he has no family or close friends for you to contact, and he refuses to give you his wife's contact details, what do you do at the end of the interview when it is time for him to leave your office?

the mix and this becomes one of the most challenging populations to work with in the criminal justice system. Anti-social personality disorder (ASPD) is most commonly found among offender populations because the symptoms or behavioural consequences of this disorder often lead to criminal charges from incidences of aggression, poor impulse control, and intensely anti-social acts that have a negative impact on others. This disorder is particularly hard to treat. Yet there is some evidence to suggest that the following interventions are of some merit: motivational interviewing, cognitive behavioural therapy, dialectical behaviour therapy, and medication to control certain symptoms of arousal and impulse control (Gordon 2009). The most important things a practitioner can do when working with people with personality disorders are boundary setting and role clarification, as manipulative behaviours and lying are common.

A point of difference between personality disorders and mental health disorders relates to pharmacological treatment. The types of licit drugs that are often used to address mental health issues like anxiety and depression can be quite problematic when used for people with personality disorders, depending on the individual. Benzodiazepines ('benzos') are a legal prescription drug most commonly used in mental health and alcohol and other drugs services for helping a person to detox. One of the adverse side effects for the general population is that this category of drugs is highly addictive and should not be used for more than a few days or weeks at a time. For people with personality disorders, the potential side effects of these prescription drugs may be a lot worse. Benzos have been associated with reduced impulse control, lack of inhibitions, and increased levels of violence for people with personality disorders (Gordon 2009). There is also an increased risk of sedation and overdose if a client combines benzodiazepines with antidepressants. A client with a personality disorder who is taking benzos, needs to work with their doctor to slowly reduce their dosage. If they are accessing illicit versions of the drug, they will need to contact a local withdrawal management service for assistance with medical detoxification. Practitioner awareness of these issues is valuable, particularly in residential or institutional settings where staff may be overseeing rehabilitation as well as monitoring treatment compliance, as the prescribing doctor may not be fully aware of their diagnosis or ongoing psychological state.

Table 7.4 illustrates the contrasting differences between the various types of personality disorders, with some presenting a far greater concern and risk to themselves and the workforce, and others simply requiring monitoring and awareness of how the disorder affects their behaviour.

It should be acknowledged that some of this terminology and associated interventions may be unfamiliar for non-clinical practitioners. Yet the supervision considerations should not be dismissed as only applicable to clinicians. Some of the most central competencies and approaches in working with personality disorders

**Table 7.4**  Supervision considerations for offenders with personality disorders

| | |
|---|---|
| **Paranoid personality disorder** | Paranoid personality disorder involves a pervasive and unwarranted tendency, beginning in early adulthood, to interpret the actions of others as deliberately threatening and demeaning. Cases with this personality disorder are sometimes argumentative, hostile, irritable or angry. Often they experience lifelong problems with working and living with others. They may need help framing their perceptions more realistically and not projecting their own hostile or unacceptable feelings onto others. |
| **Borderline personality disorder** | Because of their unpredictable and impulsive behaviour, persons with borderline personality disorder are often in a state of extreme crisis, involving problems with finances, health, relationships or other areas of their lives. Prognosis for treatment is extremely poor. These cases may play the treatment provider and the officer against each other. At the beginning of treatment, schedule a meeting with all parties to discuss treatment goals. Remain vigilant for manipulative gestures throughout supervision. Recurrent suicidal threats and behaviour or self-mutilation are common in severe cases. Hospitalisation may be required when a person is excessively self-destructive.<br><br>Focus your supervision on defining acceptable and unacceptable behaviour and parameters of compliance and providing structure that will enable the individual to comply. These cases demonstrate poor judgement in relationships and frequently change partners. Females with this disorder are often seductive and may have trouble maintaining appropriate boundaries. Thus it is often best to have another officer accompany you on home contacts. |
| **Histrionic personality disorder** | Persons with histrionic personality disorder sometimes appear to be in crisis because they are excessive in their expression of emotion. They are sensation seekers who may get in trouble with the law, abuse drugs, or act promiscuously. Cases with histrionic personality disorder have superficial relationships, although they have strong dependency needs. Seductive behaviour is common. Discourage it by defining the parameters of the officer–client relationship throughout the supervision period. To the extent possible, make home contacts in teams. |
| **Narcissistic personality disorder** | The individual with narcissistic personality disorder is often arrogant, aloof, superior and condescending. He or she is likely to play power games with the officer, and winning any of these games will only reinforce the narcissistic behaviour. In addition, these cases have fragile self-esteem and are prone |

*Table 7.4 continued*

| | |
|---|---|
| | to suicide. Individuals with this disorder respond negatively to ageing and are susceptible to mid-life crises because they place excessive value on youth, beauty and strength. Major depression can occur. Because they frequently experience interpersonal problems and exploit others to achieve their ends, rely on supervision strategies more than treatment to manage risk. Set, clarify and enforce limits on behaviour. |
| **Avoidant personality disorder** | The person with avoidant personality disorder avoids social contact for fear of rejection. Many persons with avoidant personality disorder are able to function as long as they are in a safe, protected family environment. Should this support system fail, however, they may experience anger, depression or anxiety. Individuals with this disorder respond poorly to the slightest perceived rejection or criticisms. |
| **Dependent personality disorder** | Cases with this disorder will most likely have a long-standing relationship with one person upon whom they are grossly dependent. If anything should happen to that person or to the relationship, the individual might develop depression. Be aware of the status of this individual's relationship with his or her significant other and remain alert to the signs of possible depression or suicide when the relationship is unstable. A person with a dependent personality disorder may be involved in an abusive relationship. The abuse may increase as the person becomes more self-sufficient through therapy and begins to display what the abusive partner perceives as independent or defiant behaviour. |
| **Anti-social personality disorder** | Anti-social personality disorder is characterised by an inability to conform to social norms and a continuous display of irresponsible and anti-social behaviour. It is common for people with this disorder to have been bullied, threatened or intimidated as a child, and to have a history of misconduct themselves as an adolescent. Some mental health providers find anti-social personality disorder difficult to treat and may refuse to take a referral. Prognosis for successful treatment is extremely poor. Rely on supervision strategies more than treatment to manage risk. Some persons with this disorder may be very charming and manipulative. Set, clarify and enforce limits on behaviour. Monitor these cases for drug and alcohol use and anti-social acts such as physical fights and assaults, association with criminals, and reckless or drunk driving. This personality disorder is most common among prisoner populations. |

*Source*: Drawn from Federal Judicial Center (2003: 52–6).

are the most simple. For example, consistency, honesty and fairness are paramount, as an offender with a personality disorder may be, consciously or subconsciously, monitoring for loopholes or lax boundaries for different reasons. When unwell or unstable, a person with anti-social personality disorder may wish to manipulate or exploit workers, whereas a person with histrionic personality disorder may be looking for 'the love of their life' and contradictory or incoherent professional boundaries may send the signal that you are interested in becoming a part of what is often a tumultuous and crisis-ridden life narrative. Self-disclosure and sharing about oneself is often unwise, but this can be countered by adopting a team approach where the offender with a personality disorder is not dependent on any one worker. Practitioners have been urged to be extra respectful and calm, particularly when this is perceived to be undeserved: 'don't expect to like people with personality disorders or to be liked by them' (Sainsbury Centre for Mental Health, n.d.). Heightened awareness of the individual offender's vulnerability, amid chaotic or exigent circumstances, will ensure duty of care to a group that presents some of the most challenging needs and problematic behaviours in the criminal justice system.

### Intellectual disabilities and acquired brain injury

We turn now, briefly, to a third area of mental impairment. Intellectual disabilities are a condition that a person has usually been born with that affects their cognitive functioning, whereas an acquired brain injury is something that may have resulted from an accident, trauma or head injury, leaving a person with cognitive impairment after having been healthy before this point. Box 7.1 provides an exploratory snapshot of one particular type of crime – arson – which is committed in higher rates by people with intellectual disabilities, psychiatric disorders and personality disorders.

More thorough research investigating the links between intentional fire-setting behaviour and psychiatric and intellectual impairment is required, because these two factors are not causal in their relationship and potential influencing characteristics and situational factors are many.

Thorough assessment is essential to understanding the level of risk of reoffending, as well as ascertaining an intellectually disabled offender's capacity for independent living in the community, or if incarcerated, transition back into the community. Spheres of activity and life domains for assessment are set out in Table 7.5.

Box 7.1

*Arson and adult offenders with intellectual disabilities or psychiatric disorders*

*Definition and prevalence*
Every hour of every day in Australia at least one arson fire is lit, and rates are increasing (Doley 2003). For one year alone, 323,900 intentional fires were lit in the United States, at a cost of over $1.1 billion in property damage alone, excluding costs from loss of life and livelihood (Hall 2007). Defining the crime of arson often involves four main elements (Bryant 2008: 3):

- *The setting or starting of fire* – fire is a fundamental element of arson and without the setting of fire, arson does not exist.
- *Intention or wilfulness* – all definitions of arson exclude fires that are started by natural causes or accidents.
- *Malice* – most definitions of arson incorporate an element of malice, thereby excluding fires that are started intentionally but with positive or legitimate intent.
- *Property* – most definitions require that some kind of property or object is burned.

Recidivism rates vary depending on research study, but are thought to be around 40–60 per cent (Muller 2008). Interestingly, arson is not usually a stand-alone or isolated type of criminal offending, people who commit arson may also participate in violent offences or other crimes.

*Arson and offenders with intellectual disabilities*
When the offender characteristics of arsonists are studied, arson is committed in higher rates by adults with intellectual or developmental disabilities as compared to the general population. An argument has been put forward that, for adults with mild learning difficulties, pathological arson may be 'an adaptive response to circumstances that are difficult to tolerate and which the individual does not have the necessary skills to resolve by appropriate means' (Kelly *et al.* 2009: 17). Other reasons highlighted in research investigating why people with intellectual disabilities may engage in arson include revenge, anger, a cry for help, poor communication skills, general feelings
*continued*

of frustration, a desire to feel powerful, a desire to be seen as a hero, peer pressure or being open to suggestion, depression or psychotic illnesses, and an interest in watching fires (Devapriam *et al.* 2007).

### Arson and offenders with a mental illness or personality disorder

Another characteristic associated with adult arsonists is higher rates of mental illness or personality disorders, particularly when psychosis is involved (Enayati *et al.* 2008; Anwar *et al.* 2009). 'Pyromania' is a clinical label used to describe the psychiatric condition of impulsive and compulsive fire-lighting. It involves 'the tension or arousal experienced by the individual prior to the deliberate firesetting act combined with a general fascination with fire and its trappings as well as a feeling of relief or pleasure when setting the fire or afterwards' (Doley 2003: 798).

### Treatment options for adult arsonists with complex needs

An important proviso to state at the outset is that, when choosing tools or interventions, treatment options need to be appropriate for the cognitive capacity, IQ and level of insight of the individual offender. That notwithstanding, there is evidence to support the efficacy of cognitive behavioural therapy-based group interventions aimed at reducing fire interest and changing attitudes towards fire setting (Taylor *et al.* 2002). Other interventions holding some promise for mentally or intellectually disabled arsonists include counselling, education, social skills training, family support and intervention, and short-term psychotherapy or cognitive analytic therapy (Lowenstein 2003; Hall *et al.* 2005). However, clinical supervision is recommended for any therapeutic worker involved in interventions with arsonists with complex needs, as they represent a challenging population in the criminal justice system and wider community.

Eliciting a detailed history will, in the process of hearing and exploring the person's narrative, uncover patterns and triggers, as well as other important knowledge for practitioners. This can, in turn, inform offender management and strengths-based rehabilitation activities and service provision tailored to meet the needs and responsivity of the individual offender.

**Table 7.5** Spheres of assessment and examination of the intellectually disabled offender

| | |
|---|---|
| **History of current offence** | Nature, circumstances, impulsive/planned, motive, contextual factors, e.g. life events, conflicts, pressures. |
| **Previous offence history** | Include incidents not prosecuted. Dates, nature, outcome. |
| **Neuropsychiatric and medical history** | Full details of other conduct/behaviour disorders, epilepsy, mental illness, medical problems, hospitalisations. |
| **Personality** | Features, friends, interests, relationships, gangs, pathological type. |
| **Family and background factors** | Family history of mental illness, mental retardation, delinquency, criminality or other psychopathy. |
| **Mental state examination** | Intellectual level and functioning, mental illness, fitness to plead, concept of right and wrong. |
| **Physical examination** | Note particularly any minor physical defects. |
| **Psychometry** | IQ, educational attainments, adaptive behaviour, structured analysis of offence behaviour. |
| **EEG and brain scan** | If organic pathology suspected. |
| **Chromosome studies** | If behavioural phenotype suspected. |

*Source*: Leonard *et al*. (2005: 110).

## Responding to drug issues and substance misuse in the criminal justice system

While substance use disorders are classified as a mental health disorder, and there are fairly high rates of overlap, it should be acknowledged that substance misuse and drug-related offending does present a related but different set of supervision considerations from that of cognitive impairment. We turn now to a discussion of the various criminal justice approaches to drug-related offending.

As we have indicated throughout the scope of this book, drug issues often present in relation to criminal offending, as rates are particularly high among police detainees (see Table 7.6) and inmates alike.

Similar to the information in Table 7.6, other international research suggests that between 50 and 80 per cent of prisoners in Europe and the United Kingdom have a history of substance misuse prior to incarceration (Zurhold *et al.* 2004; Boys *et al.* 2002).

The response of criminal justice institutions in many jurisdictions has generally been weighted towards a harm minimisation model in recent years (which parallels the trend towards non-adversarial justice noted in Chapter 2). This is evident in policies and programs relevant to police, courts and corrections. The broad areas include:

- Police diversion
- Court-based diversion programs
- Drug courts
- Compulsory drug treatment correctional centres.

The key concepts driving these initiatives are 'diversion' (not from the system, but to alternative programs within it) and 'therapeutic jurisprudence' (where the law itself functions as therapist to address underlying problems). The point of intervention is at least twofold (among other things): to provide for a reduction in or cessation of drug use; and to provide for a reduction in or cessation of drug or drug-related offending.

**Table 7.6** Detainees' prevalence of alcohol and other drugs use in previous twelve months by gender in Australia

| Type of substance | Women | Men | Combined |
|---|---|---|---|
| Cannabis | 60.8% | 66.1% | 65.3% |
| Alcohol | 58.7% | 67.6% | 66.2% |
| Amphetamine/methylamphetamine | 55.2% | 46.4% | 47.8% |
| Heroin | 25.3% | 17.9% | 19.0% |
| MDMA (Ecstasy) | 18.0% | 21.0% | 20.5% |
| Benzodiazepines | 16.4% | 12.3% | 12.9% |
| Cocaine | 11.0% | 10.4% | 10.5% |
| Morphine or other opiates | 15.3% | 10.6% | 11.3% |
| Street methadone | 6.9% | 4.9% | 5.2% |
| Hallucinogens | 3.1% | 5.4% | 5.0% |
| No drug/alcohol used | 10.1% | 9.5% | 9.6% |

*Source*: Loxley and Adams (2009).

The reason for the various changes and reforms in criminal justice pertaining to drugs has to do with the nature of the clientele themselves. Data collected about police detainees, for example, illustrates this point. The above tables indicate the rather huge problem of co-morbidity among those presenting to the criminal justice system. For instance, psychiatric well-being is intertwined with drug use, and these in turn are linked to issues of accommodation and income.

In a nutshell, the issues arising from the drugs/crime nexus include the fact that poly-drug use is prevalent among those most deeply implicated in the criminal justice system. The extent and nature of drug use is profoundly socially patterned, with the most public and harmful uses associated with low socio-economic background and those with few social resources. Again, it needs to be emphasised that harmful and problem drug use is intrinsically tied into issues of co-morbidity – that is, the overlapping problems of homelessness, abuse, family difficulties, mental illness and deteriorating physical health.

Prison drug programs usually encompass several different types of strategy. These include, for instance:

- *Supply reduction strategies* – drug detection dogs; urinalysis programs.

- *Demand reduction strategies* – detoxification; opioid maintenance therapies and pharmacotherapy; inmate programmes/counselling; drug-free wings/units.

- *Harm reduction strategies* – harm reduction education; illicit drug peer education; BBV testing (blood-borne viral infections); HBV vaccine (Hepatitis B); condom provision; bleach/detergent provision; naloxone.

Dealing with drugs and substance misuse in a prison context, however, frequently entails a series of interrelated problems. This can pose major institutional and operational challenges, which need to be balanced with the human rights of prisoners and staff (see Chapter 6). These issues are raised in Scenario 7.2.

One final point for caseworkers and counsellors is to remain aware of any issues of boundary maintenance that may arise. Enmeshment and unhealthy boundary crossing between client and worker can sometimes occur when a person is experiencing ongoing chronic difficulty. When working with people with complex needs,

## Scenario 7.2

### Drug use in prison

According to Dolan and colleagues (2007), drug use in prison represents three kinds of risk: risk to public health (issues of the spread of blood-borne viruses, increased health risk behaviours like unprotected sex, and higher risk of overdose upon release due to different drug strengths); risk of reoffending (drug users have higher rates of recidivism); and risk to the security of the prison (issues of drug dealing, bullying, drug-related violence and assaults, corruption of prison staff).

*Scenario*
Evaluate the strengths and weaknesses of offering the following prison harm reduction services, taking into consideration the best interests of prisoners, front-line staff and senior management:

- Detoxification and medical withdrawal management.
- Pharmacotherapy and maintenance prescribing of methadone, buprenorphine or naltrexone.
- Drug-free units and therapeutic communities offering rehabilitation inside the prison.
- Needle exchange and the offering of clean injecting gear to prisoners.
- Peer mentoring and providing overdose prevention 'save a mate' training to prisoners.

*Questions*
Making use of the discussion notes provided in Appendix 1, answer each of the following questions:

1 Discuss the opportunities and benefits involved in offering these different services in prison.

2 What are some ethical issues that arise? Can you think of any instances or examples from this list of options that might lead to conflict of different perspectives or values? Do any of the above send out mixed messages or are they pragmatic and responsible?

3 What safety and security issues arise in terms of risk management (a) for staff, and (b) for offenders?

4 In your view, which of the above options would have the biggest influence on worker–offender relationships and inmate risk management? (Perhaps give thought to issues of stigma and identification as a drug user, confidentiality and information sharing among workers, offenders and peer mentors, as well as opportunities for added therapeutic dimensions.)

it is important to liaise closely with a clinical supervisor to have an independent perspective on healthy boundaries and helping practices. How long and for what purposes agencies keep clients with acute needs on their books is worthy of critical and ongoing reflection from the point of view of best practice service provision and the best interests of the client.

## Special populations in the criminal justice system

In addition to living with health conditions, there are other groups within the criminal justice system that may form vulnerable populations or groups requiring specialist support (see the United Nations Office on Drugs and Crime 2009). These include:

- Culturally and linguistically diverse (CALD) offenders and foreign prisoners
- Indigenous people
- Young offenders
- Female offenders
- Religion and spirituality
- Gay, lesbian, bisexual and transgender offenders
- Sex offenders.

### Indigenous offenders

Canada, Australia and New Zealand are three key jurisdictions dealing with the pressing and concerning issue of the over-representation of aboriginal people in the criminal justice system. In Canada, approximately 18 per cent of prisoners in federal correctional facilities are indigenous, compared to a rate of 2 per cent of the adult population in the general community (Trevethan *et al.* 2002). Further analysis of the composition of the 18 per cent shows that the majority of aboriginal offenders in the Canadian correctional system are young, single, uneducated and unemployed males who are more likely to be incarcerated for violent offences and to have higher rates of identified personal need (emotional issues, 96 per cent; substance misuse, 92 per cent) (Trevethan *et al.* 2002).

Responses to indigenous offending in Canada are coordinated using a national approach under the auspices of the national Strategic Plan for Aboriginal Corrections. Under the direction of this plan, some promising reintegration programs and accommodation initiatives are taking place, with consultation and operation mutually dependent on a proactive and respectful relationship between aboriginal communities and correctional authorities, including the following (Correctional Service of Canada (CSC) 2010):

- *In Search of Your Warrior Program* – a high-intensity program that addresses violent criminal behaviour. Developed by the Native Counselling Services of Alberta, it is currently implemented in the Prairie, Pacific and Quebec regions.

- *The Mama Wi Program* – a family violence treatment program developed by an aboriginal social service agency in Manitoba. The program is currently implemented in the Prairie region and it is being adapted for general application.

- *A National Aboriginal Offender Pre-Orientation Program* – intended to increase inmates' preparedness to benefit from other programs offered by CSC, determine cultural and criminogenic needs and start the education of aboriginal offenders about corrections, aboriginal heritage, and healing opportunities.

- *A National Aboriginal Healing Program* – identifies and encourages traditional cultural methods of living in balance, and is currently being developed in collaboration with Native Court Workers and the Aboriginal Healing Foundation. This program is in institutions for aboriginal offenders and aboriginal communities will have access to the program for delivery in their communities.

- *Aboriginal Healing Lodges* – meeting some of the aboriginal specific accommodation needs of aboriginal federal offenders, and these are offered and operated in partnership with aboriginal communities.

- *Aboriginal Community Reintegration Program* – practical support to assist the conditional release of federal offenders back into aboriginal communities (First Nation, Metis, Inuit and Urban).

Aboriginal communities have access to funding to cover trans-portation expenses, community resources and the preparation of reintegration circles for the eventual release date.

In addition to this, there is an identified Aboriginal Corrections Continuum of Care model, developed as a new approach to addressing aboriginal offender needs. Implementation of the continuum of care includes a diverse profile of staff and community members, including elders, aboriginal liaison officers, aboriginal correctional program officers, pathways healing units, healing lodges and aboriginal community development officers (Correctional Service of Canada 2006). This continuum of care model is yielding preliminary, yet promising, results in terms of lowering recidivism rates.

In Australia, the over-representation of indigenous people in the criminal justice system has been persistent and severe, and needs to be understood within the context of colonial and neo-colonial politics. Since the initial British invasion of 1788, the indigenous peoples of Australia have been subjected to myriad interventions, exclusions and social controls. This is not simply a historical legacy; it is part of the fabric of everyday life for many indigenous peoples today. Colonialism has had a severe impact on indigenous cultures and ways of life, as have the continuing effects of discriminatory policies and practices on indigenous life chances within mainstream social institutions. The negative impact of constant state intervention into the families and communities of indigenous peoples should not be underestimated. The Stolen Generations Inquiry estimated that between one in ten and one in three aboriginal children, depending on the period and location, were removed from their families between 1910 and 1970; most indigenous families have thus been affected by this phenomenon. The earlier policies of forced removals continue to have contemporary effects.

The nature of state intervention – whether for welfare or criminalisation purposes – has had a profound effect on indigenous ways of life, their relationship to authority figures such as the police, and to the experiences of young indigenous people as they grow up in a (post-)colonial context. One legacy of colonialism has been heightened levels of intra-family conflict, including child sexual abuse. The issue of indigenous family violence is prominent today in Australia and has led to massive state intervention in places like the Northern Territory. Our concern here is not with the nature of the intervention, nor with the documentation of family violence. Rather, it is simply to say that such violence necessarily has a major impact on young indigenous people who witness and/or are on the receiving end of the violence.

Compounding the stresses of dispossession and marginalisation on many indigenous families and communities has been the removal of children from indigenous households, alluded to above. To these observations, however, we can also add that for many of those who were removed from their parents, the role of parenting has subsequently been quite foreign, and in many cases individuals have also suffered from lack of communal support in child-rearing. This can lead to instances of neglectful parenting, abusive relationships and poor role modelling. The nature and quality of parenting is thus partly shaped by the nature and dynamics of family formation as determined by oppressive state policies and interventions. For young people, this can have major repercussions in terms of upbringing and modes of conflict resolution. Bear in mind, as well, that there are huge pressures on indigenous children growing up in what is still a very difficult social climate.

As pointed out in Chapter 1, there is a close relationship between social marginalisation (incorporating racial discrimination and economic and social exclusion) and criminalisation (which constitutes one type of state response to marginalisation). For present purposes we can consider some of the cultural and social consequences for indigenous young people, given the high rates of incarceration in particular (see White 2009). First, prison is not a strange place to many indigenous young people. High rates of incarceration for both young and older members of their communities means that contact with the criminal justice system is routine and expected, rather than unusual and foreign. Bad blood between authority figures is historically grounded, and is still played out today in contemporary social relations. This has a major impact on how young indigenous people see themselves. It also has significant implications for the labelling of indigenous young people in the public domains of the streets, malls and parklands.

Second, for some young indigenous people, prison is a place you *want* to go to. It can be a rite of passage for some young people. Importantly, especially given the statistics on youth detention, in prison indigenous people are frequently in the majority, and at the very least have large numbers. They are the strong ones. They also learn the language of the prison and detention centre. Such language can be both alien and attractive to the young people on the outside. This in turn can contribute towards a gang culture and gang mentality among some indigenous young people.

Having said this, it is important to add that popular images and representations of indigenous young people tend to overemphasise criminal activities and substance abuse while ignoring the significant proportions of young people not implicated or engaged in these activities. Other distorted or one-sided representations are apparent as well. There is, for example, the underlying assumption that all indigenous young people, regardless of family background, have similar issues and life chances. This assumption leads to little appreciation of social differences within the indigenous population, apart from social differences that separate the indigenous and the non-indigenous. The former are evident with regard to class, gender and ethnic differences within communities (for example, tribal and family associations, as well as language), which manifest themselves in diverse ways, depending upon immediate social context.

Various strategies have been advocated to improve the post-release outcomes of indigenous offenders through changing and adapting existing reintegration programs (Willis 2008: 5–6):

- Incorporating an understanding of indigenous society and its collectivist approach, and the resistance of many indigenous people to disclose information about themselves, rather than rely on programs developed from a western perspective that emphasises self-disclosure, self-awareness and individual responsibility.

- Recognising the place of violence in indigenous communities and how it contributes to offending.

- Applying holistic methods that address the mind, body and spirit.

- Enhancing those elements that appear to make programs effective, such as skill development and education, by making them more directly relevant to the life experiences and circumstances of indigenous people and their communities.

- Increasing responsivity and participation by addressing issues such as anxiety, anger and resistance, which can interfere with indigenous prisoners' willingness and capacity to participate in programs.

- Making programs more enjoyable and encouraging through visual content and physical activities.

- Overcoming language and literacy barriers for those offenders with limited English language skills.

- Involving elders and indigenous facilitators in the development and delivery of programs.

- Addressing the grief and loss that consumes many indigenous people.

- Adequately responding to mental health problems.

- Achieving reintegration for those serving short sentences and on remand who rarely receive correctional programs and services.

Respect for culture and cultural difference does not only apply to indigenous groups. It has application in other ways as well.

### Culturally and linguistically diverse and foreign prisoners

There is not the adequate space to analyse or explore the issues facing this group, but it is becoming a matter of increasing prominence, particularly as European nations see an increase in the numbers of foreign prisoners incarcerated. As illustrated in Table 7.7, an emerging issue in corrections is relating to the increasing cultural, linguistic and ethnic diversity of prison populations, with some countries like Greece housing a prison population with rates that are close to a one in two ratio of prisoners being foreign.

**Table 7.7**  Comparative percentage of foreign prisoners by country

| Type of data | England and Wales | United States | Italy | Greece | New Zealand | Australia |
|---|---|---|---|---|---|---|
| Foreign prisoners (% of prison population) | 13.6% | 5.9% | 37.1% | 43.9% | 19.7% | 20.1% |

*Source*: International Centre for Prison Studies (2009).

Prison is a confronting and difficult life experience for all, yet for culturally and linguistically diverse prisoners it can be worse, with issues stemming from misunderstanding by other inmates and by staff.

This population are particularly disadvantaged because of discrimination, limited awareness of legal rights, lack of access to legal counsel, lack of social networks and economic marginalisation ... Despite the high proportion of foreigners in prisons worldwide, and their special needs, in the majority of countries there are no policies or strategies in place. (UNODC 2009: 79)

A lot of front-line workers in corrections have not been provided with cultural competency training and are often unfamiliar with protocols around the appropriate use of interpreters for prisoners where English may be their second or third language. Even where a prison may have a policy requiring the use of an interpreter, the pragmatic harsh reality is that this service will often not be used when it matters the most and cannot be available all the time.

### Female offenders

The fact that the system is by and large oriented towards men has fundamentally shaped its institutions, programs and objectives along masculine lines. This has a number of implications with regard to how we develop policies and practices that specifically meet the needs of women, especially young women who are in the early stages of contact with the criminal justice system. Table 7.8 illustrates the proportion of females incarcerated in different countries in the western world.

Alder (1997: 51–5) has argued that to understand the place of crime in young women's lives it is necessary:

- To consider the inappropriateness of the victim–offender dichotomy.
- To understand the diversity of young women's experiences.
- To recognise the significance of economic factors in young women's lives.

**Table 7.8** Comparative data on prisoner gender differences by country, 2006

| Type of data | England and Wales | Scotland | United States | Australia | New Zealand |
| --- | --- | --- | --- | --- | --- |
| Incarcerated females: (total and percentage) | 4,056 6% | 385 5% | 112,498 7% | 1,630 7% | 461 6% |
| Incarcerated males: (total and percentage) | 63,626 94% | 6,820 95% | 1,458,363 93% | 22,795 93% | 7,477 94% |

*Source*: Adapted from Australian Bureau of Statistics (2006); Ministry of Women's Affairs (2006); United Nations Office on Drugs and Crime (2008a).

There is a range of social conditions that increases the likelihood of contact with criminal justice agencies, such as inadequate accommodation, family breakdown and abuse, and unemployment. Indeed, it is even more difficult with young women than with young men to separate victimisation-related issues from offending.

Gender-specific services need to be matched by sensitivity to gender-specific issues in the lives of young female offenders. For girls and young women, this can sometimes lead to paradoxical situations. For instance, and as discussed in Chapter 6, on the one hand there is ample evidence that female offenders disproportionately suffer sexual abuse, and that issues such as homelessness and drug misuse are frequently linked to prior situations of abuse at home. On the other hand, a focus on meeting the needs of young women as victims or survivors of abuse can lead to one-dimensional intervention that continually pathologises girls and young women, locking them into a master status that emphasises their victimhood. For those working with young women, it is essential to work with the 'whole person', not just around certain aspects of their experience. This is important to connecting with the young women and providing a more rounded and encouraging avenue to desist from offending (see Baines and Alder 1996; Farrow et al. 2007).

In terms of community services and programs for female offenders in the community, research from England and Wales has identified nine key precepts and lessons for good practice in providing for women in the community (Gelsthorpe et al. 2007: 54).

1 Provision should be women-only to foster safety and a sense of community and to enable staff to develop expertise in work with women.

2 Aim to integrate offenders with non-offenders so as to normalise women offenders' experiences and facilitate a supportive environment for learning.

3 Foster women's empowerment so they gain sufficient self-esteem to directly engage in problem-solving themselves, and feel motivated to seek appropriate employment.

4 Utilise ways of working with women that draw on what is known about their effective learning styles.

5 Take a holistic and practical stance to helping women to address social problems that may be linked to their offending.

6 Facilitate links with mainstream agencies, especially health, debt advice and counselling.

7 Ensure that there is the capacity and flexibility to allow women to return to the centre or program for 'top-up' or continued support and development where required.

8 Ensure that women have a supportive milieu or mentor to whom they can turn when they have completed any offending-related programs, since personal support is likely to be as important as any direct input addressing offending behaviour.

9 Provide women with practical help with transport and childcare so that they can maintain their involvement in the centre or program.

A key message across different jurisdictions is that female offenders have specific needs, and that courts and corrections have a special role in dealing with those women who are brought into contact with the criminal justice system.

## Paradoxes and controversies

Many workers engage in ongoing discussions, accompanied by a sense of internal conflict, around how to balance or prioritise the complex needs of offenders with competing organisational constraints and policies. Perpetual controversies centre on the fact that often the very thing that will reduce harm for the individual offender is the opposite of organisational practice and ideology, and poses problems in the wider context of prevention. The use of condoms and needle exchange in prisons provides one case in point, although there are many other examples where what works for a client may go against institutional policy.

Practitioners also have to weigh up issues pertaining to 'equality' and 'difference' in working with specific groups of offenders. To some, provision of specialist assistance and the taking into account of particular attributes may be interpreted as 'special treatment' within a corrective services context. Decisions in relation to specific individuals and population groups have to take into careful consideration the history of the offender, the specific circumstances that shape how they live their lives (including ascribed characteristics such as gender or acquired characteristics such as a drug habit), key principles of fairness and justice, and the type and availability of services relevant to the needs and aspirations of the specific offender.

Development of appropriate responses to the phenomenon of complex needs requires positive strategies based on 'sameness' or 'difference' principles depending upon the situation. The issue is not one of different treatment for different people but of how best to mobilise expertise and support in ways that will best deal with the substantive issues at hand. Treating persons who are severely impaired by acquired brain injury in the same way as those who are not is clearly counterproductive. On the other hand, all offenders can lay common claim to certain human rights that are universal in nature and ought to obtain in all circumstances regardless of offender background. Clarification may be needed as to when rehabilitation requires treating people the same, and at other times and in other respects, differently.

## Conclusion

Consideration of the complex needs of offenders needs to take into account emergent issues that will in all likelihood be exacerbated rather than diminished in the coming years. Increasing numbers of prisoners are growing old within prison, for example. This means that prison gerontology (the science of dealing with ageing as a biological phenomenon) has to be taken seriously. What will be the capacity of an ageing correctional workforce to adequately support the needs of an ageing prison population? In a similar vein, how will correctional institutions respond to the different vulnerable populations requiring specialist services or separate accommodation, especially as these groups may get bigger?

Another issue is that the changing nature of drug use on the streets (for example, the advent of ecstasy and 'ice' in recent years) and in the home (such as prescription drugs) has huge ramifications for who goes to prison and what occurs in corrections generally. Acquired brain injury and issues surrounding intellectual disability and mental illness likewise persist as crucial issues within a corrective services as well as social welfare context. The challenges of working with offenders are, indeed, very complex.

## Discussion questions

1 What are some of the main health problems or challenges experienced by prisoners and how does this affect their experience of prison?
2 What are some of the issues faced by female offenders? What are some strategies or approaches practitioners can use to work with and support women?
3 Describe an innovative program or strategy that has been used to support indigenous offenders, using a real example from Canada, New Zealand, Australia or the United States. What principles and practices have contributed to this success?

## Further reading

Andersen, H. (2004) 'Mental health in prison populations: a review – with special emphasis on a study of Danish prisoners on remand', *Acta Psychiatrica Scandinavica*, (110): 5–59.

Bewley-Taylor, D., Hallam, C. and Allen, R. (2009) *The Incarceration of Drug Offenders: An Overview*. London: International Centre for Prison Studies.

Correctional Service of Canada (2006) *Strategic Plan for Aboriginal Corrections 2006–07 to 2010–11*. Ontario: Corrections Canada.

De Viggiani, N. (2007) 'Unhealthy prisons: exploring structural determinants of prison health', *Sociology of Health and Illness*, 29(1): 115–35.

Peters, R. and Osher, F. (2004) *Co-occurring Disorders and Specialty Courts*, 2nd edn. New York: The National GAINS Centre.

Sheehan, R. and Flynn, C. (2007) 'Women prisoners and their children', in R. Sheehan, G. McIvor and C. Trotter (eds) *What Works with Women Offenders?* Cullompton: Willan Publishing.

## Key resources

Lewis, S., Raynor, P., Smith, D. and Wardak, A. (eds) (2006) *Race and Probation*. Cullompton: Willan Publishing.

Ministerial Advisory Committee on AIDS, Sexual Health and Hepatitis (2008) *Hepatitis C Prevention, Treatment and Care: Guidelines for Australian Custodial Settings*. Canberra: Australian Government Department of Health and Ageing.

Moller, L., Stover, H., Jurgens, R., Gatherer, A. and Nikogosian, H. (2007) *Health in Prisons: A WHO Guide to the Essentials in Prison Health*. Copenhagen: World Health Organisation Regional Office for Europe.

Osher, F., Steadman, H. and Barr, H. (2002) *A Best Practice Approach to Community Re-entry from Jails for Inmates with Co-occurring Disorders*. New York: National GAINS Centre.

United Nations Office of Drugs and Crime (2009) *Handbook on Prisoners with Special Needs*. New York: United Nations.

# Chapter 8

# Difficult work: managing risk, violence and crisis

I didn't want to go to the [prison hospital], because I was still so ashamed about what had happened to me, but I had to. They gave me a test, and that's when I got the devastating news. I am HIV positive ... Fighting for my life is now my full time job. They took my life, but they didn't take my ability to live my life. Every day I wake up and I'm just grateful that I'm still here.

> (Male prisoner, rape survivor, quoted in
> Just Detention International 2009: 8)

You can have the best programs in the world, you can have the best legislation, fantastic policies and procedures, but if you have got staff who are disillusioned, who are being paid badly, who are not trained and who are under so much pressure that they leave here, then you've shot yourself in the foot.

> (Community corrections officer, quoted in Astbury 2008: 38)

## Introduction

The very nature of working with offenders on a daily basis involves the possibility of difficult situations arising. Critical incidences and complex situations can be triggered with little or no warning, requiring worker responses that may have lasting consequences for themselves, the offender and the organisation. Responding to actual or attempted suicide or self-harm is an example of a client behaviour that involves acute risks, duty of care issues, and the emotional drain of difficult work on practitioners.

Difficult work has a number of interrelated dimensions. It involves difficult work with clients, and difficult work with colleagues and other collaborators in working with offenders. It involves difficulties associated with the everyday and more mundane aspects of the job, such as working with clients with mental illness or acquired brain injury. It involves dealing with tense spectacular events, such as prison riots or clients 'going off' during a scheduled meeting.

Difficult work can also present difficulties for individual workers. For instance, self-care and violence prevention strategies are essential to avoid burnout. Working with offenders is intensely personal work, and it is important to recognise the toll that such work can have on practitioners. This is important for each individual worker, but also those around them, especially supervisors and managers. Helping offenders rests upon a platform of being able to help each other in times of need, as well as part of everyday work life.

## Manipulation and violence

Our first example of difficult work revolves around the way in which some offenders attempt to manipulate situations and people to their advantage. Bearing in mind the social backgrounds, criminal histories and institutional settings related to correctional service provision it is not surprising that critical vigilance and resilience are a must for those who work with offenders. Manipulation can be subtle or seemingly minor but can become a breeding ground for unhealthy dynamics that impinge upon professional authority and boundaries (see Scenario 8.1).

Being subject to manipulative behaviour is basically an occupational hazard of working in corrections. However, such behaviour can have major consequences in terms of worker status and reputation, capacity to execute rehabilitative strategies, and potential conflicts involving workers and offenders. One outcome of manipulative behaviour may well be an escalation in the possibility of violence, among prisoners and between prisoners and prison officers.

As with many issues within coercive institutional and organisational settings, and involving involuntary clients, there are complexities of situation that create stresses and strains for everyone concerned. This can manifest itself in forms of anti-social and violent behaviour that are unsuitable (on the part of everyone engaged in the offender–

## Scenario 8.1

## Manipulation

### Prisoner profile
* Criminal history

Inmate Troy is serving a prison sentence for kidnapping; he had parole but breached his parole conditions. He was accused of being the criminal mastermind of a small group of highly effective thieves.

* Correctional history

During his imprisonment, Troy has spent a small amount of time in detention for various prison offences. He is rumoured to have made over one million dollars' worth of drug deals during his imprisonment, approximately twelve years. He generally presents no problems for correctional staff but intelligence suggests he is a 'bullet maker'. This phrase refers to someone who rarely becomes involved in incidents but controls others, getting them to do their dirty work. He is adept at manipulating people to get things that he wants, and persistent rumours credit him with having corrupted at least two staff members – rumours that have been substantiated.

### Situation

Troy is having a discussion with you about the type of coffee that he likes to drink. He comments that he can smell the coffee that you are drinking. He says that he doesn't believe that it's the standard prison coffee and smells like 'Maccona'. You tell him that his nose has not deceived him and that it is in fact 'Maccona'. He asks what type of 'Maccona' it is. You tell him that it is 'Maccona Mystique'. Troy tells you that he hasn't tried that particular flavour and then asks you if he can have a spoonful to try it.

### Questions
1 What do you say to Troy?
2 What should you be mindful of?
3 What do you think you can do to protect yourself from manipulation, both subtle and overt?

practitioner nexus) even if understandable given certain underlying factors.

## Violence in prison

The threat of violence is ever present when working with offenders, stemming in part from histories of violence among offenders but also related to issues such as co-morbidity, acquired brain injury, onset of dementia (in the case of elderly prisoners, for example) and so on. Violence can also feature among staff, as workplace pressures and inappropriate coping mechanisms (such as alcohol and drug use or unchecked anger, or even overzealous or heavy-handed 'takedowns') can affect well-being, group morale and psychological states.

Violence involves different participants (prisoner to prisoner, prisoner to staff, staff to staff). It can involve different sorts of activity (pushing, spitting, throwing objects, striking, attack with a weapon, exposure to threats, intimidation, bullying, manipulation, victimisation). The scale of violence also varies, from one-on-one assaults through to hostage-taking and riots.

So too the response to the threat and actual incidence of violence ranges from contingency planning related to occupational health and safety considerations through to institutional strategies for de-escalation and conflict resolution. Importantly, how one responds to violence and violent situations is partly driven by the precautions and resources put into place beforehand. For instance, the creation of specialist tactical response units that feature heavily armed and combat-trained personnel is likely to foster reliance on coercive responses above others; alternatively, responses that are less paramilitary look to alternative means to resolve conflict and relieve tension, using applied force only as a last resort.

How authorities intervene in any given situation has ramifications for future events. In some cases how we deal with difficult situations may well perpetuate or ignite further crisis and violence. For example, in an Australian medium-security men's prison complex, following one siege involving three inmates the whole of that prison complex was locked down for 23 hours a day for many weeks over the summer of 2009. It took institutional legal action and political intervention before the lock-down order was eventually lifted. This particular response to the original event fuelled widespread inmate resentment and set the stage for more violence and distrust, because of the injustice of the imposition of a mass punishment that affected those who had done nothing wrong. Legitimacy and respect are essential in maintaining good order and favourable everyday relationships. The message of this story is that you should not exercise authority in ways that ignore or bypass a relational ethic based upon a culture of respect and appreciation of human rights. Table 8.1 highlights a one-year snapshot of violent incidents, injuries and assaults in Canadian prisons.

The level of violence reported will vary from place to place and from jurisdiction to jurisdiction. This is due to factors such as the institutional approach adopted in dealing with questions of security and risk, and the mechanisms put into place that might reduce the possibility of violence. At a general policy level, for example, a human rights approach to security, good order and control, and discipline and punishment generally incorporates prevention and intervention strategies based upon international human rights conventions and laws. These are meant to provide a basic guide to standards of care within corrective service environments (see United Nations 2005). The emphasis is on humane practices and coercion as

**Table 8.1** Institutional incidents, assaults and injuries in Canada, 2007–08

| Type of data | Total number (one year) | Rate (% of total population) |
|---|---|---|
| Major institutional incidents | 112 | 0.6% of 20,021 offenders |
| Staff assaults by inmates | 214 | 1.8% of 11,841 staff |
| Inmate assaults by inmates | 497 | 2.5% of 20,021 offenders |
| Staff injuries due to assaults by inmates | 45 | 0.4% of 11,841 staff |
| Inmate injuries due to assaults on inmates | 496 | 2.5% of 20,021 offenders |

*Note:* 'Major institutional incidents' include staff murders, inmate murders, hostage-taking/forcible confinement, escapees from institutions or escorts, suicides, as well as any assaults on staff, assaults on inmates or inmate fights that result in a major injury.
*Source:* Adapted from Correctional Service of Canada (2008).

a last resort. By contrast, punitive institutions such as high-security Supermax facilities are inherently brutalising in their peculiar forms of institutionalised violence (see Carlton 2007). Dealing with potential security threats, threats to good order and imposition of disciplinary punishment thus varies according to the nature of the institution and the broad penal mission.

As mentioned earlier in the book, the sheer number of prisoners in the system also has a major impact upon prison life. Too many prisoners translate into both uncomfortable and potentially explosive living conditions, as well as the inability of prison officials to implement proper and adequate rehabilitation strategies. As shown in Figure 8.1, the phenomenon of overcrowding is neither novel nor does it appear subject to easy remedy in prisons in England and Wales. Yet, the consequences for clients and workers alike are enormous.

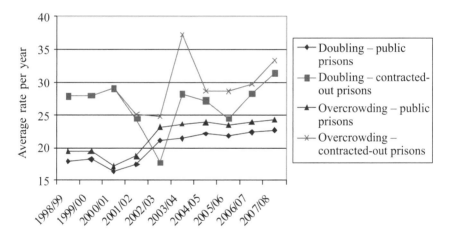

**Figure 8.1** Average rates of doubling and overcrowding in public and contracted-out prisons in England and Wales – a ten-year trend
*Note*: These rates are the averages of all public prisons and all contracted-out prisons.
*Source*: Adapted from HM Prison Service (2009a).

At material and experiential levels, the kinds of things that influence how an offender responds to the prison environment include the following:

• *Crowding* – cell size, and total prison population in relation to capacity.

- *Denial of responsibility* – in most prisons the inmates are told when to get up, wash and do everything else, and even their lights are commonly controlled by an officer from outside the cell.

- *Type of work* – menial, repetitive and/or uninteresting.

- *Social isolation* – correspondence and a drop-off in number of outside visitors over time.

- *Families* – difficulties for families on the outside, single parenting, and poverty.

- *Relationships* – little choice in 'new' friends, or escape from them.

- *Control and intimidation* – strip searches, cell searches and dependence on 'privileges'.

- *Deterioration* – increased introversion and increased self-directed hostility.

The interface between prison environment and outside community is complicated by the nature of coercive internment in the first place. It is also made worse by procedures – such as strip searches – that reinforce the isolation and abuse of prisoners and their family members. Prison workers are inevitably seen as part of the problem rather than the solution in such instances. This has direct impact on the kinds of services and programs on offer, and the reception by inmates of these.

There are a range of situational crime prevention measures which, if adopted, could well reduce the likelihood of violence and other kinds of unsuitable behaviour within secure settings (see Wortley 2002). For example, negotiation with prisoners and grievance mechanisms, personal control over lights and heat, ensuring mixed-aged populations, allowing personal decorations, noise-absorbing surfaces and so on are seen as measures that could reduce factors that precipitate transgressions of various kinds within prison. Similarly a wide number of opportunity reduction strategies can be adopted, such as drug testing, staggered cell release, vandal-proof furnishings and denial of parole. Yet all of these measures depend to some extent upon a commitment to developing an approach that simultaneously attempts to control prison disorder through 'tightening up' and hardening the prison environment on the one hand, and 'loosening up' and normalising it on the other. It also very much depends upon institutional resources, level of staffing, capacity of the facility versus number of prisoners, and the profile of both offenders and prison staff alike.

Much like the rest of the world, sometimes the most significant clues of looming unrest come from the most ordinary of sources. One of the most pragmatic signs that trouble is brewing is when prisoners in a certain wing or unit appear to be hoarding or stockpiling food, toiletries or other meagre luxuries they can purchase from the canteen. Local knowledge and intuition about situations, however, is also derived as much as anything by the relationship that staff have with prisoners.

### Violence in community settings

Issues of institutional violence need to be acknowledged in tandem with a similar risk experienced by outreach workers in the community. It is just that the nature of potential harm may differ because of the setting. Similar to prisons, various crime prevention measures can be instituted that will increase the safety of workers with offenders in the community (see Box 8.1).

---

**Box 8.1**

*Strategies for preventing client-initiated violence in outreach or community settings*

Probation and parole officers and outreach workers may spend significant amounts of time working off-site, requiring personal intuition and professional discretion to maintain healthy boundaries and personal safety. Where possible, it may be helpful to ensure that clients with the potential for aggression or violence are required to come to the worksite or a neutral professional workspace for an interview or interventions; however, this is not always an option. The following guidelines are simple reminders of how to keep safe when working in the community:

- The days, triggers and situations where violence is more common should be identified and patterns are monitored.
- Records are kept of names, contact numbers and home addresses of off-site staff.
- Detailed timetables are kept of where staff are, whom they are with, how long they should be, and when they are expected to be back. Diaries are kept at the central worksite of: client name, car registration, medicare or health benefits number,

---

and driver's licence numbers and the reason that the worker is visiting the client/accompanying the client to another destination.

- Before any off-site visit, a code word, phrase or sentence is agreed that can be incorporated into a telephone conversation to indicate danger.

- Clients are assessed for violence potential before staff visit them off-site. Additional precautions are made, and records kept, if staff are likely to be unwelcome at the site to be visited, or if the client has some history of aggression; for example, staff go in pairs or alert police prior to the visit taking place, in cases of high risk.

- Procedures are in place for staff who feel at risk, change plans, or are delayed. Procedures are in place *and followed* if staff cannot be contacted or do not return/check in when expected.

- Off-site clients are visited in daylight only, where possible.

- Off-site staff are issued with personal alarms, mobile phones and public phone change/card. Mobile phones need to be well charged and have good coverage. Work cars should be used for off-site visits; avoid using a personal vehicle. The cars for off-site visits should have sufficient fuel, with spare in case staff are lost, particularly if visiting rural areas.

- When a worker arrives at a destination, parking location is assessed for the nearest exit route. Staff always park cars in well-lit areas. Lock-up procedures are followed for cars, car keys, alarms and safety equipment.

- When staff knock on the door, they stand to one side and not in a position where the opening of a screen door can trap them. On arrival, staff ensure the client(s) knows who they are and why they are there. Staff wait to be asked inside, and let the client lead the way. Staff put their belongings in an easily accessible space, always close to them, in case they need to leave quickly.

- If there are people hanging around the car as a staff member is leaving, they do not go and ask them what they are doing.

*Source*: Adapted from Mayhew (2000a: 67–8; see also Mayhew 2000b, 2000c).

*Guidelines for interviewing/treating a high-risk client in a community organisational setting*

As has been acknowledged throughout the book, a significant amount of work and intervention with offenders is done by the voluntary and community sector. The following tips have been devised from applied research by the Australian Institute of Criminology (Mayhew 2000a: 66), and are particularly relevant to workers in the healthcare sector and community forensic and residential rehabilitation settings:

- Make sure the interview or treatment is not conducted in isolation and others know where you are and who you are interviewing. Use a room in which you are visible to others, for example, glass (security) windows, but where confidential discussions cannot be overheard. If this type of room is not available, schedule someone else to check in occasionally with minor queries by phone or in person.

- Do not arrange to meet anyone when you know you will be alone in the building, and make sure the client knows their presence has been recorded.

- Ensure that there is a duress alarm system of some sort.

- Stay near the door – preferably have a room with two doors – but do not block the client's exit if they want to leave quickly.

- Keep equipment in the room to a minimum as many things can be used as a weapon. Make sure the room is well lit.

- Keep waiting time to a minimum. If the interview is delayed, ensure that the client is informed.

- Shake hands and introduce yourself by first name and explain your job task. Use language the client will understand.

- If you are escorting a client to a room, walk beside them on the same level, in front going upstairs, and behind them going downstairs.

- If the client is reacting badly to you because of your age, sex or class, try to match the client to a more appropriate staff member (if the client agrees).

- If the client has a history of aggression, find out about prior incidences to aid your interview process.

- Attempt to have equal seating with the client, at an angle, and leave greater inter-personal space with aggressive people. Maintain eye contact. Adopt a relaxed posture rather than closed arms. Maintain empathy and do reflective listening.

- If the situation is escalating, take a break to defuse aggression. At the first sign you are in distress, staff should know who will respond and what immediate action to take.

- Try to solve some problems immediately to demonstrate that you are trying to find solutions. If you are governed by rules of some kind, try to explain them.

- Avoid provocative expressions such as 'calm down'. Never get drawn into aggression or agitation. Avoid tapping pens, fiddling or doodling.

These tips illustrate basic and yet important considerations when planning to interview a client with the potential for aggression. Practitioners need to be aware of prior assessments of dynamic risk factors and of risks to personal safety. Assessment, however, is a continuous process, that should happen wherever necessary, formally and informally, and as circumstances change. Services that have offenders as their main client group may also offer specialist training and intervention in preventing client-initiated violence in the workplace.

Creative programs offer an interesting therapeutic alternative for violent male offenders, going beyond the preoccupation with risk, to achieving self-expression and constructive use of time in prison (see Innovative practice 8).

## Other types of harm

Violence comes in many shapes and forms. Among those most prevalent among offender groups are harms perpetrated against another such as rape, harms associated with living in a coercive environment, and harms directed at oneself.

### Sexual assault and prison rape

Sexual assault is a sensitive issue that can relate to offenders as victims or perpetrators, and also staff as victims or perpetrators. In

## Innovative practice 8

### Acting out: prison theatre and drama therapy for violent male offenders

With the assistance of a pilot project and the commitment of a passionate creative director, Lebanese prisoners staged an adaptation of the play *12 Angry Men* in late 2009. Inside Roumieh Prison, Lebanon's biggest high-security jail, notorious for bloody riots and inhumane conditions, prisoners used the performance to raise issues and question the justice of Lebanon's prison system – to an audience of government and judicial officials. One of the inmates taught himself to read so he could take part. Another prisoner, Hassan, convicted of double murder, spoke of his emotion about simply being heard: 'After the premiere, I cried. For the first time in my life' (quoted in Antelava 2009)

In Romania, prisoners received a standing ovation from an audience of 400 at a prestigious Bucharest theatre for their performances of original plays for the two-day 'Exit' festival organised by NGOs and prison officials. Teodorescu (2009) relays inmates' comments about the opportunity to act and, in the process, being shown respect and recognition: One prisoner, Zota, said that people knowing you are an offender 'destroys your confidence. But now I feel like a new man. Theatre has taught me to be more social; I have more courage dealing with people.' Kocze, a prisoner convicted of murder, said 'Theatre has taught me to control myself, which is important because that is why we are in prison, we just can't control ourselves.'

In Israel, the population of Hermon Prison predominantly consists of violent offenders with histories of misuse of alcohol and other drugs and/or domestic violence. Hermon's drama therapy groups make use of movement, voice, games, improvisation, picture cards and masks to stimulate increased self-expression, as well as deep insight into troubled lives. Drama therapists regularly witness 'recreations of childhood so painful that no words on paper can reproduce them ... Time after time, the linkage between childhood trauma and the adult's use of drugs, used to dull the mental pain of repressed memories, can be observed' (Goldring 2001).

the prison context particularly, inmate-on-inmate sexual assault is a serious problem that faces acute under-reporting. Stigma and shame play a major role, as do issues of protection and fear of further victimisation.

Sexual violence and rape have received particular attention in the United States over the past few years, due in part to very high rates of incarceration, increasing prison populations and disturbing accounts of prison rape. In 2003 a piece of legislation called the Prison Rape Elimination Act was brought in to address the prevalence and incidence of sexual assault in correctional facilities. This new initiative was aimed at increasing the quantity and quality of data collection across the nation and different types of correctional facilities and jurisdictions, providing funding for program development and research, and endorsing a national commission to develop standards and accountability measures. The Bureau of Justice Statistics was delegated the responsibility for collecting and compiling data on issues such as inmate-on-inmate non-consensual sexual acts (rape), inmate-on-inmate abusive sexual contacts, staff sexual misconduct, and staff sexual harassment.

Data provided on inmate-on-inmate sexual violence for the year 2006 revealed (Beck *et al.* 2007: 4–7):

- More than one perpetrator was involved in 10 per cent of the incidences.

- Males constituted 82 per cent of the victims and 85 per cent of the perpetrators.

- Victims were on average younger than perpetrators; 44 per cent of victims were aged 24 or younger and 81 per cent of perpetrators were aged 25 or older.

- Incidents of sexual violence occurred most often (more than 70 per cent of cases) in a victim's cell, and 17 per cent of cases occurred in common areas such as showers or dayrooms/lounges.

- Sexual violence was more common in the evening (between 6 p.m. and midnight).

- Incidences of sexual violence among inmates, when reported, are typically reported (in 83 per cent of cases) by a victim or another inmate and not by a correctional officer or other staff.

- In relation to sexual misconduct or harassment by staff, there were significant gender differences depending on the type of facility.

In state and federal prisons, 65 per cent of inmate victims were male while 58 per cent of the staff perpetrators were female. In local jails, 80 per cent of the victims were female, while 79 per cent of the perpetrators were male.

- In most incidences of staff sexual misconduct or harassment (76 per cent), victims received no medical follow-up, counselling or mental health treatment.

Information resources are starting to emerge in the US directed at offenders and victims of sexual assault in prison, as well as the practitioners who support them. Two examples are the 72-page prisoners' handbook on identifying and addressing sexual misconduct, *An End to Silence* (Smith 2002), and the Pennsylvania Coalition Against Rape (2006) guide, *Meeting the Needs of Prison Rape Victims*, to assist sexual assault professionals, counsellors and chaplains.

It may be discerning to conclude this section with a reminder to practitioners of not indirectly supporting the 'master status' of 'prison rape victim' longer than is necessary to support a person's recovery. Stories of hope can emerge in recovery from hellish circumstances, as outlined in this narrative from one prison rape survivor to encourage others who have been through similar suffering and trauma:

> I was gang raped at 17, on my first day in general population in a Michigan prison. Even though I felt hopeless at the time, I want you to know that there is hope. I was able to go on and live a healthy and productive life. I graduated from college, became a successful businessman, and I now advocate for the rights of prison rape survivors. I tell you this not to impress you, but to impress upon you that you too can recover from the horrific ordeal you have endured. (quoted in Just Detention International 2009: 1)

The experience of rape can be highly traumatic. Apart from this specific kind of harm, there is also the issue of how corrective services might respond to issues of trauma more generally.

### Supporting a person who has experienced a traumatic event

The experience of trauma and the diagnosis of post-traumatic stress disorder (PTSD) are fairly common among clients of alcohol and other drugs services and mental health services, as well as in offender populations. The following suggestions should be prefaced with acknowledgement that despite how common it is, trauma remains a nebulous and complex issue, and should only be addressed by qualified practitioners. However, there are some helpful guidelines for non-specialist community service workers and criminal justice professionals who may have to support the person in the intermediary to accessing clinical assistance (Mental Health First Aid 2007: 28):

1 *Let the person tell their story if they wish, but do not push them to do so if they don't want to.* People who experience a traumatic event have their own pace for dealing with the trauma. In trying to help such a person it is important to let them set the pace and not force the issue. Urging someone into a discussion of a traumatic event may actually re-traumatise a victim. (Research has shown that a routine session of critical incident debriefing does not reduce the risk of post-traumatic stress disorder developing after a traumatic event.)

2 *Be a patient and sympathetic listener, before giving any advice.* Make personal contact and listen non-judgementally before making any recommendations for help.

3 *Validate the person's stress reactions as being normal responses to abnormal events.* Explain that stress reactions are normal for days or even weeks after a trauma and that people usually have a normal recovery of their emotions. These stress reactions include shock, fear, grief, emotional numbing, indecisiveness, worry, unwanted memories, fatigue, difficulty sleeping, being easily startled, distrust and irritability.

4 *Encourage the person to reach out to other people who can provide support and share feelings about what is happening.* Encourage traumatised people to talk with family, friends and work colleagues, following their own instincts on how much they say and with whom they talk. Don't tell the person to stop reliving the trauma or to forget the trauma and get on with life.

5 *Advise the person not to use alcohol or drugs to cope.* Instead advise them to use simple relaxation methods and to do healthy activities they enjoy.

6 *If the stress reaction persists for more than a month, encourage the person to seek professional help.* If the person continues to experience stress reactions or severe distress that interferes with normal functioning after a month following the trauma, encourage the person to seek professional help, if not already sought.

*Self-harm*

Self-harm is a behaviour that involves self-inflicted or deliberate actions to harm oneself. It is sometimes called 'self-mutilation', 'cutting', 'parasuicide' or 'self-injury'. These actions include (but are not limited to):

- Cutting
- Burning
- Punching, kicking, or head-butting an object (such as a wall) to cause injury
- Deliberate and excessive scratching of skin or carving patterns or wounds into skin
- Pulling out hair
- Self-inflicted physical injuries resulting in bruising
- Overdoses (that are not intended to result in death)
- Deliberate use of everyday items (such as a car) to inflict injury to oneself
- Injecting substances (for example, poisons) or swallowing objects (razor blades, glass).

People who are long-term injecting drug users may have collapsed veins in most of their limbs, and resort to injecting in the groin; in extreme cases it is increasingly common for people to inject into their eye area.

Self-harm in a prison environment can be particularly confronting, as inmates who are in an acute state of distress may resort to desperate and violent measures, including lighting fires or setting fire to themselves, spreading faeces over themselves and/or their cell, cutting or removing parts of their body (hair, nails, eyes, ears), or using objects in their cell (the toilet, or the bed) to inflict injuries such as broken bones, attempted drowning or suffocation. Nearly all correctional facilities have monitoring protocols and 'suicide rooms' that can also be used to observe and monitor an inmate who is at heightened risk of harming or killing themselves.

Self-harm may or may not be an attempt at suicide. It is not helpful to refer to self-harm as 'attention seeking'. Often it is a behaviour within itself that is motivated by wanting to get release or get some help. Empathy and non-judgemental responses play an important role in communicating with a client who harms themselves.

From the point of view of a practitioner, self-harm can be quite upsetting or disturbing. It is important that you are comfortable enough to acknowledge and process the feelings and triggers that may come up for you as a worker. Case review and clinical supervision sessions may offer opportunities for problem-solving and debriefing.

There are many reasons why people self-harm; each individual will have different reasons. However, the following are some indicators that may have a contributing role (adapted from Child and Adolescent Mental Health Services 2008). The person may:

- Be under stress or in crisis
- Experience extreme issues with self-esteem and may feel self-hatred
- Have been bullied or a victim of harassment
- Be going through some grief or loss
- Be coping with a relationship break-up
- Have been a victim of abuse
- Be experiencing problems at home, work, or school
- Be coming to terms with their own sexuality
- Be coping with a serious illness or disability, or another disorder (such as bulimia)
- Lack coping mechanisms and skills to assert themselves in positive ways.

According to the Australian National Training Authority (2003: 1), self-harm is

> often used by a client as a mechanism for coping with, or gaining control over feelings of anger, sadness, helplessness, guilt, self-hatred, pain or tension. The physical pain caused by self-harm can also block memories or flash backs of traumatic events, such as sexual abuse. Inflicting harm on a particular part of the body can temporarily disperse or release feelings or memories for a client, subsequently providing them with a sense of control.

*Communication skills: responding to someone who is deliberately injuring themselves in a community setting*

If you suspect that someone is deliberately injuring themselves, you need to discuss it with them. You may have noticed suspicious injuries on the person's body; do not ignore them. Avoid expressing a strong negative reaction to the self-injury and discuss it calmly with the person. It is important that you have reflected on your own state of mind and are sure you are prepared to deal calmly with their answer when asking the person about their self injury.

It is important to reiterate that self-harm is a coping mechanism, and therefore 'stopping self-injury' should not be the focus of the conversation. Instead, look at ways to relieve the distress. Do not trivialise the feelings or situations that have led to the self-harm. Do not punish the person, especially by threatening to withdraw care.

If you have interrupted someone in the act of deliberate self-injury, intervene in a supportive and non-judgemental way. Remain calm and avoid expressions of shock or anger. Express your concern for the person's well-being. Ask whether you can do anything to alleviate the distress. Assess whether any medical attention is needed.

Try and remove the means for self-harm, and talk with the person about how they can plan to keep themselves safe. Explore different alternatives and options that they could do every time they want to hurt themself. Most services have a self-harm policy, and the protocols listed should be followed. Our role as workers is one of first aid and immediate safety, whereas the client may also need to be referred to a specialist mental health service. The emergency services should always be called if the person is confused, disoriented or unconscious, or if they have bleeding that is rapid or pulsing.

Even though any self-harm is upsetting and of serious concern, it may be necessary to work with the client to come up with harm minimisation strategies to reduce the amount of self-harm if a person is not going to stop it completely.

A useful tool that is increasingly being used in the field deals with issues relating to self-harm: a client safety contract (see Appendix 2 for a *pro forma* version of this). This involves the client actually signing a therapeutic contract that says that they will not engage in harmful behaviours over the course of their service provision. These sorts of contracts have been surprisingly successful in reducing levels of self-harm.

People who self-harm have genuine difficulties coping. All self-harm deserves serious assessment by practitioners who are qualified in medicine, psychiatry or clinical psychology. We can help clients, but we cannot work through the deep-seated issues behind the self-harm on our own. If you have concerns about potential for self-harm by a client, ensure that they are encouraged to seek support and input from a GP or mental health service or, alternatively, a prison health service.

*Suicide*

Many factors are involved in why a person may think about suicide. Different types of warning signs and situations to look out for are listed in Table 8.2.

**Table 8.2** Potential warning signs that a person might be considering suicide

| SEE: what is their behaviour like? | HEAR: what are their conversations like? |
|---|---|
| • Previous suicide attempts<br>• Moody, crying a lot, or withdrawn<br>• Taking less care of themselves and their appearance, lack of motivation<br>• Engaging in risky, careless or self-destructive behaviour<br>• Increased substance use<br>• Losing interest in things or activities previously enjoyed<br>• Giving away possessions<br>• Expressing thoughts about death through drawings, stories, songs, art | • Talking of feeling hopeless, helpless or worthless<br>• All alone, not very connected<br>• Don't want to be a burden<br>• Have no purpose<br>• Want to escape<br>• Nobody can help<br>• Not sure whether can cope any more<br>• Talking or joking about suicide<br>• Can't stand the pain<br>• Saying goodbye to others |
| **SENSE: how does the person feel?** | **LEARN: what is happening in their life?** |
| • Desperate<br>• Hopeless<br>• Sad, fragile or depressed<br>• Numb and disconnected<br>• Ashamed or feelings of guilt<br>• Agitated or restless<br>• Irritable<br>• Anxious<br>• Distress followed by a sense of calm | • Has experienced some recent loss (a loved one, a job, loss of family contact)<br>• Major disappointment (major rejection, missed job promotions, failed exams)<br>• Change in circumstances (retirement, redundancy, incarceration, children leaving home, financial problems)<br>• Has experiences of abuse<br>• Has a mental or physical illness<br>• Recent suicide of loved one or friend |

*Source*: Adapted from Lifeline Australia (2005).

The World Health Organisation (2000) has compiled a resource that is specifically targeted at suicide prevention in prison, and a similar publication was designed in the United States (see Hayes 1995). Both resources are particularly instructive in guiding institutional responses and understandings, with Hayes particularly vehement of the dominant attitude among prison staff that attempted suicide is 'manipulative' or 'attention-seeking' behaviour:

> Correctional, medical and mental health staff should abandon the effort to classify suicidal behaviour according to expressed or presumed intent, particularly since the tendency of persons to minimize the seriousness of their suicidal intent after the fact is well known across community, hospital and other health settings. There are no reliable bases upon which we can differentiate 'manipulative' suicide attempts posing no threat to the inmate's life from those true 'non-manipulative attempts' which may end in a death. The term 'manipulative' is simply useless in understanding, and destructive in attempting to manage, the suicidal behaviour of inmates (or of anybody else). (Haycock 1992, cited in Hayes 1995: 6)

While the actions and behaviour of individual prisoners is of their own agency and choosing, senior management within prisons have an overwhelming duty of care to ensure safe and humane facilities (including mitigation of hanging points), something that is still not as embedded in prison architecture as it otherwise should be. Scarce finances and fiscal limitations are not an adequate response to excuse ageing facilities with ample opportunities for self-harm and suicide, as the preservation of life and safety should be of paramount priority for senior management, even within the perennial context of limited resources. Too often in too many jurisdictions responses have only been prompted by coronial deaths in custody inquisitions. On the ground, front-line prison staff retain responsibility for being the eyes and ears in intuitively responding to at-risk prisoners, whether overtly suicidal or not.

Research into prison suicide in federal prisons in the United States highlights common risk factors based on probabilities and demographics (Hayes 1995: 53–6):

- *Gender* – the vast majority of prisoners who commit suicide are male.

- *Age* – age is not seen as a strongly predictive factor, that notwithstanding, the 31–40 year age bracket may be at higher risk.

- *Psychiatric history* – the research found that half of all prison suicides involved a person with a mental illness, meaning that the other 50 per cent did not have a psychiatric history. Within the percentage with a mental illness, the most common diagnosis is a psychotic disorder, followed by mood (depressive) and anxiety disorders.

- *Means/method* – the most common means used was that of strangulation, mainly by hanging, followed by jumping from buildings, overdoses and shootings.

- *Location/prison accommodation* – the most common location was a locked unit or a cell, followed by suicide in common areas such as showers or stairways.

- *Length of sentence/type of prisoner* – one of the most at-risk groups identified in this research is that of remandees or unsentenced prisoners. Other at-risk groups are prisoners serving over 20 years and those housed in high-security facilities.

Staff support options such as management, clinical supervision and debriefing (when needed) are beneficial, in that a wise sounding board may help ease stress or overwhelming feelings of responsibility or helplessness. Working with clients who are suicidal is a formidable responsibility, requiring a strong sense of personal insight to avoid burnout.

For workers in a community setting, in Table 8.3 we provide a guide to protective principles and proactive practices for responding to a person who is at risk of suicide. Once again, the client safety contract in Appendix 2 may provide a useful mechanism or resource in regard to these issues.

## Practitioners and self-care

Dealing with difficulties is not only about dealing with offenders and their issues. Difficult work also involves practitioners trying to navigate through a sea of workload demands, high caseloads, working with colleagues and managers who themselves can be difficult to

**Table 8.3** Protective principles and proactive practices for responding to a person who is at risk of suicide in a community setting

| Compassion: protective principles | Action: proactive practice |
|---|---|
| **Communication** | **Ask** |
| *The client*: when you are observing the person and interacting with them, watch both their verbal and non-verbal communication. What are they saying? What are they not saying or avoiding? | If you have observed potential warning signs and the client is communicating in a way that suggests they might be thinking about killing themselves, actually ask them directly about suicide and if they have got a plan. Try to find out where they are at, and the means they might intend to use. |
| *You*: be aware of the way you are interacting and connecting with them. Use your communication style to tell the client in different ways that you care and are concerned. | |
| | An important predictive factor is whether a person has thought about and attempted suicide before. If an opportunity arises, ask them about this too. |
| **Care** | **Assess** |
| *For the client*: empathy is vital throughout the whole process. If the client does not feel that they can be honest or relate to you, then they may keep vital information to themselves. Tell them you care. | *Their behaviour and thinking* – what the person is doing and saying. Assess their level of suicidal ideation and actual planning in terms of specificity and level of lethality. |
| *For yourself*: Avoid making promises that you will keep it a secret and be the only one who knows. This would be a very heavy burden to bear, especially if the person takes their life. | *The environment and potential risks* – the client's circumstances. What is the impact of their physical surroundings? (access to means, being alone, access to alcohol/drugs). |
| Keep safe and look after yourself. Acknowledge that this is a difficult situation for you as a worker. | *Safeguards and protective factors* – what is keeping them alive? (company of a friend, hope of a future event or goal, wanting to stay alive for children's sake). |

*Table 8.3 continued*

| Collaboration | Act |
|---|---|
| *With the client*: adopt a collaborative partnership approach, such as, what can 'we' do about it? For suicide prevention to work, the person at risk needs to be active in planning for their own safety.<br><br>*With others*: it is important that you explore with the client who they would consider or allow to be part of their support network. Together you may identify different people that can help, for example, a family member, friend, a GP or a suicide prevention service. | Discuss with the client what actions you can take in the here-and-now to keep them safe. Remove the means to commit suicide, and avoid the client spending time alone. The next two to three days are crucial. The client may wish to contact a 24-hour crisis helpline. You may need to contact their GP or ring a mental health services triage service.<br><br>Collaboratively put together a safety action plan, with practical strategies and actions that you and the client can take to keep them alive. |

work with, and constantly grappling with work-related issues such as information sharing.

### Stress and worker self-care

Stress is commonly expressed as a range of psychological, physical and behavioural symptoms. Different people experience stress in different ways. Table 8.4 portrays symptoms and early warning signs that indicate that a worker may be experiencing significant stress or issues in the workplace.

Burnout is 'a form of chronic strain that develops over time in response to prolonged periods of high stress' (NCETA 2005). The consequences of stress and burnout can include a negative influence on a worker's health, possible relationship problems at home and at work, reduced job satisfaction, increased absenteeism, and lower retention rates. The first step in managing stress is to acknowledge that it exists (Lifeline Australia 2009).

Skinner and Roche (2005: 34, from Edelwich and Brodski 1980) cite the following ten common irrational beliefs in the health and human services sector.

1 It is an absolute necessity for me to be loved and appreciated by every client.
2 I must always be in the 'good books' with my supervisor.
3 I must be thoroughly competent and successful in doing my job to be considered worthwhile.
4 Anyone who disagrees with my methods is bad, wicked or ignorant and therefore becomes an opponent to be scorned, rejected or blamed.
5 It is reasonable for me to become very upset over clients' problems and circumstances.
6 It is awful and catastrophic when things are not as clients and the organisation would like them to be.
7 Unhappiness is caused by clients or the organisation, and I have no control over my feelings.

**Table 8.4** Symptoms of worker stress and burnout

| Work performance | Physical symptoms |
|---|---|
| • Declining or inconsistent performance<br>• Loss of enthusiasm or motivation<br>• Accidents or uncharacteristic mistakes<br>• Increased time at work<br>• Lack of holiday planning/leave requests<br>• Indecision<br>• Memory lapses<br>• Criticism of others<br>• Unable to concentrate or relax | • Nervous, stumbling speech<br>• Sweating<br>• Tiredness or lethargy, sleeping problems<br>• Frequent headaches<br>• Hand tremors<br>• Rapid weight loss or weight gain<br>• Upset stomach<br>• Lack of interest in appearance/ hygiene<br>• Increased smoking and alcohol or other drugs use |
| **Withdrawal behaviours** | **Emotional reactions** |
| • Reluctance to give support to co-workers<br>• Arriving late or leaving early<br>• Extended lunch breaks<br>• Increased absenteeism<br>• Reduced social interaction | • Crying, moodiness or irritability<br>• Overreactions to problems<br>• Temper outbursts or aggressive behaviour<br>• Sudden mood swings |

*Source*: Adapted from Skinner and Roche (2005: 41).

8 Until clients and the organisation straighten themselves out and do what is right, I have no responsibility to do what is right myself.

9 There is a right, precise and perfect solution to human problems and it is catastrophic if that solution is not found.

10 Dangerous and fearsome things happen to clients, which are a cause for great concern and should be continuously dwelled upon.

The human services sectors are renowned for involving work that can become complicated quite quickly, placing workers in unique and challenging situations that do not always have clear-cut answers. Given the overarching context of the human services as usually being overloaded and under-resourced, there are times when front-line workers can experience strain and stress that is far above the normal threshold or equilibrium of the work–life balance. Terms such as 'compassion fatigue', 'secondary trauma' and 'vicarious trauma' are used to describe a common phenomenon across the workforce, highlighting the role of governance and structural determinants in sustaining a healthy (or unhealthy) workforce (Figley 1995; Baruch 2004). A qualitative study done in the United States identified the three main reasons for burnout among prison caseworkers as being low salaries, lack of support from management, and stress (Carlson and Thomas 2006). None of this comes as a surprise. In more serious or extreme cases, criminal justice workers may develop their own mental health conditions, particularly anxiety disorders such as post-traumatic stress disorder from stressful or dangerous work experiences, leading to compensation claims and burnout.

### We are only human: managing our own frustration and reactions

There is a plethora of guidance about how to maintain an empathetic and compassionate therapeutic practitioner–client relationship, and this book is no different. Yet this advice is largely (as it should be) client-centred.

This not withstanding, practitioners rarely raise their own voice on these issues as they pertain to themselves. For workers, it seems that the 'to do' list is as sizeable as the 'thou shalt not' list of professional *faux pas*. But, in the bid to appear an esteemed professional, sometimes work cultures do not allow space for the 'what about me?' questions, or to discuss weaknesses or mistakes. So there remains an elephant in the room: difficult work may naturally elicit strong emotional reactions by workers. Yes, the clients are important, but we are too. What do we do with our own anger? How do we maintain a therapeutic alliance with clients who have abrasive personalities, problematic anti-social behaviours, and sabotaging or destructive responses to their rehabilitation? How should we respond to increasingly frustrating cases that push our buttons or trigger unexpected offence or fragility in us as workers? What should be done when we are battling with our own judgement of what a client has done or who they are as a person? Criminal justice professionals daily support offenders who may have done things that, in our own minds, are unthinkable.

Acknowledging these private practitioner battles and struggles as valid is the first step. The second step is encouraging responsibility and preparation for maintaining our own professional boundaries and personal growth.

If we gain insight into what makes us upset as workers – our own triggers – we can then prepare, respond and grow. The following anger reduction strategies have been proposed for practitioners (adapted from Kassinove and Tafrate 2002: 260–70):

- *Engage in self-monitoring of anger episodes.* Is your anger related to clients with specific types of pathology or problems? Do you react more strongly to some types of client statements, behaviours or body language? Pay attention to your own body language, tone of voice, feelings, and how you communicate with them.

- *Supervision and feedback from other professionals.* Discuss difficult cases with supervisors or skilled colleagues who are willing to accept different points of view and who are themselves relatively comfortable with anger.

- *Experiment with different styles of responding to difficult client behaviours.* Balance empathetic listening with more authoritative or firm communication. Try different styles and notice the way clients respond. If clients react more positively to your interventions, they are less likely to trigger anger in you. Also, engage in problem-solving. Think about alternative responses and strategies, creative responses to the problems that are currently a source of frustration.

- *Skill building – develop advanced therapeutic skills and techniques.* For whatever types of client interactions you find to be challenging, there are skills that can help you maintain a productive collaborative relationship. For example, perhaps you feel angry when clients are verbally hostile or insulting. In this case, it may be beneficial for you to develop an increased variety of de-escalation and conflict resolution skills, allowing you to accept verbal barbs and be assertive without reacting strongly. Professional books, education and professional development seminars and training, and supervision can all increase skills. Unfortunately, as practitioners we sometimes put our own development at the end of the list. Make it a priority to increase your competencies.

- *Avoidance and escape.* Some anger and frustration could simply be avoided by deciding not to take on additional cases. Limits can also be set on the number of clients seen with particularly difficult problems. Since these clients may demand more time and practitioner skill, such limits allow for more thoughtful attention to their problems. When working in criminal justice settings, sometimes clinical judgement needs to involve swift exit to avoid injury.

- *Practise forgiveness/apologise to clients.* Since anger negatively affects interpersonal relationships, it is important to rebuild connections that have been damaged by bad feelings. Our clients do some pretty bad things and we may respond with annoyance, anger or outright outrage. Forgiveness and letting go occur when it is recognised that clients are not 'evil' but rather they are pawns of their learning history, biology, social world and genetics. Letting go any vestige of global condemnation we may have for their acts will allow us to develop a better anger management program for them, and more professional responses for ourselves. Apologising communicates a number of important messages. First, it models taking responsibility for your own actions. Second, apologising shows that you are a fallible person who accepts making mistakes. It also sends the message that you care about the client's concerns and are empathetic, even when you might be at fault. Ultimately, apologising prevents resentment from building up and repairs alliance ruptures.

- *Foster a realistic and accepting, flexible, and less demanding philosophical view of your clients.* Of course, acceptance is hard when we find our clients engaging in self-defeating choices and being unresponsive to our interventions. Although we may use all the tools at our disposal, have much clinical experience, examine the research evidence about specific interventions, and consult with colleagues, it is still difficult to know in the early stages of treatment which of our clients will do well. In terms of practitioner–client interactions, we need to remember that clients often 'march to their own drummers' and *their* difficulties are *their* struggles. We as practitioners simply move along with them.

Responding to difficult clients and doing difficult work is an ongoing learning process, requiring a sense of resilience to help navigate the constellation of issues that come up in the lives of our clients and, at times, in our own lives as well. Scenario 8.2 provides an opportunity for further planning, problem-solving and strategising to respond to difficult situations and prevent worker burnout.

The most important resource that a service has is its workers. Staff support mechanisms can be put in place to provide organisational support for each worker, for example, clinical supervision and management support. The value of a wise sounding board may help us to keep a balanced perspective on the proportionality and importance of different issues that arise, avoiding feelings of isolation or being overwhelmed. Just as clients are able to access ongoing support after they have been through traumatic events and difficult circumstances, so too workers should be able to step back or entirely step out of difficult work when circumstances such as violence or crisis take their toll. Working with respect means that we are heard too, and that we can offer our colleagues respect by walking with them through their responsibilities and routines. Notions of human capital and social capital remain just as relevant for the workforce as they do for those with whom we work.

## Paradoxes and controversies

Experience and research have shown that in the corrections area difficult situations and working with difficult people are inevitable. Given this, one potential source of tension is how far we ought to go in taking pre-emptive action and how much we should rely upon reactive intervention. Strategic planning is essential to forestall possible and foreseeable risks. However, we cannot plan for everything. On the one hand, it is important to be flexible when things happen. On

### Scenario 8.2

#### Reducing stress, preventing burnout

A combination of *workforce development* and *self-management strategies* are needed to begin to address adequately problems with retention and burnout among practitioners in criminology and corrections. The former points to strategies involving professional development and staff support options (training, capacity building, and seeking assistance from co-workers, managers, clinical supervision, employee assistance programs), and the latter relates to personal strategies involving self-care and coping strategies that are intrinsic to the individual in how they reduce stress, cope with work demands, and maintain an appropriate work–life balance. Both encourage planning and ideas, but the first draws on resources and supports external to the individual and the second focuses on internal capacity and ability. Using the two blank columns in the table, think of appropriate ways to deal with these issues in response to the scenarios described.

| Scenarios | How should I approach this? What staff support options are available in this instance? | Stress prevention and self-care strategies – planning to look after myself |
| --- | --- | --- |
| 1 Your team leader has extensive experience in front-line work, but limited skills in management and administration. You get on well with him, but find some of his decision-making frustrating. Lately, he has moved away from direct client contact, instead overseeing assessments and allocation of clients. For several weeks, your caseload has been filled with at-risk clients (personality | | |

*continued*

disorders, trauma) and those with anti-social tendencies – clients who are testing your boundaries. Your work days are becoming stressful due in part to ongoing unwise caseload allocation, without the professional support to match.

---

**2** Recent changes to quality assurance processes brought in by the government have resulted in front-line workers needing to take increasing responsibility for added record-keeping and administration. You work for a community sector organisation that does not have a dedicated quality improvement officer. You are struggling with the level of reporting involved, specifically the complicated reporting templates and statistics. Getting the paperwork finished by the government's deadlines involves longer hours at work, which is affecting your family time.

---

**3** You are working as a parole officer in a community corrections agency. You are required to visit the house of a female offender, pregnant and in her late twenties. Her male partner is concerning you because he has a history of being violent, possessive, and is well known in criminal justice circles. The female client has been non-compliant twice in the past month when you requested meeting in a public place. She cited relationship problems, social phobia and lack of transport as reasons for not leaving the house. Her GP confirmed the social phobia. The female client has just raised a complaint with your manager that you don't seem responsive to her needs, because you do house visits for other clients. She has promised that her partner won't be at the house when you visit.

the other hand, to prepare facilities and to construct interventions entirely around 'risk aversion' can stifle interaction and create an atmosphere of mistrust. Doing nothing is sometimes the best thing to do rather than assuming or anticipating something that may in fact not occur. Taking anticipatory action may lead to unnecessary intrusions in lives and situations.

Building a sense of community and shared purpose, developing relationships based upon respect and trust, and ensuring facilities are compliant with basic health and welfare standards are some of the best preventive measures one can take. Having a plan to deal with emergency and stressful situations, and engaging in ongoing training and discussion of how best to cope with difficulties can provide a sound basis for responding to things when they do happen.

Importantly, from a practitioner's perspective, we need to recognise that come what may, 'shit happens'. Expect the unexpected, but do so in the knowledge that whatever happens, we need to develop confidence in agencies and the people in them by providing them with the skills, capacities and training to handle whatever comes their way. Accepting the reality and being flexible can go some way to help us to navigate whatever circumstances we find ourselves encountering in the workplace.

## Conclusion

This chapter has covered a wide range of issues that add stress to an already difficult job. However, as indicated in the examples, there has also been a lot of work done on these questions, which provides a guide to useful practice. One of the key messages of the chapter perhaps is that practitioners need to consider how we might best support each other in achieving institutional goals and maintaining our personal and professional well-being. Related to this, it is important to develop strategies that will assist workers with offenders in dealing with public pressures and outside criticisms of the work undertaken. Supporting clients and supporting practitioners are simultaneous and essential aspects of working with offenders.

## Discussion questions

1  What are some approaches and strategies that can be used to prevent and reduce suicide in prison?
2  What causes prison riots? What are the roles of practitioners in responding to riot conditions?
3  Suggest strategies and approaches that an organisation could implement to increase staff support and reduce stress and burnout. Also, what practical responses can an organisation implement to support workers in maintaining healthy professional boundaries?

## Further reading

Carlson, J. and Thomas, G. (2006) 'Burnout among prison caseworkers and correctional officers', *Journal of Offender Rehabilitation*, 43(3): 19–34.

Carlton, B. (2008) 'Understanding prisoner resistance: power, visibility and survival in high-security', in T. Anthony and C. Cunneed (eds) *The Critical Criminology Companion*. Sydney: Hawkins Press.

Gutheil, T. and Gabbard, G. (1993) 'The concept of boundaries in clinical practice: theoretical and risk management dimensions', in G. Adshead and C. Jacob (eds) (2009) *Personality Disorder: The Definitive Reader*. London: Jessica Kingsley Publishers.

Liebling, A., Durie, L., Stiles, A. and Tait, S. (2005) 'Revisiting prison suicide: the role of fairness and distress', in A. Liebling and S. Maruna (eds) *The Effects of Imprisonment*. Cullompton: Willan Publishing.

Rynne, J., Harding, R. and Wortley, R. (2008) 'Market testing and prison riots: how public-sector commercialization contributed to a prison riot', *Criminology and Public Policy*, 7(1): 117–42.

## Key resources

Hayes, L. (1995) *Prison Suicide: An Overview and Guide to Prevention*. Massachusetts: National Institute of Corrections, US Department of Justice.

Just Detention International (2009) *Hope for Healing: Information for Survivors of Sexual Assault in Detention*. Los Angeles: Just Detention International.

Mayhew, C. (2000a) *Preventing Client Initiated Violence: A Practical Handbook*. Canberra: Australian Institute of Criminology.

Mayhew, C. (2000b) *Preventing Violence Within Organisations: A Practical Handbook*. Canberra: Australian Institute of Criminology.

Schwartz, J. and Barry, C. (2005) *A Guide to Preparing for and Responding to Prison Emergencies*. Washington, DC: US Department of Justice, National Institute of Corrections.

Vess, J. (2006) 'Preparing practitioners for assessing and managing risk', in K. McMaster and L. Bakker (eds) *Will They Do It Again? Assessing and Managing Risk*. Lyttleton: Hall McMaster and Associates.

World Health Organisation (2000) *Preventing Suicide: A Resource for Prison Officers*. Geneva: Department of Mental Health, World Health Organisation.

# Chapter 9

# Continuums of care and collaborative alliances

We really need to understand that they [police] are a different system and we [social workers in community agencies] are a different system. We need to mutually respect each other's work, as we don't do the same kind of stuff. There is a need to know the differences, the role division, and accept that we have a very different mentality, different policies … But we need to keep talking so that everyone can explain their own position and perhaps we can come to a compromise.

(Social worker, quoted in Buchbinder and Eisikovits 2008: 6)

## Introduction

Collaboration and partnership is essential in supporting offenders across the continuum of care, from the point of their entry into the criminal justice system through to the point of their exit and reintegration into the community. Collaboration also means being able to work with other practitioners within and across different institutions and sectors. Collaboration is not just about individual client referral pathways (referring a client to someone else), therefore, but encompasses the bigger picture of working across the broad human service, corrections and education sectors in an integrated way (working closely with those to whom we refer our clients).

This chapter provides an examination of issues pertaining to information-sharing, partnerships, strategic planning, accountability and evaluation. The notion of learning how to speak each other's language is an important aspect of collaboration, especially given the many different disciplines and occupations involved in working with offenders. The exercise of role delineation and interdisciplinary collaboration needs to be mutually respectful, as illustrated in a practitioner observation (cited in Cameron *et al.* 2007: 4): 'In integrated teams, people can get a bit precious about their roles.'

It is this preciousness that it is necessary to avoid, yet it is understandable why there might be existing tensions or turf wars in the correctional and community sectors. Fundamentally, it is essential to recognise that multidisciplinary collaboration is not that different from working with offenders, in that it also involves role delineation, goal-setting, motivation for change, strong social networks and working with respect. As with offenders, some agencies are more successful at collaboration than others. In part this stems from a clear idea of who is taking responsibility for what, when and why.

In its most basic sense, collaboration simply refers to people or agencies working together for a shared purpose. In this chapter we explore various dimensions of collaboration. We begin by emphasising that collaboration is at the heart of the contemporary models of working with offenders. It is an essential part of this work. As such, learning to work collaboratively is not a luxury or something we should do reluctantly. It lies at the very foundation of attempts to assist offenders. The chapter then discusses issues relating to stakeholder participation, the importance of strategic planning and the practical barriers and opportunities posed by collaboration.

## Institutional realities of collaboration

Throughout this book we have stressed that the key models of intervention today all incorporate the ideas of pathways, continuums of care and individualised interventions that cater to the needs and circumstances of the client. This is expressed in the language of (integrated) offender management and the concept of corrections as problem-solving.

The logical institutional implications of the contemporary philosophies that underpin offender intervention are that people and agencies have to work closely together to achieve client outcomes. This involves both vertical and horizontal forms of collaboration. For example, within a prison context, collaboration means that prison officers, therapeutic staff, senior managers, teachers, nurses and doctors, case managers and support staff – that is, all of those employed within the *institutional hierarchy* – work in unison and with a shared purpose around prisoner issues. Simultaneously, these staff need to be able to collaborate with the many outside persons coming into the prison, such as drug and alcohol counsellors, youth workers, representatives of welfare agencies and government bureaucracies, sex offender specialists and so on – that is, those who offer skills *across institutional settings*.

Collaboration is not only about with whom one works, it also implies a temporal element. For instance, the notion of integrated offender management hinges upon doing what is best for the client over *a defined period of time*. In particular, it relates to preparing offenders (for the prison, for community-based service, for parole, for probation), working with offenders in specific environments (the prison, the community, the rehabilitation centre), and ensuring that offenders have adequate support post-release or post-program. In other words, the continuum of care extends from the first formal point of contact of the offender with the criminal justice system, through to the point of official release of obligation (and beyond, since services can still be provided on a voluntary basis to those who have completed their 'time' under the supervision of corrective service officers).

'Corrections as problem-solving' and offenders as 'on a pathway' are concepts that demand the engagement of many different practitioners and agencies. Along the way, there will be different types of intervention, ranging from individualised case management to referrals, to case conferencing and multidisciplinary teams. Throughout this process, the offender too will need to be at the centre of consultation and participation in the continuum of care and associated alliances.

### Ethics and understanding in collaboration

Ethics is not simply about 'correct procedures'; it is about human relationships. The ethics of collaboration is about 'trust', 'honesty', 'reciprocity' and 'reliability'. It means treating people fairly and openly and implies a commitment to the physical, psychological and emotional well-being of everyone concerned. It is about how we relate to the 'subjects' of the intervention and to the roles and responsibilities of those undertaking the intervention.

Practitioners need to be conscious of the following issues in relation to their own roles and expertise:

**Innovative practice 9**

## Animal therapy and 'Pups in Prison' in Australia and North America

Various animal therapy initiatives are under way in Canada and the United States, including visitation programs, wildlife rehabilitation programs, livestock care programs, assistance animal training, husbandry, and pet therapy (Correctional Service of Canada 1998). Important outcomes of animal therapy are improvements in self-esteem, encouragement of non-threatening, non-judgemental affection and loyalty, the bestowal of responsibility, hope and something to look forward to, diversion and reduction in isolation and loneliness through ongoing companionship (Correctional Service of Canada 1998). The types of animals include dogs, cats, birds, guinea pigs, horses, farm animals and wild animals.

In Tasmania, Australia, the 'Pups in Prison' project is a collaborative initiative of Assistance Dogs Australia and the Tasmania Prison Service. Apart from the obvious therapeutic value, prisoners are provided with work skills and training throughout the sixteen months it takes to train a puppy, receiving input from correctional staff and external trainers, as well as broader recognition of community contribution in support of people with disabilities. Lisa Singh, the former Minister for Corrections, commented on the practicality and social capital inherent in this new venture:

> We have received a lot of community support for the Pups in Prison program ... The inmates have welcomed the opportunity to take part in the program which will teach the dogs important skills such as opening and closing doors, retrieving essential items and turning light switches on and off ... These dogs become crucial to the daily routines of their owners, who are often confined to wheelchairs. (Singh 2010)

The pups go home with staff on weekends to get a taste for life as an assistance dog in the wider community. Launched in 2010, the newly established working relationship between the two stakeholder agencies will be an interesting collaborative interface for evaluation in the future.

- Conflict of interest
- Capacities and levels of competence
- Mechanisms to deal with potential harm or wrongdoing
- Knowledge of codes of conduct
- Consideration of the social composition of the collaborating team
- Storage of materials and data associated with the collaboration
- Confidentiality and anonymity
- Fair, honest, comprehensive and accurate reflection and reporting on the collaboration process.

We also have to be aware of the fit between organisational values and certain ethical stances. This can be a source of conflict if potential differences are not acknowledged or accommodated early on. There is a need for clear understanding of the others' values when it comes to maintaining an ethical working partnership in the case of, for example, a prison and an external service provider for injecting drug users, or between law enforcement officers and a local community agency that is working with an offender.

Institutional and organisational cultures shape practice in different ways and in different directions. It is important to recognise that this is so, and to be sensitive to how it may impact upon potential collaboration between agencies that have quite different approaches and legal mandates. The circumstances under which offenders on parole are breached is a case in point: government-employed community corrections officers have a specific obligation to report breaches (it is built into the job description); workers in non-government organisations may be less concerned about reporting breaches by offenders who occasionally transgress the conditions of their order (since their brief is not that of compliance enforcement as such, but rehabilitation). Who breaches or reports an offender and when and how they do so can become a bone of contention if the ground rules for collaboration involving government agencies and NGOs are not worked out ahead of time.

Working with offenders means engaging with many different people with a wide variety of experience and expertise. It also means involvement in processes that should build a sense of coalition or shared purpose through heightened transparency and consultation. This is about building collaborative alliances. Generally speaking, the key players should include:

- Offenders, offender families and advocates, victims (experts by experience)

- Practitioners and agencies (experts by profession)
- Academics and research teams (experts by investigation)
- Authority figures and community leaders (experts by governance).

Preliminary meetings of these respective experts might discuss the following kinds of issues:

- Roles and responsibilities
- Structure and accountability
- Confidentiality
- Project genesis and outline
- Preliminary scoping document
- Establishing a Reference Group comprising experienced people across sectors to support the project
- Guidelines on reporting requirements
- Intellectual property rights.

An important aspect of collaboration is unpacking the meaning of 'collaboration' at the earliest point in time. Different people may understand the term to mean different things. It is important, therefore, to define what we mean by collaboration in any given circumstance.

For example, Carnwell and Carson (2005) distinguish between 'partnerships' (who we are) and 'collaborations' (what we do). In so doing, they describe different types of partnership, ranging from those based on a particular project or particular social problem, through to ideological and ethical partnerships that involve shared perspectives and specific viewpoints. Collaboration is seen as the process of working together in a particular kind of partnership. It is one of several such methods of partnership, which may also include the more loosely constructed 'networking' (exchange of information for mutual benefit), through to 'coordinating' (exchanging in-formation and altering activities for a common purpose), and 'cooperating' (exchanging information, altering activities and sharing resources), as well as 'collaboration' (all of the above, plus enhancing the capacity of the other partner(s) for mutual benefit and a common purpose) (VicHealth, n.d.).

Importantly, different professions and occupational groups may define 'collaboration' in quite different ways (see, for example, Woodside and McClam 2006). Nurses who work in prisons, for instance, may be used to 'traditional' multidisciplinary collaborations

249

with Professions Allied to Medicine (PAM), but the PAM model is very different from one involving broader agency collaborations that include social, business, voluntary and charitable services (Whitehead 2006: 127). The reality that prison-based healthcare has implications for the whole of the immediate community, as well as family and relatives (consider, for example, Hepatitis C and its prevalence within prison environments) means that a wider notion of collaboration is crucial to viable offender services, including health services.

Different occupations and professions use different language. But language itself embodies specific understandings of the world and particular ways of intervening based upon these understandings. Professional training in social work, psychology, youth and community work, nursing, and rehabilitation counselling will yield overlapping but different social constructions of the 'problem' and its 'solution'. Employment as a caseworker in a non-government agency, holding a job within a government prison or providing occasional professional services for offenders influences how we see our main job function and imbues each intervention with its own values and primary purpose. Discerning where practitioners are coming from is valuable when establishing the first lines of communication.

Addressing complex needs and complicated social issues requires a lot of work. It demands that people collaborate on many different levels if substantive social and personal change is to be achieved. Part of the process of collaboration is identifying where different parties are coming from, in order to assess where, collectively, we might be going. Scenario 9.1 illustrates how language, and the different perspectives embedded in each way of speaking, can enable or inhibit this process of communicating and sharing viewpoints and visions. The rest of this sub-section provides a rough sketch of views from 'above' and 'below' as these pertain to practitioners. The intention is to highlight, in schematic and exaggerated form, key differences in perception and perspective. The point of this is to provide a better understanding of work context within which collaboration is meant to take place, and to highlight differences that may shape the nature and dynamics of collaboration. Our example is based upon working with youth at risk.

Those who are 'above' include managers, policymakers, academics, politicians and directors – basically those whose job it is to identify strategic issues, to develop institutional policy and/or to direct broad operational plans. Those who are 'below' include youth and community workers, front-line professionals, case managers, direct service providers and front office workers – basically those whose

## Scenario 9.1

### *We talk all the time, but we don't speak the same language*

The use of language is essential to communication across different parts of the criminal justice system, yet it is often taken for granted that we each know what the other means. Acronyms are used for everything, and yet they can sometimes be confusing. Healthy dialogue is premised upon shared meaning and understanding.

*Exercise*
Define and discuss the meaning of the following terms and acronyms used by different stakeholders. Which terms or acronyms are you unsure of? Which terms in particular might be interpreted to mean different things, depending on occupation and jurisdiction/country?

| Offenders/ clients | Front-line therapeutic workers | Correctional managers | Law enforcement and criminal courts |
|---|---|---|---|
| Dogs | Relapse | Evidence-based | Recidivism |
| Screws | prevention | practice | Demand |
| Rock spiders | Cost-benefit | Duty of care | reduction |
| Grievous bodily | analysis | Quality | Therapeutic |
| harm | Criminogenic | assurance | jurisprudence |
| Bup | Throughcare | Prisonisation | Diversion |
| | Inpatient | Workforce | Situational |
| | withdrawal | development | crime |
| | unit | Clinical | prevention |
| | Enmeshment | supervision | |
| | | | |
| THC | CBT | IOM | CMD |
| OD | LS/CMI | KPI | DTO |
| IDU | BBV | NOMS | HDO or HDC |
| | SASH | HMP | CPTED |
| | ATOD | CCTV | DUI |
| | DSM-IV | | |

job it is to work directly with clients in some way, both at a generic level (telephone referral, first point of contact) and in regards to specific interventions (group facilitator, intake and assessment worker, counsellor). Looking at issues and interventions from more than one angle is healthy and constructive so long as it is accompanied by dialogue about differences in viewpoint and attempts to find the suitable middle ground.

There is sometimes a disjunction between the expectations from 'above' and the realities of working 'below'. These are summarised in Table 9.1. A key point here is that the theoretical models, and abstract pronouncements about putting principles into practice, too often ignore those who are central to the success (or otherwise) of the intervention – the practitioners. Yet, we cannot afford to sidestep the fact that things such as staff burnout and high turnover of practitioners will have immediate and direct impacts on the best-laid plans. A key message here is that practitioners, too, need to be taken care of, as discussed in Chapter 8.

At the end of the day, the whole point of intervention is to assist the client. But again, one's views of the client may vary depending upon one's location in the intervention process and institutional hierarchy. Sometimes the organisational imperative is pre-given, in the sense that state laws and government policy may decide for us what the orientation is to be. For example, the breaching of people for social security offences and the breaching of offenders on community service orders are command-driven from the top. How managers and practitioners actually respond to these imperatives is partially 'negotiable' depending upon how decisions are made and discretion is used at the street level. Nevertheless, the dynamic between differing views of the client, and approaches to client needs, will shape the nature of the service provision generally.

It is important to take the differences and tensions between viewpoints seriously. What can appear to be patronising in one context (such as broad statements about doing things 'for their own good') may in fact be an essential starting point in another (for example, dealing with someone with co-morbid health issues, over which they have lost personal control). Again, identification of differences (which at times may seem extreme) provides the basis for listening, learning and finding balance in how we intervene in the lives of our clients.

The point of understanding the diverse viewpoints is to assist the process of engaging with the challenges of working with communities and clients. Fundamentally, if we want to *change* complex situations, then we have to *engage*. As part of this, we need to join up with

**Table 9.1** Views of practitioners

| From above | From below |
|---|---|
| • Strategy and policy cascades downwards to the workers, even when managers are often hamstrung by inadequate budgets. | • Excessive workloads – too much to do, too many people to assist, too many reports to write. |
| • Emphasis on addressing all of the dynamic risk factors simultaneously, since this relates to agency mission. | • Lack of adequate resources, training and funding – unsupported workforce. |
| • Emphasis on multi-agency collaboration and memorandums of understanding. | • New models of working with offenders increase the intensity of the work, and the extent of the work. |
| • Emphasis on case management (of individuals) and throughcare principles (guiding processes). | • Stress is a major problem. |
| • Emphasis on 'what works', as a measurable outcome. | • Lack of direction or direct leadership from the top, very little policy impact from the bottom. |
| • Emphasis on the practitioner changing the offender. | • Failure to acknowledge 'risk' and 'protective' factors affecting *practitioners*' lives and work. |

others who share a commitment, a personal interest, in making things different and better. Yet, collaboration must be undertaken in ways that are cost-effective and time-limited (see Woodside and McClam 2006). It must also involve participatory models that truly engage practitioners and their clients.

An example of how to be inclusive in collaborative practice is well illustrated in the case of those practitioners who are working with issues of violence in family relationships. A strong sense of egalitarianism is evident throughout.

Harnessing the therapeutic potential of multiple observers and multiple perspectives, we develop our ideas in conversation with each other in front of the family, inviting them to comment and add to what we have said; the therapist invites reflections from the in-room consultant on what transpires between the family and therapist, and all participants are encouraged to adopt the roles of both listener and speaker and to comment on the differences and similarities in perceptions. The in-room consultant uses the role to acknowledge success where it may have been overlooked, i.e. in the written documents, to ask questions and offer suggestions, to introduce new ideas and to ask confrontative and challenging questions in ways that facilitate constructive problem-solving. We have few rules, which include always being brief, not using too many ideas, being tentative and always encouraging our clients to comment on our ideas. (Vetere and Cooper 2001)

Engaging clients in the collaborative process is also integral to the forging of a 'therapeutic alliance' in cases of one-to-one and group work with clients. This refers to the idea of learning from a client's experiences, developing a mutual understanding of the meaning given by a client of their behaviour in any given situation, and for the practitioner to learn what to do from the client (see Kirby 2001). Such an approach assists the client in developing a sense of control, to be involved as an active participant, to have a positive relationship with the practitioner and to view the overall process as revolving around human relationships (rather than bureaucratic guidelines and administrative purposes).

Working collaboratively involves not only understanding perspectives from 'above' and 'below', but ensuring that people at all levels are actively engaged in the collaborative process. Again, effective collaboration involves interventions over time, and working vertically and horizontally across and within relevant institutions.

## Collaboration involves planning

If collaboration is to make any sense at all, then it must be related to the specific principles and objectives of a particular program or project. In other words, collaboration must make reference to the broad social vision that underpins any initiative, and the specific intent and focus of the intervention. *Stories from the field* 9.1 reflects on some of the barriers and contextual considerations that might inhibit full participation in planning from all collaborating parties.

### Central questions for collaboration in the planning stages

The first phase of collaboration is a time to reflect on what it is we are trying to achieve and who is going to be involved in the collaboration process. Before beginning, therefore, we need to be clear about the answers to a series of central questions:

- *What?* Identify what precisely is to be the point of the collaboration (the focus of collaboration in relation to programs, services, processes, outcomes).

- *Why?* Clarify the purposes of the collaboration and the kinds of issues you want to address (the reasons for collaboration in relation to existing uses of resources, effects of a program and so on).

- *Which?* Establish the criteria that will be used to serve as 'benchmarks' for the assessment of whether or not the collaboration is working (in relation to the object and purposes of the intervention).

- *Who?* Identify the key persons or 'stakeholders' who will be involved in, or affected by, the collaboration (such as caseworkers, service agency personnel, funding bodies, client advocates, clients, peak bodies and sector representatives).

- *How?* Identify the main sources of information, methods of data collection and how these are collected (for example primary or secondary sources), and resources that can be drawn upon in carrying out the intervention (includes both information sources and agency resources).

- *When?* Develop timelines for completion of any particular intervention, and as part of this set out when specific tasks are meant to be carried out and by whom (broad schedule of activities and target dates including milestones).

### Stories from the field 9.1

#### 'Plan' is a four-letter word? Barriers to transparent collaborative planning

Hannah Graham

The following points are personal observations from work with the community sector establishing and formalising partnerships between NGOs and government agencies, as well as broader practice wisdom that I have drawn upon in discussions about putting together this book. Collaboration and evaluation are pragmatic topics that lend themselves to frank and fearless discussion, as the following barriers and issues are widespread across various sectors.

It is common for organisations to undertake training needs analyses and plans, as well as evaluation plans, usually on the grounds

*continued*

of meeting the expectations of funding bodies. Yet collaborations and partnerships can and do operate informally and even formally with limited futures planning. Operational and strategic reasons why this may be the case include the following:

Stakeholders are often coy about promising things into the future in a new relationship because there is a 'wait and see how it all goes' mentality. This may be wise but when taken too far may undermine the very reason for setting up an interface between players. In some more problematic cases, a memorandum of understanding (MOU) can end up, metaphorically, feeling like a prenuptial agreement (that is, risk mitigation exercise in case it fails) rather than a positive opportunity for healthy interdependence in the context of a trustworthy partnership.

There may be hesitance to plan because of an unspoken fear of being controlled or the most vocal and bossiest stakeholder taking over, which is a possibility, and others left thinking, 'what have we got ourselves into?' There may also be imbalance between how much each stakeholder really wants or needs the partnership, creating political or power dimensions to the relationship, particularly if one of the stakeholders is a government agency with links to the funding source.

More seasoned workers may have some quiet apprehension if a new partnership, and associated collaborative activities, is being planned by people who are new to the area being covered or who do not have front-line practitioner experience in service delivery. This is a valid suspicion, as unfortunately it is common for new (often young or inexperienced) project officers or policy officers to be delegated administrative planning duties that have real world outcomes. Yet the people doing the planning may not be responsible for the work involved or they may not stick around long enough to see the plans materialise into a reality. Causes of this may include burnout, parental leave, ulterior motives of temporary commitment due to ambition and ladder-climbing, or just routine corporate restructuring and internal staff movements.

From an organisational perspective, it is difficult for managers to engage in planning and make solid and specific commitments into the future in the context of time-limited competitive funding arrangements. A worst case scenario, albeit a common one, is where stakeholders are forced to compete for the same scarce resources and funding rounds, which does little to assist longevity of trust and collaboration. Instead it may turn into a problematic sense of a 'marriage of convenience', for example, being forced to keep secrets from each other and, in extreme cases, undermine or sabotage the other's chances of success if they impinge on one's own. Unfortunately, as long as there are competitive funding arrangements, empire-building will remain alive and well, whether we like it or not.

From a systemic perspective, effective planning and long-term insight can be inhibited by the very nature of the sector in which a practitioner works. For example, even the best-placed plans may be wasted or affected when key stakeholders experience incidences or situations that suddenly hijack their time and focus. One example is if a community corrections agency may be experiencing workforce development issues with a sudden spate of employment vacancies or stress leave so that even the most committed practitioners are recalled to return to help cope with caseloads displaced by the decision by others to quit suddenly or take time off.

A second example that is common to crisis services and corrections is when the nature of the service delivery (helping offenders or clients in crisis) results in the service itself being thrown into crisis. For example, a residential rehabilitation program may be affected by chaotic and disruptive manipulative behaviour by a client with a personality disorder, resulting in an aggressive critical incident and repeat harassment and threats of the staff, clients and property, lock-down, debriefing and follow-up procedures. This is even more common in correctional environments where security is paramount, and therapeutic imperatives and progress can evaporate when security concerns take over. A successful recreational pilot program using a sports oval inside a prison may be shut down after a security breach, resulting in inmates being reclassified, use of the oval temporarily banned and permission to use the sports equipment revoked in fear of use against staff as a weapon. Where does this leave the evaluation planning for this program? How will a case be built to continue this program out of pilot phase if it didn't get the chance to discover its full potential in the first place? A systemic reliance of acute care and provision of emergency-focused services means that planning for long-term reintegration and rehabilitation outcomes may be affected by a sector itself addicted to crisis.

These barriers highlight the urgency and importance of open and honest planning because any successful partnership demands future planning for collaborative and joint activities. There are times and situations where planning might need to legitimately be put on

*continued*

> hold, but there is an urgent need for thorough planning and good communication to supersede sectors and services with a history of episodic crisis or turnover. This is the only real hope of moving on in our own recovery as a sector towards an integrated approach to reintegration and recovery-oriented systems of care.

The first step is to examine the nature of the project or policy requiring a collaborative effort. The idea of *scoping* refers to the review of the specific aims, targets and strategies of a particular program or project. We need to know at the outset, for example, why the policy, program or project was adopted or introduced. The scoping process involves identifying the values, focus and activities associated with the project or program.

As part of the scoping and planning process, for example, we might consider what is currently available for prisoner support and where the existing or potential service gaps might be. Scenario 9.2 provides a *pro forma* template to map the kinds of information that would need to be collected as part of this scoping exercise.

An essential precondition to collaboration is the undertaking of a preliminary analysis of the context within which the intervention will take place. This has a number of dimensions.

### Internal focus

Collaboration requires human and material resources. Key questions and issues here include:

- Available resources (such as computers, stationery, telephones).

- Budget (relationship of financial resources to the kind and extent of intervention required or desired).

- Culture of the workplace and specific values and principles that might underlie the intervention process (perspectives on aims and objectives).

- Staff skills (technical expertise, in areas such as interviewing, telephone contacting, computer analysis, report-writing).

- Staff morale (collaboration as adding to stress or as means of relieving tensions).

- Availability of outside financial assistance and human resources (*via* direct funding bodies or other sources).

## Scenario 9.2

### Mapping key stakeholders: identifying local post-release prisoner services

*Exercise*

Using the template, map out existing current services that are available locally, and make an ideal list to identify gaps and what services are needed in the future.

| Need | Current | Ideal |
|------|---------|-------|
| **Accommodation**<br>Crisis/temporary<br>Familial<br>Rental<br>Permanent | For example crisis accommodation is provided by a specific non-government organisation. | For example halfway houses. |
| **Employment**<br>Job search<br>Volunteering | | |
| **Financial**<br>ID process<br>Banks<br>Credit cards<br>ATMs<br>Welfare benefits<br>Debts<br>Family payments | | |
| **Transport**<br>Movement<br>License | | |
| **Life/social skills**<br>Sustenance<br>Shopping<br>Food – quality, selection, preparation<br>Bill paying<br>Budgeting<br>Technology<br>Interpersonal skills | | |
| **Communication**<br>Telephone<br>Internet | | |

*continued*

**Health (physical, mental, emotional)**
Medicare care card
Access to GP
Alcohol/drug treatment
Gambling
Anger management
Counselling for depression, anxiety, isolation

**Education**
Literacy
School/TAFE/university
Vocational training

**Legal aid**
Family
Child support
Parole issues

**Family support**
Parenting
Referral
Relationship counselling
Finances

**Pastoral care**
Guidance
Mentors
New friends

**Community connectedness**
Relations (victims)
Compensation (counselling)
Reconciliation (mediation)
Community restoration (welcome participation)

**Recreation and leisure**
Participation
Spectator
Hobbies
Pubs/clubs

*Source:* White and Heckenberg (2006: 22).

- Timing of collaboration activities (relative to agency peak periods of activity or service provision, and to grant application deadlines).

### External focus

Collaboration also must make reference to, and be undertaken in the light of, developments outside of the specific agency context. Background information could be sought on questions and issues such as:

- National and state/provincial policy initiatives and programs relevant to the specific activity of the agency (specific initiatives and demonstration projects from elsewhere).

- Policy changes at the national, state/provincial and local level that may have a bearing on agency work and the intervention process (funding allocations, priority projects).

- Social and community issues in the local area (based on events, media reports, statistical trends).

- Relevant literature on activities related to the initiative (needs studies, consultation reports, other evaluation reports, research articles).

- Identification of main opportunities raised, and threats posed, by the collaboration process and potential findings (such as funding bodies, government agencies, community groups).

- Social mapping of local conditions and local factors that may influence specific project development, and intervention processes (information on the physical environment, demographic data, role and activity of authority figures such as the police).

This type of preliminary analysis should provide some idea of the current 'state of play', and perhaps the kinds of things that need to be addressed before collaboration can properly be undertaken. Once an assessment is made of the context of collaboration, and what may be required to be done before, or as part of, the collaboration process, then the planning process can begin in earnest.

### Administrative issues: turning the questions into answers

Undertaking collaboration can be a relatively simple process, or a fairly complicated process, depending upon the aims of the intervention and the number of people involved as both participants and organisers. There are a number of administrative issues that need to be worked out before the collaboration begins and for effective collaboration practice to occur.

### Conflicts over purposes

It is essential at the start of an intervention to clarify what the intervention is intended to do, and for whom it is being undertaken. It is necessary, therefore, to define the aims and objectives of the intervention in relation to particular conceptions of the program, project or strategy at hand and, if need be, to establish a hierarchy of aims and objectives in cases where there are multiple aims. The collaborating team has to be clear as to which aims are to receive priority, and which are of less importance.

### Nature of multi-agency relationships

As part of the administrative structure, it is important to be clear as to the nature of any multi-agency partnerships or relationships. There are several ways in which these relationships may be construed: as strategic partnerships that involve a formalised relationship between parties that are built upon group decision-making and adherence to the decisions by the group as a whole; or multi-agency cooperation, where the emphasis is on communication with interested parties, in a consultative manner, but such that decision-making is by and large restricted to the core intervention group.

### Being flexible and responding to change

How well a collaborating group responds to unforeseen difficulties or opportunities is partly a matter of administrative flexibility. The possibility and likelihood of changing details and scope of the intervention needs to be acknowledged from the beginning, and the coordinating group needs to consider ahead of time what kinds of implementation contingency plans may be required in order for this to occur. It is important, as well, to see issues of flexibility in terms of delegated authority. For example, a steering committee or coordinating group may wish to set broad parameters on the scope and aim of the intervention, but leave the details and process aspects up to the direct project coordinators.

### Who is to lead the process of collaboration

While collaboration is about a form of partnership and participatory action, this does not mean that there is no central leadership. Indeed, the first administrative priority is to determine which agency is to be the 'lead agency' and/or which person is to assume the central coordinating role for the collaboration. As part of this, we need to negotiate the role of the leader, and how this role can both support the other participants and how participants can support the coordinator. Basically we need to know who is ultimately in charge, what it is that they are in charge of, and how each specific agency and practitioner fits into the overall picture.

*Constructing the file*
Collaboration in the context of working with offenders inevitably involves case notes and the sharing of information between agencies and practitioners. This means that the offender's file is constantly being added to by many different people, each with their own perspective on the client's needs and issues. The use to which the file is put is never socially neutral insofar as 'the file' will very much influence the pathways and choices to be made available to that person. Those who collaborate over a specific client, therefore, have an ethical and professional duty to ensure that case notes are as objective and constructive as possible, and that the language used therein is clear to those coming from different fields of expertise (see Chapter 4).

Collaboration should always be carried out in relation to some kind of strategic plan. That is, it must be related to aims and objectives. While good intervention is not determined by one's resources, it is nevertheless bounded by the resources at one's disposal – one can only work with offenders according to the limits and possibilities offered by the resources available. This, too, should be reflected in strategic planning.

## Barriers to collaboration

Exhortations to work together have long featured in government pronouncements about efficiency and effectiveness in corrections and many other spheres of government activity. So why is collaboration so difficult, and the field littered with so many failed attempts? There are a range of reasons for this.

Even when organisational structures and administrative processes can be worked out to practitioner and management satisfaction, big issues remain with regard to the toll that such intervention takes on practitioners. For example, case management is closely tied to efforts to coordinate service provision in relation to specific clients. But it is the role of the practitioner to do the coordinating work, not the human service agencies and correctional institutions. Organisationally, this can be seen as devolution of responsibility to the ground level stemming from cost pressures within corrective services as a whole. Thus, as an American commentator observes:

> … any major expansion of existing services is unlikely, yet those that exist are inadequate, particularly in the areas of housing, substance abuse treatment, and employment. Recognizing this, policymakers, program administrators, and advocates hope case managers can ensure that clients receive the most appropriate set of services from existing resources, with the maximum possible benefit. (Marks 1994: 6)

Whatever the various rationales for the introduction of case management and other methods of hands-on intervention requiring collaboration, there can be no doubt that the net result is more work for practitioners. This work rests upon a platform of renewed emphasis on involving multiple agencies in client service provision. Scarce resources and multiple client needs demand that practitioners work across organisational boundaries.

At the coalface of practice, serious questions can be asked about workloads (number of cases, working with people who demand more intensive service provision), workplace support (high staff turnover, professional development opportunities), and workplace dynamics (low morale, stress). Much of the rhetoric associated with rehabilitation includes reference to concepts such as 'resilience' and 'capacity building'. How are these attributes to be fostered in those who are meant to deliver them to others?

In addition to work-related demands on practitioners, Australian workshops with workers from a wide range of government and non-government agencies revealed the following list of barriers to collaboration:

- *Locality* – physical location, geographical isolation, accessibility.

- *Funding and resources* – costs, resources under pressure, under-staffing, time constraints.

- *Governance, leadership and accountability* – missions (public safety vs clinical or rehabilitative).

- *Relationships, information sharing and communication* – confidentiality.

- *Conflicting cultures* – stereotypes (lock 'em-up vs bleeding heart), stigmas (sociopath vs crazy).

- *Processes*.

- *Workplace dynamics* – fraternity (for example boys' club of policing; professional club of experts).

On the other hand, a number of opportunities for effective collaboration were also identified (White and Heckenberg 2006; see also Burke 2001; Delaney *et al.* 2003):

- *Leadership and accountability, high levels of commitment* – assigning authority or responsibility for overall coordination.

- *Shared vision and resources* – setting of goals for collaborative effort, formalisation of procedures and sharing of resources (financial, personnel, other).

- *Diversity in decision-making* – identifying stakeholders and engaging diverse stakeholders.

- *Relationship and information sharing* – individualisation of service provision to suit the client, not systems.

- *Improved service delivery and advocacy* – coordination, cooperation.

- *Evaluation and monitoring* – sustaining partnerships through change.

These general observations dovetail with the collaboration experiences of others working broadly on criminal justice issues. For example, a report on the United Kingdom National Strategy for Neighbourhood Renewal (2000: 8) found deep-seated problems when it came to collaboration. Key issues included:

- *Lack of priority* – where no agency or government has a specific requirement to reduce anti-social behaviour.

- *No clear responsibility* – where no one government department or local authority or community group is clearly responsible for pulling together collaborative efforts.

- *Lack of information* – where little information is collected, and where it has been is patchily shared.

These problems were seen in turn to cause:

- *Poor implementation* – there is a lack of effective joint working, including sharing of information, confusion over perceptions of the problem and attitudes and knowledge of available measures.

- *Real policy gaps* – strategies have not focused on strengthening communities' resistance to anti-social behaviour through addressing underlying causes and changing perpetrators' behaviour.

As observed elsewhere (White 2002) 'If it is everybody's responsibility, then it is nobody's. Part of the difficulty with multi-factoral analysis, leading to multi-pronged approaches, involving multi-agency collaboration, is determining whose problem it is in the end.' Clearly, if effective work is to take place across a range of institutions and agencies, then issues of priority and coordination need to be addressed. Leadership is central to this process. This once again ought to direct our attention to the crucial questions guiding collaboration and the importance of strategic planning, as described in the previous section.

### Evaluating collaboration

One way to gauge the success or otherwise of collaboration is to evaluate it. Evaluation is the process of determining how a particular initiative is working and what might be done to improve its chances of success or indeed to stop it altogether. Adopting a 'program logic' approach, which uses and measures things such as inputs, process, outputs and outcomes may be beneficial for evaluation of a more in-depth nature (see Kellogg 2004).

Evaluation is never simply a technical exercise, or something for which there is a simple recipe. It requires honest reflection about aims and objectives, conscious thinking about outcomes and processes, a professional approach to the gathering of information, clarity in presentation of findings, and a culture of constant appraisal. Evaluation of collaboration can be used to articulate three things:

1 *Activities* – to identify the specific mechanisms designed to achieve the objective of increasing collaboration with relevant agencies in order to address multiple criminogenic factors of offenders (for example, activities geared towards enhanced collaboration between program leaders and with offender management team, with custodial staff, and with generic providers of services).

2 *Performance indicators* – to measure the success of each of these activities (for example number of meetings held with various

stakeholders, number of referrals to and from relevant agencies and groups, interviews with offenders and ex-offenders, feedback from agencies regarding extent and nature of collaboration, feedback on quality of working relationships that have been developed).

3  *Outcomes* – to gauge where there is increased collaboration between relevant agencies, and whether there is an increase in referrals to and from agencies as a consequence of the collaboration.

Monitoring of performance is an essential part of teamwork and the team-building associated with collaboration. It provides lessons of failure as well as pointers to success. As such, evaluation is a vital part of ensuring that collaboration itself is actually working.

## Paradoxes and controversies

The biggest question when it comes to collaboration is the matter of who is doing what and to whom they are accountable. We need to determine the specific roles of case managers, program managers, program facilitators, and those working most closely with the offender, and the role of the leader of collaboration efforts in relation to each person and agency involved in a particular intervention. Even the language used to describe different positions can be confusing: a 'case manager' in a prison context can refer to a prison officer with certain responsibilities to coordinate action around a particular offender, while simultaneously a 'case coordinator' might be a non-custodial professional officer whose job is to map out the sentence plan for each individual client. Who wears what title, and does what activity, needs to be sorted out if smooth collaboration is to take place.

Sorting out roles and 'leadership' functions can also be complicated by strong and conflicting personalities, and power imbalances (within and between organisations, and between people). Moreover, adopting the rhetoric of collaboration (similar to that of 'empowerment') may in itself seem sufficient for funding bodies, bureaucratic institutions and practitioners, especially if collaboration itself is not subject to rigorous evaluation and sustained efforts at renewal. Rhetoric without action can be divisive and counterproductive; in the words of a senior practitioner, 'In spite of all the exhortations for joint working and the rest of it, there are a whole set of pressures that are designed to drive people apart. It is a paradox of the government's position and it filters through all the way' (quoted in Webb and Vulliamy 2001: 320).

Simply going through the motions is not conducive to building partnerships and sustained relationships of trust, and will not do much to provide for concrete and measurable outcomes.

From a practitioner's point of view, collaboration may be welcomed or feared depending upon the level of time, energy, staffing and resources expended relative to outcomes. There has to be a pay-off if collaboration is to work. Otherwise, people will disengage from processes regardless of formal agreements and memorandums of understanding. Where there are successes, there can be a sense of reward and it can lead to broader organisational culture change and cross-sectoral development.

## Conclusion

This chapter has provided an introduction to the concept of collaboration as this applies to the continuums of care involved in working with offenders. The benefits of collaboration for clients are nicely summarised as follows:

> First, clients receive services from several professionals working together. The greater the sum of expertise, creativity, and problem-solving skill applied, the more effective the planning and delivery of services will be. Each professional can perform his or her responsibilities better because of having participated in the process of setting goals and priorities as well as planning. Because of the team, the professionals also have a better sense of the client as a whole person and a clearer conception of how their own particular treatment is integrated into the larger plan. (Woodside and McClam 2006: 233)

Indeed, the benefits flow through to all of those involved in the collaboration since by its very nature collaboration is about sharing – of knowledge, of ideas, of responsibility, of problems, and of solutions. Any form of integrated offender management program ultimately has to be based upon precisely this kind of cooperation among agencies and practitioners.

## Discussion questions

1  Focusing particularly on strengths-based rehabilitation, give examples of what an effective collaborative continuum of care might involve.

2 What are some of the key barriers to collaboration between 'inside' workers and 'outside' workers, and between government and non-government workers?
3 List examples of the types of activities and elements that should be included in an evaluation of a collaborative partnership. What kind of information or data would be needed to assess the quality and progress of these different activities?

## Further reading

Burke, P. (2001) 'Collaboration for successful prisoner reentry: the role of probation and the courts', *Corrections Management Quarterly*, 5(3): 11–22.
Delaney, P.J., Fletcher, B.W. and Shields, J.J. (2003) 'Reorganizing care for the substance using offender – the case for collaboration', *Federal Probation*, 67(2): 64–8.
Ellwood, R., Murphy, K., Hanson, D., Hemingway, C., Ramsden, V., Buxton, J., Granger-Brown, A., Condello, L., Buchanan, M., Espinoza-Magana, N., Edworthy, G. and Hislop, T. (2009) 'The development of participatory health research among incarcerated women in a Canadian prison', *International Journal of Prisoner Health*, 5(2): 95–107.
Vetere, A. and Cooper, J. (2001) 'Working systemically with family violence: risk, responsibility and collaboration', *Journal of Family Therapy*, 23: 378–96.
Whitehead, D. (2006) 'The health promoting prison (HPP) and its imperative for nursing', *International Journal of Nursing Studies*, 43: 123–31.

## Key resources

Home Office (2009) *Partnership Working Crime Reduction Toolkit*. Online at: http://www.crimereduction.homeoffice.gov.uk/toolkits/p00.htm (accessed 1 November 2009).
LaVigne, N., Davies, E., Palmer, T. and Halberstadt, R. (2008) *Release Planning for Successful Reentry: A Guide for Corrections, Service Providers, and Community Groups*. Washington, DC: Urban Institute Justice Policy Centre.
Rinehart, T., Laszlo, A. and Briscoe, G. (2001) *Collaboration Toolkit: How to Build, Fix and Sustain Productive Partnerships*. Washington, DC: US Department of Justice, Office of Community Oriented Policing Services.
Roman, C., Moore, G., Jenkins, S. and Small, K. (2002) *Understanding Community Justice Partnerships: Assessing the Capacity to Partner*. Washington, DC: Urban Institute Justice Policy Centre and the National Institute of Justice.
United Nations Office on Drugs and Crime (2008b) *Handbook on Prisoner File Management*. New York: United Nations.

# Chapter 10

# Pathways and possibilities: the process of reintegration

I would like to do things like you do. Like vote. I've never voted. I would like to do something like that. Take time and go to the library... And work. I want a savings account.
(Prisoner, quoted in Pettus-Davis *et al.* 2009: 378)

## Introduction

Reintegration is a process, not a program. Re-entry is a crucial point of intervention and support on the part of practitioners and agencies, but it is an even more fundamental transition for the offender and the communities they return to. Questions of responsibility, on the part of society and on the part of offenders, need to be discussed as part of this transition. This chapter deals with post-release issues and pathways, and the issue of recidivism or repeat offending. An important area for consideration is that of offender programs that involve engagement on matters dealing with victims and victimisation. Working with offenders will only be successful in a generalised way if reintegration and rehabilitation are embedded in communities as well as in the work of offenders and the practitioners who work with them.

Institutionally, a rehabilitation orientation within corrections will best work under conditions where there are few people in prison, supported by a wide range of positive programs and services, and placing the bulk of offenders in community-based alternatives to imprisonment. Rehabilitation needs to focus on the 'whole person': the offender is also a mother or father, son or daughter, worker, sportsperson, card player, friend and neighbour. We are all multifaceted and complex humans. Offenders, especially, have complex issues and problems, and offending itself often stems from complicated and overlapping causes.

Working with offenders should focus on working with individuals rather than systems. In other words, the centre of attention should not be on this or that program or service, but the individual who requires our assistance. This translates into a tailored approach that should follow the person as they move *through the system* and that is flexible enough to adapt to changed life circumstances of that individual. The point of intervention should be to build capacity – to participate, to make decisions, to be well, to define and live a good life. For this to happen there has to be investment in people (meeting social needs) as well as systems (fulfilling organisational missions).

If one of the goals of justice is to prevent future offending, then it is clear that much more needs to be done at both practitioner and system levels.

We began this book by alluding to two core problems that persistently beset the corrections field. The first problem relates to the fact that prisons fail. The second problem is that the offenders are victims too and that this needs to be built into any response to crime and anti-social behaviour. In the following pages we once again return to aspects of these questions, in particular the issue of reoffending, and the place of victims in offender rehabilitation.

## Recidivism and responsibility

The impetus for criminological and policy development in the areas of rehabilitation, therapeutic justice and restorative justice stems in part from the sheer volume of people going through contemporary corrections systems worldwide, and the effects of this on future offending. Specifically, it is well known that putting someone into prison increases the likelihood of them reoffending. With prison numbers going up, the question is how crime and victimisation can be reduced if we are simultaneously preparing the ground for yet more of the same into the future. One answer to this is to prevent them from coming back. This can be achieved by offering offenders alternative pathways out of the system and incentives to engage in pro-social rather than anti-social behaviour.

Recidivism can involve repeating the same kinds of offences (such as drug dealing), an escalation in the kinds of offences (for example, from graffiti to robbery) and an increase in the number of offences. It is a common phenomenon among those who end up within the more punitive parts of the correctional system.

The accompanying table provides some indication of how entrenched the problem of recidivism actually is. Table 10.1 demonstrates that a sizeable proportion of prisoners return to prison within two years of release. The figures go up when we consider individuals who may not return to prison but who nevertheless return to some part of the corrections system. Perhaps the most revealing aspect of Table 10.1 is that the majority of offenders in prison for serious offences have been there before.

In Australia and New Zealand this is particularly striking in the case of indigenous people who, for both male and female prisoners, have a disproportionately high rate of recidivism (see Australian Institute of Criminology 2008; Nadesu 2009). The indigenous Maori people of New Zealand constitute half of the prison population and are reimprisoned at a rate of 58 per cent (Nadesu 2009). This 'massive over-representation' has raised questions about the social and cultural appropriateness of current risk management focused approaches to corrections and the impact this might have for the reintegration of indigenous offenders back into their communities (Ward *et al.* 2006).

The question, therefore, is not how to get people inside a prison – it is how to keep them out of prison once they have served their term. The answer lies both in preventing people from being put into prison in the first place (through various diversionary schemes and therapeutic justice measures), and in building platforms for them upon release that enable them to lead crime-free lives. In either case, the emphasis is on 'rehabilitation', since this is about changing the offender and the offender's circumstances in ways that will allow them to desist from offending.

Practitioners, of course, have a crucial role to play in this process. They are the front-line workers whose job is to do what they can to smooth the pathway towards a non-criminal future. Along the way, however, it is necessary to recruit many others in the quest for a better society.

The successful reentry of offenders into the community is neither a linear process, nor one that can be accomplished by a single agency. It requires collaboration and commitment from literally anyone concerned about public safety, as well as commitment to

Table 10.1  Prior incarceration and recidivism rates for Australian states and territories

| Type of data | NSW | VIC | QLD | SA | WA | TAS | NT | ACT[1] | Total |
|---|---|---|---|---|---|---|---|---|---|
| Prior imprisonment (number and percentage) | 5,508 52.4% | 2,202 52.1% | 3,232 58.3% | 1,060 54.6% | 2,037 54.1% | 342 66.4% | 662 69.5% | 161 64.4% | 15,154 54.9% |
| Percentages of prisoners released 2005–06 returning to corrections within two years: | | | | | | | | | |
| Prison | 43% | 35.6% | 33.6% | 33.2% | 37.1% | 36.0% | 44.8% | N/A | 38.2% |
| Corrective services[2] | 45.2% | 42.4% | 42.0% | 44.7% | 44.7% | 42.5% | 48.3% | N/A | 44.0% |

*Notes:*
1 Including ACT prisoners located in NSW facilities.
2 Corrective services in this regard includes prison sentences and community corrections orders.
*Source:* Australian Commonwealth Government Productivity Commission (2009).

ensuring that victims' rights are consistently enforced and victim services are consistently provided. It requires communities – including crime victims – to be open to, and involved in, partnerships that provide a wide range of opportunities for offenders to return to the community as focal members who, given the chance, can be held accountable for their actions, and be monitored and provided with supportive services to reduce their chance of recidivism and become productive and responsible members of society. (Seymour 2001: 2)

Interestingly, it is important not only to concentrate on those who do not succeed in the post-release process, but to realise that for every person who does not do well, there are many others who in fact do not return to prison or community corrections. Their stories are worth investigating and telling as well. Indeed, we need to collect more information and anecdotes about these 'forgotten' former participants in the criminal justice system.

The point of working with offenders is to improve their life chances, to prevent further offending, and to ensure that future victimisation does not occur. Many offenders who have been to prison, however, end up back in prison. Most offenders currently in prison have been there before. There are both complex and simple reasons why this is so. The complexities stem from individual biographies and the complicated lives characteristic of many offenders (involving among other things drugs and abuse). The simple reasons refer to the basics of life: employment (gainful, meaningful, available); accommodation (stable, homely, available) and relationships (loving, intimate, supportive). In either case, the role of practitioners is to do what they can to provide transitional support to assist people to forge a good life for themselves. As shown in Box 10.1, however, release is frequently only the start of yet further problems for ex-prisoners.

In the end, desistance from offending is a long and arduous task for many offenders. Like quitting smoking, it can occur in fits and starts. It requires support and commitment. It requires patience. It requires empathy, hope and respect. It also means taking responsibility.

## The duality of responsibility

Both society and the offender benefit from sharing social and moral responsibility for offending. Here it is useful to introduce the concept of the 'duality of responsibility' (White 2008b). On the one hand,

Box 10.1

*Setting them up to fail? Post-release issues of debt and poverty*

Apart from accommodation and the urgency of finding food and shelter, one of the most pressing issues for a newly released offender or, indeed, many offenders on probation, are those of a financial nature. In the absence of securing stable, legitimate sources of income, debt and poverty are, for many, a perennial ghost haunting individuals in the here and now and, by doing so, often limiting their future.

*Accruing debt while doing time – the controversy of child support*
The numbers of parents in prison and the economic disadvantages of their children is an ongoing source of dispute, with legal and ethical debates raging about whether prisoners should pay child support while incarcerated and the pros and cons of the resulting scenario of facing significant repayments upon release into the community (see Griswold and Pearson 2005a, 2005b; Cammett 2006; Smith *et al.* 2007). Child support requirements for parents in prison differ depending on jurisdiction, for example, in the United States different states adopt entirely different approaches, which are subject to change. In 2003, separate decisions by the Supreme Court of Pennsylvania and the Supreme Court of Wisconsin overturned long-standing case law that prisoners cannot be expected to pay child support, with the counter-argument that imprisonment is a foreseeable result of criminal activity and therefore financial obligations should continue (Pearson 2004). The result is that, despite prison wages being overwhelmingly insufficient to pay child support, incarcerated parents were expected to repay their accumulated arrears upon re-entry to the community, with the Wisconsin father owing US$25,000 (not including interest). Balancing financial obligations to family with the impetus to protect the future prospects of successful reintegration (resulting in greater ability to provide) is an ongoing problematic challenge for the correctional, judicial and family services sectors.

*'A saving grace': bank accounts and financial advice for prisoners*
On the topic of financial responsibility more generally, a profoundly simple initiative is yielding promising returns

*continued*

for individual offenders and the community in England. A savings account is something widely taken for granted and yet, astonishingly, 69 per cent of all male prisoners at HMP Forest Bank Prison, the site of the new cooperative project, have never had a bank account (Allison 2008). For people without proof of identity or of their current (often unstable) accommodation address, and with the added issue of a criminal record, getting a bank account can prove to be quite difficult. The project allows prisoners to access pre-employment training, get a new savings account, set up mechanisms for direct debit for bills payment, and automatically portion off percentages of their wages into savings. An eighteen-month study found recidivism rates of participants in this scheme are being halved – only 37 per cent have returned to prison compared to the national average of 67 per cent (Allison 2008). While desistance is a nebulous, multifaceted and highly individual process, promoting adoption of 'the good life' may start with addressing simple issues of access and equality, like overcoming economic barriers that set offenders up to fail.

offender rehabilitation is a societal imperative, to help balance the social disadvantages and personal injuries suffered by many offenders. Society will benefit by giving something to the offender in order for them to go beyond offending.

On the other hand, a vital part of responsibility is to acknowledge the doing of harm, and that you have actually hurt somebody. This is a process that can take a substantial amount of time; if an offender ever reaches that point, it is a transition from denial to acceptance and remorse. As one prisoner comments, '[Back then] I was still beginning to open up to myself. First of all you have to see your own evil before you can really share about it. Obviously I thought I was alright before all that, meaning the crime etc. Looking back, I see what a pathetic bastard I was' (quoted in Jensen and Gibbons 2002: 222).

Taking responsibility requires the individual offender to have an interest in making things right, in repairing the harm, in addressing the wrongs. The offender has to give something to society, to someone else, for the sake of doing the right thing.

The first year inside, because of my strong moral value system growing up in the country, I beat myself up for a good year, maybe even a little longer. But, about that time I realized that maybe up till then it served a purpose, for me. But beyond that it was serving no purpose because it was self defeating. It was just self defeating behaviour, self defeating thinking … To move past that, I couldn't retract what I had done; I couldn't take the harm back … I had to move on. So, I did … I was doing good, in my mind, I was taking advantage of the lost years and that is all I could do. I could firmly commit myself not to harm anyone ever again. That's all I could do to make it better. (Prisoner, quoted in Jensen and Gibbons 2002: 222)

This prisoner did go on to take advantage of the 'lost years' and successfully completed a university degree while holding down a full-time job in prison industries (Jensen and Gibbons 2002).

The duality of responsibility implies a 'both ways' sense of responsibility. As such, and as discussed in Chapter 2, it also embodies the notion that justice is an active social process that demands commitment from everyone. A key focus therefore is on building capacity for victims, offenders, families and communities to enjoy their lives to their fullest extent. In this project, the prison has to be reconstituted as a site for empowering rather than brutalising people. The emphasis has to be on prison as a last-resort circuit-breaker, an opportunity for positive intervention arising out of the crisis of arrest (see Denckla 1999–2000). This requires the development of spaces in which to give and forgive, grow and choose to desist from offensive lives – such as prison education mentor schemes, volunteer work brigades, social skills workshops, drug rehabilitation programs, life narratives, arts and music. It demands intensive engagement with supportive staff, informed by a rehabilitation ethos and the promotion of good life aims, who deal with whole persons.

Making rehabilitation work is also about work at the local level. Repairing harm, for example, can and should involve communities, and a range of restorative justice measures involving community-based agencies and victims. Problem-solving starts at 'home' and in one's relationships and communities. Hence the rise of and importance attached to therapeutic justice and specialist courts. Moreover, resistance to rehabilitation and restorative justice measures can itself be traced to impersonal and formalised systems of justice. That is, victim and community frustration and insecurity is an outcome of distant processes and lack of direct engagement in justice. Community justice panels are just one proposed remedy to this phenomenon (Commission on English Prisons Today 2009). Another example is youth restorative projects that enhance the *participatory* elements of standard restorative justice forums (by engaging youth in the decision-making processes directly) and the *purposive* elements of standard restorative justice forums (by mobilising discussions and resources around social justice issues) (Hogeveen 2006).

Imprisonment without the capacity for giving and forgiving (both to and by individual offenders within the prison) substantively fails to address and, indeed, actively impedes the development of social and personal responsibility in relation to offending, and working towards a life free from offending. More community-based interventions involving individually tailored responses, including giving and forgiving strategies, therefore need to be devised and supported. In its entirety, there is a need for a truly progressive justice system – one based on small steps, achievable goals, offering capacity for social recognition, in a suitable time frame. The emerging evidence base seems to support this, positioning forgiveness as a key concept yet to be fully operationalised through the criminal justice system (see Bibas and Bierschbach 2004; Karremans and Lange 2005; Bibas 2007; Strelan *et al.* 2008; Witvliet *et al.* 2008).

Relapse is a process not an outcome and so we should not be too dismayed if someone reoffends. For practitioners and offenders, a culture of learning and continuous improvement is important. Most offenders offend again and most in prison have offended before, so there is obviously something wrong with the prison system and it is not deterring people. Generally it is creating the conditions for future offending. It is better to believe in and work on the premise that the change will mostly occur in the community, not in the prison.

## Working things out

The role and place of work is a central issue when it comes to consideration of topics such as community reintegration and rehabilitation. The availability and type of work within prisons, for example, varies greatly (see Table 10.2) even though it is well established that employment and housing are the two key things that most influence how well and how quickly offenders can settle back into conventional society.

Prison work is not always a 'good thing'. The purpose of prison work varies according to corrective services policy, resources available and the local context. It has various dimensions (White 1999):

**Table 10.2** Prisoner employment rates by jurisdiction in Australia, 2007–08

| Prisoner employment | NSW | VIC | SA | WA | QLD | NT | ACT | TAS | National |
|---|---|---|---|---|---|---|---|---|---|
| Commercial industries | 44.7% | 36.4% | 22.2% | 12.8% | 26.9% | 3.6% | – | 18.3% | 31.1% |
| Service industries | 34.9% | 49.7% | 47.4% | 64.4% | 40.8% | 85.7% | – | 51.3% | 46.2% |
| Work release | 1.1% | – | 1.5% | – | – | 0.9% | – | 0.4% | 0.5% |
| **Total** | **80.6%** | **86.1%** | **71.1%** | **77.1%** | **67.8%** | **90.2%** | – | **70.1%** | **77.8%** |

*Note*: ACT is remand only.
*Source*: Adapted from Australian Commonwealth Government Productivity Commission (2009).

- *Inmate management* – keeping prisoners occupied and 'out of trouble'.
- *Disciplinary punishment* – part of the penalties of prison life.
- *Deterrent punishment* – hard, boring and monotonous work to deter future offences.
- *Institutional operations* – maintenance of infrastructure and routine services.
- *Rehabilitation* – provision of work experience and occupational skills.
- *Commercial profit* – competitive advantage in commodity production.
- *Cost reduction* – state and private costs of housing prisoners.
- *Public interest* – performing labour for community purposes.

### Scenario 10.1

### Balancing issues of duty of care with rapport with a female offender

You are interviewing an offender for a report prior to her release from prison. She has become eligible for parole after serving an eighteen-month prison term for social security fraud. During the interview you establish that her reason for failing to report her income to social security was that she was in a relationship with a highly abusive partner who refused to work, and forced her to claim parenting benefits as well as working part-time. She has four children so had to provide for them as well as her partner. She identifies that while her children had witnessed her partner severely beating her, he had never laid a hand on the children.

When asked about who has been caring for the children while she was incarcerated, she states that her partner has been caring for them, and that he now receives the parenting payments from social security. She advises that while she is not worried about him being physically abusive towards the children, she is aware that the children are afraid of him, having witnessed him being very violent towards her in the past. She asks you not to write this information in her pre-parole report, and specifically requests that you do not tell anyone, as she is fearful that her children will be taken from her, and that her partner will seek revenge on her when she is released from prison.

### Question
How do you respond to the possible issue of the children being

abused (emotionally if not physically) without disturbing the rapport you have developed with the offender, keeping in mind that it is likely that you will have to supervise her if she is released on parole?

Prisoners are sometimes forced to undertake work in a regime designed to instil discipline in time and place terms (see Foucault 1995). In this sense, prison labour itself is basically a repressive mechanism of control and punishment. This is particularly evident in the chain-gang mentality of some US prison schemes, which is about stripping human dignity and using demeaning work as a means of humiliation. Work, in this context, is integral to punishment (rather than to rehabilitation or reparation) and is intended to inflict pain of some sort (both emotional and physical). Demeaning work is also symptomatic of a lack of innovation on the part of corrective services in forming partnerships with external organisations that might provide more innovative prison industries. It is a punitive response to complex and entrenched social problems (White and Coventry 2008).

While less punitive, other types of prison work often involve work teams undertaking negative tasks, such as menial work, dirty work and work that nobody else wants to do. Ironically, such work frequently mirrors the work experiences and employment prospects of prisoners when they are on the outside. Even these kinds of work can be of advantage to prisoners, however, with many jurisdictions in the US exchanging 'good time' work credits to ease off sentence time.

Work within a community corrections context usually involves activities that have been mandated through either court processes or some form of restorative justice mechanism (such as juvenile conferencing). Like prison work, the type of work undertaken within a community context can be inspired by many, and competing, motivations and rationales.

There are large questions about the use or value of prisoner work, whether this is related to time in prison or engagement with community corrections (White 1999). While many work assignments could be considered to be of a negative kind, there are other types of work, arguably of a more constructive type, including:

- Construction of walking trails
- Construction of children's playgrounds and public bridges
- Vegetable harvesting

- Painting and undertaking minor repairs to an aged care facility
- Maintenance of cemeteries and public parks
- Restoration of railway tracks
- Removal of graffiti.

In 1985, for example, prisoners from Risdon Prison in Tasmania supplied meals on wheels to pensioners, and constructed outdoor settings for children (Evans 2004: 71). In 2008, the Department of Corrective Services in Western Australia (WA) celebrated the tenth anniversary of work camps in that state (WA Department of Corrective Services 2008). The express purpose of the work camps is to foster reparation and rehabilitation, 'providing prisoners with the opportunity to get involved in meaningful work in a community environment, repay a debt to society, develop vocational and personal skills, and for those prisoners nearing the end of their sentence, increase their chances of making a successful transition from prison to the community on release' (WA Department of Corrective Services 2008: 13).

The role and place of work also can be conceptualised in terms of reparation directly relevant to victims, and to victimisation generally as a problem that ought to be addressed by offenders.

### Victims and offender rehabilitation

If you are employed in this field you have to work with people, and those who have done 'good' and 'bad' throughout their lives. Offenders by and large are victims themselves, of violence, of abuse, of bad circumstances. The issues are well known. They consist of self-medication, working in the sex industry to pay for drugs, engagement in illegal activity and perhaps violence. There are high unemployment rates, low education levels, abusive histories, and the list goes on.

As stated previously, there is a social responsibility to deal with the fact that offenders are victims. The flip side, however, is that they are harming other people and have done harm. They are perpetrators of crime. As such they have a moral responsibility to victims; even though they themselves are damaged, it does not give them the right to go around inflicting harm on others. Often they do not know the harms they have caused, or they do not want to know what they have done. This can take the form of rationalising the harm (for example, victims can afford being burgled as they have house insurance).

In our view, people need to gain knowledge and be more aware of victimisation. This has a number of different dimensions. For example, many offenders are simultaneously victims, and vice versa. For those who work with offenders, it is important to gain a sense of victim needs (including offenders who have been victimised), and the social processes that go into the social constructions of victimhood (see White and Perrone 2010; White 2010). We also need to raise awareness of victimisation as an integral part of an anti-recidivism strategy.

Learning to give is an important step in offender rehabilitation. This requires development of spaces in which this might occur – as in the case, for example, of prison education mentor schemes, or volunteer work brigades that assist with disaster relief efforts (such as responding to cyclone damage in far north Queensland). Learning to give is also about learning more about the harms that one has been implicated in. Morality – in this case referring to the development of a moral sense – is learned behaviour. And moral lessons can be learned from those who have been harmed by offenders.

One of the great misfortunes accompanying victimisation is that all too often the emotional needs of the victim are forgotten in the criminal justice process. To some extent this is a matter of providing adequate counselling and other support services, to guide victims through the difficult stages of transition and victim recovery. It is also vital that *offenders* be given the opportunity to be exposed to the victims' plight.

> No one can fully understand the victim's feelings or experience. Thus, one must allow victims to speak from the heart and let them know that we are listening with the heart as well. They have things to say that we might not understand; they often need answers to irresolvable questions; they have expectations that might not be met. We have to assume that what they say is important for us to hear and that we learn from our hearing it. Sometimes victims prove remarkably frank, blunt, or direct. It is important to respect these exchanges and the victim who shares them. (Nicholl 2001: 27)

There are two key issues here. One is how best to give victims a forum in which they can most positively voice their feelings. The second is how to arrange for offenders to 'hear' the victims' voices, without compromising their own safety, future opportunities and rehabilitation processes. Options can range from face-to-face meetings between individual victims and individual offenders (in the community, or in prison confines), family or juvenile group conferences that involve family members and support people, through to 'surrogate victims' in the form of panels of victims telling their stories to offenders (see Nicholl 2001). Raising consciousness among prisoners of the harms that they have caused can be achieved in different ways.

*Classes could be designed for adult and juvenile offenders*, both non-violent and violent, in diversion, probation, incarceration, detention, parole and offender re-entry settings (see Seymour 2001). The course description would include that the objectives for students would be as follows:

- To explore how they view the rights of other people.

- To raise their awareness of the long-term impact of their actions.

- To recognise their own possible victimisation as children and how that abuse might impact them today.

- To provide opportunities to help them become non-abusive parents, and good spouses/partners.

- To discuss their tendency to depersonalise the people they injure.

- To consider how they are accountable for the crimes they have committed.

*Victim impact panels* (VIP) involve a small panel of volunteer victims addressing a group of offenders, in different settings (see Fulkerson 2001). The VIP description is as follows:

- Victims and offenders are provided with an opportunity to meet in a group to discuss the nature of the harm.

- Victims are not allowed to speak on any panel in which the offender in their case is present.

- Subjects meet with a panel moderator for an orientation prior to the panel session.

- A security officer is present to ensure the safety of all victims.

- Victims get the chance to express their hurt and the effects of the harm on them.

- Offenders have an opportunity to learn from victims directly about the effects of their behaviour.

- Offenders may see things in a different light, since they are not directly threatened by their own victims, but are forced to deal with victim issues nevertheless.

*Community-based discussion groups* involve a structured program in which convicted offenders of a particular offence (such as burglary) are subjected to a probation order that brings them into contact with burglary victims (Mawby 2007). This is similar in approach to the victim impact panels described above. It has been commented that such processes are beneficial for offenders in that allowing victims to confront them about the nature of the harms perpetrated means that the normal techniques of neutralisation (such as, the victim can afford it) are challenged. The result is that offenders have to acknowledge how their actions have impacted upon 'real' victims.

Discussion of the preparation of prisoners for release, including *via* pre-release leave programs, requires that offenders at least begin to understand the impact of their actions on victims. More than this, however, many jurisdictions also now demand some kind of involvement in restitution, reparation or restorative justice activities, both while an offender is in prison and while they are on leave from prison or on parole. Where appropriate, and where suitable human and material resources have been put into place, restorative justice mechanisms can be usefully applied in relation to pre-release programs and strategies.

## Restorative forms of giving

Practical examples of how community corrections can be imbued with a restorative ethic at a concrete level are still relatively few and far between, although this is changing in some jurisdictions. The usual emphasis in community corrections work is what can be done to better supervise the offender, or what can be done to assist them to make the transition towards being a law-abiding citizen (see, for example, Nelson and Trone 2000). Restorative justice inverts this relationship by making the offender an active contributor and participant. Thus, in the UK, 'Offenders in some programs carry out work for their own communities, which can help give the offenders a sense of social responsibility and an experience of social acceptance and recognition' (Marshall 1999: 14). Seymour (2001) cites examples in the USA where the concept of 'restorative community service' has taken hold. Relevant community work has included such things as youthful offenders escorting Alzheimer's patients from a local retirement centre and their families for a day at the State Fair, through to a licensed pharmacist who was convicted of forging drug documents performing 500 hours of community service at the free clinic in the neighbourhood in which he had sold drugs.

In specific criminal justice terms, work can be viewed as serving three important social goals (White and Coventry 2008):

1 *Reintegration*
   • Preparation for release by establishing social/family bonds.
   • Lower rates of recidivism, especially for low-risk prisoners on placement.

2 *Humanitarianism*
   • Work release may soften the incarceration 'experience'.
   • Allows prisoners to gain some attachment to society.

3 *Expanding opportunities*
   • Opportunities for excitement – the thrill of discovery.
   • Opportunities for creativity – the thrill of invention.

Positive prisoner work, that avoids the pitfalls mentioned earlier, can provide inmates with an important sense of 'normality', self-esteem, and pride in a job well done, as is illustrated in Innovative practice 10.

In an examination of the role that prisoners played in responding to Cyclone Larry in Australia, it was found that, in fact, cyclone work works (see Coventry and Westerhuis forthcoming). The prisoners who volunteered to participate in the extended clean-up phase following the cyclone worked hard at their tasks. Who did what is interesting:

• 35 prisoners (almost 70 per cent indigenous) from Townsville Correctional Centre attended camps at Malanda and Innisfail.

• As of early May 2006, 1,500 person work hours were undertaken by these prisoners.

• Participation was voluntary and was restricted to those serving the tail end of their sentences at the prison farm of Townsville Correctional Centre.

• Some prisoners were deemed to be ineligible (for example, sex offenders, violent offenders).

- Prisoners worked six-hour days, six or seven days per week.

- 40–50 (approx) farmers' properties were attended.

- Work included pulling down sheds, removing trees off fence lines, cutting trees, stacking roofing tin and repairing fences.

Many of the prisoners were interviewed about their experiences (Coventry and Westerhuis forthcoming). Typical of the responses were these comments:

- 'We [prisoners] get little praise, like those on the Good Morning Shows [*sic*] flying them up here … but we CHOSE to come out and work'.

- '[The farmers] treat us like normal human beings.'

- '… giving them a hand, feeling good'.

- '… didn't treat us like prisoners'.

- 'By going out we are paying back, not just the taxpayers … we don't do it shoddy.'

- 'At Innisfail, they had a lot of pride, they bust their guts. You don't need to do that while you are in jail.'

- '[The work program] helps reintegration into the community, and makes jail time easier.'

Such positive responses from prisoners themselves reaffirm for us the importance of work to the re-entry process upon prison release. Coventry and Westerhuis tap into the emotional side of the rehabilitative process, consistent with notions about the quality of life required by all, not just prisoners re-entering communities. This small group of offenders (almost all of whom have since been released) were proud of their work, felt strongly that they positively contributed to an area in crisis after a natural disaster, and developed a sense of belonging with the Atherton Tablelands. For dairy farmers, their work thwarted the loss of herds to mastitis and the financial devastation that would have followed such a loss. For prisoners, the experiences opened the door to the outside world and how they might connect to it. Working in the Cyclone Larry clean-up was about the exertion of labour power, some skill development and the opportunity to play a constructive and meaningful role in contributing to the community – no trite outcomes.

### Innovative practice 10

### A foot in the door: pre-release vocational education and training pathways to employment

Pre-release vocational education and training courses are a valuable learning opportunity for prisoners, particularly when matched with the interests of the individual and meaningful payment in return for work. The example of Timpson, a well-known chain of shoe stores in the UK, opening a store and repairs shop in Liverpool Prison highlights how work can be made a normal part of prison life and a transition back into the real world. Jointly funded by Timpson and the Prison Service, the new branch looks exactly the same as the 650 other branches in the community, but with curtains cloaking the bars. Allison (2009) describes the bold social and commercial enterprise:

> The company is working with 22 prisons in England and Wales. In the last year, it has taken on 40 ex-offenders, with an impressive 80% retention rate. The trainees earn £16 a week – a more than respectable prison wage – with an added £10 bonus for every course passed … the undoubted star of the 13 Liverpool trainees is Mick, who is nearing the end of a seven and a half year sentence. In eight weeks, he has achieved level two grade in shoe and watch repairs, several types of engraving, and health and safety procedures … which would usually take 12 months to achieve that standard. (Allison 2009)

Upon reintegration into the community, former offenders may be employed and promoted within Timpson, with managing director James Timpson saying he believes they add an important dimension to his company: 'They have more to lose, have a strong desire to show their families and the world they can succeed, and they want to repay the trust we place in them' (quoted in Allison 2009).

## Paradoxes and controversies

Offending and victimisation are social in nature. Reform and rehabilitation ultimately have to grapple with the community context within which offending and victimisation occur. The big question here is, how do we integrate criminal justice activities into a social justice agenda that leads to meaningful societal change? The challenge is to acknowledge that institutional supports are needed for working with offenders in ways that allow them to work for their own benefit and as part of this to contribute to society.

We need to reconfigure prison and community-based work as an opportunity to 'be' someone of worth and value. That work should also bear some relation to the task of community building. In this way the minimal value of the workhouse from the granting of good time for negative work can be extended to a reconceptualised and integrated correctional approach, whereby successful reintegration is couched in terms of opportunities for important work that develops skills to counter workforce marginalisation, enriched personal identity, enhanced quality of life, positive forms of community belonging and interactive engagement. This can be called a status enhancement approach to prison labour (White and Coventry 2008). Such an approach would emphasise expansion of opportunities and the humanitarian values of social justice.

As discussed above, disaster relief has demonstrable benefits for offenders and communities alike. How then can we link the prison work agenda to that of community building as such, and not solely as disaster relief? Can 'disaster relief' be redefined to include institutional efforts to overcome social disadvantage? Unemployment, poverty and declining opportunities continue to directly affect the physical and psychological well-being of people in our communities. Such social problems are entrenched at a spatial level, and are increasingly concentrated in specific locations within our cities. Disastrous lives and living conditions equally demand relief. Community building and physical rejuvenation of neighbourhoods is a social task that likewise can be addressed through innovative social planning and creative offender programs.

## Conclusion

Working positively with offenders in prisons and in the community is vital to changing their world and assisting in the processes of wider social transformation. Insofar as imprisonment harms individuals – both those who live in prison and those who work in prison – its social utility must be questioned. Community-based programs and community-based work with offenders offer the promise for the building of safer, cohesive communities: 'There are few presumptions in human relations more dangerous than the idea that one knows what another human being needs better than they do themselves' (Michael Ignatieff, quoted in Ward and Maruna 2007: 17).

The primary concept underpinning the discussions in this chapter has been that of giving. Since there are strong connections between community circumstances that give rise to street crime (such as economic marginalisation), and the community relations that sustain them (such as group identification), community processes are also most likely to provide the best opportunities for their transformation. Giving, therefore, ought to take place in a communal context.

However, the duality of responsibility does not mean that giving itself has to be socially differentiated or that offenders need give only in relation to their particular transgressions. The *societal responsibility to the offender* is reflective of systemic or structural features of a socially divided community. Class, gender and ethnic inequalities, among others, may be immoral but the process of redress does not need to be dressed up in the language of 'desert' or 'justice'. It is a social obligation, one that warrants community resources. But it need not inadvertently stigmatise the offender through adopting the language of 'the disadvantaged', 'the destitute', 'the deserving' and 'the no hoper' to describe those who need our collective help.

The *personal responsibility of the offender* is reflective of the fact that it is they, themselves, who participated in the harmful behaviour. But giving something back to the community does not mean that the giving need be linked to the original criminal harm. This, too, could well end up as disabling and paternalistic intervention for what is best left to the offender to work through for themselves. This is worth explaining in greater detail.

Within many of us lies a certain place that is uniquely ours. It is a place that only we can go to, and a place that only rarely can we share with others. It is a place of shame, of regret, of melancholy and of despair. It is a place where our harms to others congeal, only to return to haunt us in our vulnerable moments. It is a place that is difficult to acknowledge, and even more difficult to articulate and speak about. It is a place, fundamentally, of denial.

Living, much less offending, is a very personal experience. So too is coming to grips with who we are, who we have been, and who we want to be. If life is hard to fathom for the most ordinary of us, then why do we expect the ex-prisoner to somehow magically find redemption through the programs we provide? All we can do is provide the ground upon which something new might be built, and a life resurrected.

Taking moral responsibility is not the same as publicly addressing the demons within. There are offences that offenders still, many years later, refuse to name. The shame runs too deep. *Self-denial of the specific* is important to their well-being and ability to negotiate life in the present. But this self-denial is only of the specific – they are more than happy to acknowledge the wrongness, the harms that they 'in general' have committed, and their status as offenders.

Offending, and redemption from suffering the individual and social consequences of one's offending, is very personal. It involves intimate thoughts and intimate relationships. It involves struggle for *self-respect* as much as the struggle for *social respect*. It can touch upon the darkest of personal secrets, and the most threatening of challenges to one's sense of self as a good person.

Redemption can be seen as a journey towards self-knowledge and personal betterment. The process depends upon the offender taking moral responsibility for their actions, but this in turn is shaped by the social resources available to them as provided by the outside world.

The inner struggles of the offender, and indeed of us all, do not necessarily have to be named and brought out into the open. This would, in many cases, be counterproductive. It could be too hurtful and a source of alarm and consternation – and thus a harm in its own right.

But the external world and what the offender does in this world can be a fruitful site for the reconstruction of identity and integrity. By giving freely in this world we can hold at bay the angst of the inner. By *being given the chance to give* the offender is provided with hope. The act of giving itself feels good. It is accompanied by a feeling of satisfaction. It is life-affirming. Thus, the inner world of the offender and the outer world of the society can be intricately linked by the process of giving. Our role and responsibility as citizens, as workers and as a society are to make sure that giving – in all senses of the word – is made possible. For this is how new worlds are made.

## Discussion questions

1  Discuss the most pressing needs a person faces upon release from prison. In your opinion, what are the key ingredients to effective integrated offender management and reintegration?
2  Discuss the strengths and weaknesses of arguments surrounding whether prisoners should be expected to pay or accrue child

support while they are incarcerated. What is the impact of both sides in terms of family relationships, the identity and role of the incarcerated parent, and finances?

3 What is meant by forgiveness? Discuss and evaluate some strategies and approaches through which forgiveness and giving might assist or be incorporated into the criminal justice system. Consider the perspectives and impact of different restorative practices for offenders, victims, families and communities.

## Further reading

Brown, J. (2004) 'Managing the transition from institution to the community: a Canadian parole officer perspective on the needs of newly released federal offenders', *Western Criminology Review*, 5(2): 97–107.

Denckla, D. (1999–2000) 'Forgiveness as a problem solving tool in the courts: a brief response to the panel on forgiveness in criminal law', *Fordham Urban Law Journal*, 27: 1613–19.

Maruna, S. and Immarigeon, R. (eds) (2004) *After Crime and Punishment: Pathways to Offender Rehabilitation*. Cullompton: Willan Publishing.

Ross, S. (2005) 'Bridging the gap between prison and the community: post-release support and supervision', in S. Eyland and S. O'Toole (eds) *Corrections Criminology*. Sydney: Hawkins Press.

Wright, M. (2002) 'The court as last resort: victim-sensitive, community-based responses to crime', *British Journal of Criminology*, 42(3): 654–67.

## Key resources

Burke, P. (2008) *Transition from Prison to the Community Re-entry Handbook*. Washington, DC: United States Department of Justice National Institute of Corrections.

Conolly, M. and Ward, T. (2008) *Morals, Rights and Practice in the Human Services: Effective and Fair Decision-making in Health, Social Care and Criminal Justice*. London: Jessica Kingsley Publishers.

Solomon, A., Osbourne, J., LoBuglio, S., Mellow, J. and Mukamal, D. (2008a) *Life After Lockup: Improving Reentry from Jail to the Community*. Washington, DC: Urban Institute Justice Policy Centre.

Solomon, A., Osbourne, J., Winterfield, L., Elderbroom, B., Burke, P., Stroker, R., Rhine, E. and Burrell, W. (2008b) *Putting Public Safety First: 13 Parole Supervision Strategies to Enhance Reentry Outcomes*. Washington, DC: Urban Institute Justice Policy Centre.

Willis, M. (2008) *Reintegration of Indigenous Prisoners: Key Findings – Trends and Issues No. 364*. Canberra: Australian Institute of Criminology.

# Appendix I

# Drug use in prison – discussion notes

**Medical detoxification** is the most common intervention offered in prisons. One interesting consideration is that the detox process often involves the use of licit drugs (usually sedatives, benzodiazepines) to manage withdrawal symptoms and pain and to aid sleep. These prescription medications are highly addictive in themselves, and may already be a source of substance misuse for an individual or the introduction of a new drug of choice. A second consideration is that 'prisoners who have been detoxified, and so have a reduced level of tolerance, may experience overdose if they return to using their previous doses of illicit opiates. For this and other reasons, detoxification services should lead on to other forms of support and should provide warnings of the dangers of overdose' (Dolan *et al.* 2007: 4).

**Drug free units and therapeutic communities** are intensive treatment programs for prisoners with a history of severe drug dependence, often voluntary and segregated from the general prison population. Inmates entering these units are required to 'pledge to abstain from drug use, usually in return for increased privileges such as recreational facilities or improved accommodation. Inmates are regularly urine tested and punishments for positive urinalysis include loss of privileges and expulsion from the programme' (Dolan *et al.* 2007: 5). Drug-free units in Australia are resource intensive and expensive, costing approximately the same as keeping a prisoner in maximum security (Black, Dolan and Wodak 2004, cited in Dolan *et al.* 2007). Aftercare is also essential or some of the treatment effects may be lost. There is a need for more evaluation of which specific components within these programs are most effective.

**Pharmacotherapy and methadone maintenance treatment** results in 'reduced drug use, reduced transmission of blood borne viruses, reduced mortality and reduced recidivism and re-incarceration' (Dolan *et al.* 2007: 6). Getting the dosage right is a challenge sometimes, but dispensing pharmacotherapy offers inmates increased interaction with medical staff. It is important that there is important throughcare upon release so that offenders have the opportunity to continue pharmacotherapy in the community. On the other hand, some more extreme governmentality theorists might be critical of the hypocrisy of the state in terms of pharmacotherapy as simply controlling the delivery of a state-sanctioned drug (such as methadone), which is often even more addictive than the original opiate drug of choice.

**Needle exchanges in prison** contribute to reduced sharing of injecting equipment, reduced rates of harm and blood-borne viruses, and no increases in injecting or drug use (Dolan *et al.* 2007). There are considerations around how the needles should be dispensed, either by staff or by vending machine, depending on the culture of the prison. There are also issues involved in the provision of needles that could then be used to assault other prisoners or staff. Needle exchanges should not be offered in isolation as they are a temporary harm reduction measure; complementary psychosocial interventions are essential to address the personal reasons for addiction.

**Culture clash** – harm reduction strategies 'that are used outside prison are often regarded to prison administrators and staff as undermining the measures taken inside prison to reduce the supply of drugs' (Stover *et al.* 2001, cited in Dolan *et al.* 2007: 4).

# Appendix 2

# Client safety contract *pro forma*

[NAME OF SERVICE]

**CLIENT SAFETY CONTRACT**

Client safety contracts are an important agreement because **we want you to stay safe**, which means that you are promising that you will not self-harm or attempt suicide. Self-harm means any injury you do to yourself, including: cutting, burning, scratching, swallowing or injecting dangerous substances, overdose, pulling out hair, or punching, kicking or headbutting a solid object (e.g. a wall) to cause injury. If you are a residential client and you have the means to hurt yourself (e.g. a razor, knife or rope), we expect you to hand this over to staff to keep yourself safe.

This safety contract is an agreement between

_____ a client of [insert service here], and

_____ a staff member of [insert service here].

I agree that I will not harm or hurt myself during the time that I am a client with this service.

I agree to speak to a staff member if I feel like hurting myself, or if my feelings become unbearable and I am thinking about suicide.

In case of an emergency, I agree to call 911/999 (for an ambulance) if my health is at risk.

I am aware that I can speak to my caseworker if I want to find out more about strategies that I can use as an alternative to harming myself.

**Client's signature** _____

**Staff signature** _____

**Date** _____

If you would like some advice or would like to find a service that can help, you can ring the local Mental Health Services Helpline, phone #### ### ###. This line is available 24 hours a day.

We respect your privacy. Copies of this safety contract will only be given to you, as a client, and to the practitioners involved in your care, who will store it confidentially in case notes.

# Glossary

The contents of this glossary are prefaced by the mention that these terms are not necessarily used in the same way in every country, an important proviso for a book that considers several, quite different jurisdictions.

**Aftercare** Follow-up or ongoing care and support of a person following initial provision of a treatment or service, commonly associated with reintegration. Aftercare is the final stage along a rehabilitative continuum of care, and is not necessarily always time limited but may be available for 'top-ups' or troubleshooting when a person needs support the most, regularly or occasionally.

**Bond** Also referred to as 'recognisance', bond is where the offender is required to be of good behaviour for a specified time, and may be required to forfeit a sum of money if they breach the order. The court may impose conditions such as paying compensation to the victim, or attending a drug rehabilitation clinic.

**Camps** Where the offender is placed in a wilderness or correctional boot camp of some kind with the proviso that they are meant to learn self-discipline, to be rehabilitated, and to be subjected to a rigorous schedule of activities. They include specialist camps for specific categories of offender (for example, young offenders and/ or indigenous people), as well as post-release camps that attempt to develop offender skills, knowledge and confidence after they have served their sentence.

**Classification**   The allocation of a security status to an offender within a correctional facility, with classifications usually ranging from minimum through to maximum security. This is seen to be representative of level of risk to self (at risk or protected populations) and/or others (violent inmates).

**Community corrections**   Community-based management of a variety of court-ordered sanctions that serve as either non-custodial sentencing alternatives or post-custodial sentencing mechanisms for the reintegration of offenders back into the community. Community-based correctional orders vary greatly in the nature and extent of supervision, restrictions and conditions attached.

**Community sector organisations (CSOs)**   Sometimes referred to as the voluntary or 'not-for-profit' sector, community sector organisations can be delineated as service providers that are different from government agencies and private companies (such as private prisons or private healthcare providers).

**Community service order**   Also known as a 'community attendance centre order', this is a term used extensively in Australia and other jurisdictions to describe orders where the offender is required to attend an activity centre for specialist programs such as counselling, group work, and employment skills, or they may be required to perform a certain number of hours of community work in a designated form for a designated community organisation, such as charity shops or municipal gardens.

**Co-morbidity**   A clinical term referring to the co-existence of multiple problems in the life of the individual, but most commonly used to refer to co-occurring mental illness and substance misuse.

**Conditional release order**   Where certain inmates who are deemed to be amenable to, and who would benefit from, a community-based program, especially educational and vocational programs, are granted leave to live in the general community under close supervision and with appropriate counselling.

**Consumer participation**   The process of involving a 'consumer' (current or past client or recipient of services) in meaningful consultation and decision-making about the service(s) they receive as well as organisational quality improvement and structural planning.

**Corrections**   The study of the institutions and processes involved in the punishment of offenders and their rehabilitation and reintegration, with a particular focus on prisons and incarceration.

**Criminogenic needs**   The needs in the life of an individual that are directly related to the nature of their criminal offending; for example, an offender may engage in burglary because of the pressures of keeping up with an addiction to illicit drugs. The criminogenic need here relates to the need for drug rehabilitation. By contrast, a violent offender may have need for anger management training and conflict resolution skills.

**Criminology**   The systemic study of crime, criminality and criminal justice systems. Criminology involves interdisciplinary understandings of the process of criminalisation, punishment and rehabilitation of offenders, law enforcement practices and broader processes of social control. There are various thematic areas and sub-disciplines within criminology, for example, critical criminology and cultural criminology.

**Day leave schemes**   Where the inmate is allowed to take advantage of educational or work-related activities, while still serving their sentence in some type of secure custody.

**Decarceration**   The process of deliberately trying to reduce the time spent in prison by an individual or group; a diversionary measure that represents a move away from the use of institutions.

**Desistance**   Ceasing and refraining from offending.

**Duty of care**   A legal and ethical obligation requiring a practitioner to maintain a reasonable standard of care throughout the therapeutic relationship and provision of service to a client. A key element is the responsibility to balance the rights and well-being of a client with the rights and well-being of family, other clients, the worker or organisation.

**Engagement**   A skill set that involves the development of rapport and respect, achieving insight into the offender's view of themselves, clarifying expectations and boundaries, and promoting pro-social change.

**Evidence-based practice (EBP)** Practice informed by the use of theories, interventions and tools that are supported by an ample evidence base of credible research and verified real-life practice outcomes. EBP involves the integration of individual practitioner expertise and discernment with conscientious application of the best available research knowledge.

**Good Lives Model (GLM)** A strengths-based approach to offender rehabilitation focusing on the promotion of personal development, skills acquisition, self-esteem and meaningful community contribution. This model shifts the focus away from purely focusing on risk and deficits, and instead encourages action in contributing to the quality of life for oneself, family and the wider community. The focus for practitioners is to support a person to ascertain the resources, skills, opportunities and relationships needed to live 'a good life', free of criminal offending.

**Home detention** This can take several forms, involving in some instances electronic tracking devices, or in other instances unpredictable phone or in-person checks from the appropriate correctional authority. The idea here is that the offender is restricted in their movement: they are in effect prisoners in their own homes, rather than being placed in a secure, mass correctional facility.

**Human capital** The concept of human capital broadly relates to the personal skills, motivation, capacities and knowledge that facilitate productive activity (education, employment) and can result in self-efficacy and self-esteem (McNeill and Whyte 2007). This concept is closely interrelated to social capital.

**Integrated offender management (IOM)** A holistic and integrated approach to the management of offenders that supports desistance through the assessment and tailoring of interventions to meet the needs of the individual. IOM operates within a throughcare model, promoting seamless, consistent and collaborative service coordination for the individual in prison and the community.

**Involuntary client** A person who is mandated or required to be a recipient of services or professional intervention. Examples include offenders who are legally required to undergo intervention (sex offenders, dangerous offenders with a severe mental illness) through to people who receive services or intervention as a prerequisite to obtaining or regaining something (such as parental involvement with child protection authorities out of a desire to regain custody of their children).

**Parole**   The early release of a prisoner, prior to the expiration of their sentence, subject to the supervision and conditions of correctional authorities. A parolee is still considered to be in custody while living in the community, and can be reimprisoned if parole conditions are breached.

**Person-centred practice**   A holistic approach to the delivery of interventions where the practitioner assists a client to develop pro-social behaviour, insight and empathy. Reflective listening, unconditional positive regard and empowerment are central to the therapeutic relationship.

**Prisonisation**   The changes that a prisoner experiences in prison (described as the pains of imprisonment) which socialises them into the culture and social norms of prison society. This subculture generally involves using 'inside' language, loyalty to other prisoners and a code of silence in never reporting another inmate, sources of pride and expectations around defending group membership, and antagonism towards prison staff. The process and impact of prisonisation makes adjustment to life outside the prison environment difficult.

**Probation**   Community supervision of an offender who has been convicted of a crime, often subject to specific supervision or conditions set by a court of law. A probationer is the status of a convicted person who is given freedom on the condition that, for a specified period, they are subject to supervision by authorities and to demonstrate good behaviour.

**Quality improvement**   A systematic administrative approach to enhancing and managing the quality of a service across various domains (for example, policy, fire safety management, organisational governance) through the use of standards and performance indicators.

**Recidivism**   Repeat offending or habitual relapse into crime.

**Recovery capital**   Recovery capital is a combination of two important notions: self (human capital) in community (social capital).

It involves the internal personal capacities and the external resources, relationships, services and opportunities needed to holistically support a person in their recovery. This can be applied to issues such as addiction or mental illness.

**Reintegration**   Also referred to as 're-entry' or 'resettlement', reintegration is the transition between prison and re-entry to the community, with the ultimate goals of desistance and enjoying an active and productive life independent of the criminal justice system.

**Restorative justice**   A theory of justice that conceptualises crime and wrongdoing as an act against the individual or community, rather than the state. Restorative justice promotes non-adversarial processes, which foster dialogue between the offender, the victim(s) and the community. These processes afford victims a central role in the justice processes, and seek to move beyond punitive dimensions of the law to instil a sense of responsibility into the offender. A key goal is to promote resolutions that seek to heal and repair the harm caused, reintegrate the offender back into the community, and prevent reoffending.

**Risk-need-responsivity (RNR) model**   The dominant rehabilitation model in use today, the RNR model is based on assessment and intervention to address risk, need (targeting of dynamic risk factors) and responsivity (matching the intervention to the individual). Assessment and risk management are central tasks.

**Social capital**   The relationships, resources and opportunities available to an individual to support and enable relationships with significant others and meaningful community participation. Reciprocity, trust and giving are inherent in the mutual value of these relationships and networks.

**Solution-focused practice**   A popular model of intervention focusing on discovery of solutions and positive problem-solving, rather than problem talk or a deficit focus. The individual is positioned as a system of complex and interrelated parts, and encouraged by the practitioner to explore their options, to clarify goals and to engage in personal change.

**Strengths-based rehabilitation** Encourages proactive and creative ways to work with clients to honour and tap into their skills, competencies, resilience and protective factors, as opposed to purely focusing on deficits and areas of risk. Empowerment and individual agency are central to the supportive therapeutic relationship and client outcomes.

**Suspended sentence** Where the court defers passing a sentence of imprisonment for a designated period, during which certain conditions may be stipulated. With satisfactory completion of these conditions, the sentence will lapse at the end of this period.

**Therapeutic jurisprudence** A philosophy and framework for intervention that recognises the impact that the law, courts and associated practitioners (magistrates, judges, lawyers, prosecutors) can have on the social and psychological well-being of offenders with complex needs. As its name suggests, processes of tailoring justice to balance community protection with therapeutic intervention are used to holistically address underlying factors contributing to a person's offending. Examples include drug courts and mental health diversion courts.

**Throughcare** A model of practice based on the principle of consistent and collaborative support of a person throughout the time they are involved with a service system. Throughcare involves collaboration and communication between practitioners and agencies from the point of intake and assessment through to reintegration, community outreach and follow-up.

**Victimisation** An act that attacks, exploits, injures or harms a person. Victims of crime are people who have been victimised or been subject to an illegal act.

**Workforce development** A multifaceted approach using a systems focus to address the range of factors impacting on a workforce to function with maximum effectiveness. This involves a broad approach to targeting individual, organisational and structural factors through developing the potential capacity, as well as current satisfaction and skills, of a workforce.

# References

Aho-Mustonen, K., Miettinen, R., Koivisto, H., Timonen, T. and Raty, H. (2008) 'Group psychoeducation for forensic and dangerous non-forensic long-term patients with schizophrenia: a pilot study', *European Journal of Psychiatry*, 22(2): 84–92.

Ahmad, A. (2009) 'Garden a show piece for social inclusion', *Guardian*, 20 May.

Alder, C. (1997) 'Young women and juvenile justice: objectives, frameworks and strategies', paper presented at the Australian Institute of Criminology Conference, *Towards Juvenile Crime and Juvenile Justice: Towards 2000 and Beyond*, Adelaide.

Allison, E. (2008) 'A saving grace: giving bank accounts to prisoners is an effective way of cutting down re-offending', *Guardian*, 3 December.

Allison, E. (2009) 'A foot in the door: shoe company opens prison workshop to train offenders and to provide job opportunities', *Guardian*, 11 March.

Altrows, I. (2002) 'Rational emotive and cognitive behavior therapy with adult male offenders', *Journal of Rational-Emotive and Cognitive-Behavior Therapy*, 20(4): 201–22.

Andersen, H. (2004) 'Mental health in prison populations: a review – with special emphasis on a study of Danish prisoners on remand', *Acta Psychiatrica Scandinavica*, 110: 5–59.

Andrews, D. and Bonta, J. (1998) *The Psychology of Criminal Conduct*. Ohio: Anderson Publishing.

Annison, J., Eadie, T. and Knight, C. (2008) 'People first: probation officer perspectives on probation work', *Probation Journal*, 55(3): 259–71.

Antelava, N. (2009) 'Lebanese prisoners stage drama', BBC News, 28 February.

Anwar, S., Langström, N., Grann, M. and Fazel, S. (2009) 'Is arson the crime most strongly associated with psychosis? A national case control study of arson risk in schizophrenia and other psychoses', *Schizophrenia Bulletin*, 10: 1–7.

Arun, N. (2007) '"Green" prison softens tough convicts', BBC News, 7 September. Online at: http://news.bbc.co.uk/2/hi/europe/6983186.stm (accessed 3 February 2010).

Associated Press (2007) 'Eco-prison aims to change hard core criminals: recycling, organic farming part of Norway's "human ecology" experiment', 28 August. Online at: www.msnbc.msn.com/id/20483351/ (accessed 10 February 2010).

Astbury, B. (2008) 'Problems of implementing offender programs in the community', *Probation and Parole: Current Issues*, 46(3): 31–47.

Attorney-General's Department (2004) *Revised Standard Guidelines for Corrections in Australia*. Online at: www.bfcsa.nsw.gov.au/bfcsa/CSA/downloads/GUIDEL-1.pdf (accessed July 2009).

Austin, W. (2001) 'Relational ethics in forensic psychiatric settings', *Journal of Psychosocial Nursing and Mental Health Services*, 39(9): 12–17.

Australian Bureau of Statistics (2006) *Corrective Services, Australia*. Online at: www.abs.gov.au/ausstats/abs@.nsf/ProductsbyReleaseDate/B5C8821 8BEA653C9CA2571EF007D4F95?OpenDocument (accessed 16 November 2009).

Australian Bureau of Statistics (2008) *Prisoners in Australia*. Online at: www.ausstats.abs.gov.au/ausstats/subscriber.nsf/0/F618C51B775B2CF7CA 25751B0014A2D5/$File/45170_2008.pdf.

Australian Commonwealth Government Productivity Commission (2009) *Report on Government Services: Volume 1*. Melbourne: Productivity Commission. Online at: www.pc.gov.au/__data/assets/pdf_file/0009/85392/31-chapter8-attachment-only.pdf (accessed 16 November 2009).

Australian Institute of Criminology (2008) *Crime Facts No. 168, 15 April 2008*. Canberra: Australian Institute of Criminology.

Australian Institute of Criminology (2009) *Australian Crime: Facts and Figures 2008*. Canberra: Australian Institute of Criminology.

Australian National Training Authority (2003) *Self Harm Policy Paper*. Canberra: Department of Education, Employment and Workplace Relations.

Auty, K. (2006) 'Introduction', in M. King and K. Auty (eds) *The Therapeutic Role of Magistrates' Courts*, E Law Special Series (1). Online at: http://elaw.murdoch.edu.au/special_series.html (accessed 1 August 2007).

Baines, M. and Alder, C. (1996) 'Are girls more difficult to work with? Youth workers' perspectives in juvenile justice and related areas', *Crime and Delinquency*, 42(3): 467–85.

Baldry, E., McDonnell, D., Maplestone, P. and Peeters, M. (2002) 'Ex-prisoners and accommodation: what bearing do different forms of housing have on social reintegration or ex-prisoners?', paper presented at the Australian Institute of Criminology and the Australian Housing and Urban Research Institute Conference, *Housing, Crime and Stronger Communities*, Melbourne, 6–7 May.

Barry, M. (2006) *Youth Offending in Transition: The Search for Social Recognition.* Abingdon: Routledge.

Barry, M. (2007) 'Listening and learning: the reciprocal relationship between worker and client', *Probation Journal*, 54(4): 407–22.

Baruch, V. (2004) 'Self-care for therapists: prevention of compassion fatigue and burnout', *Psychotherapy in Australia*, 10(4): 1–9.

Bazemore, G. (1991) 'Beyond punishment, surveillance and traditional treatment: themes for a new mission in US Juvenile Justice', in J. Hackler (ed.) *Official Responses to Problem Juveniles: Some International Reflections.* Onati International Institute for the Sociology of Law.

Bazemore, G. and Cruise, P. (1995) 'Reinventing rehabilitation: exploring a competency development model for juvenile justice intervention', *Perspectives*, Fall: 12–21.

Bazemore, G. and Walgrave, L. (1999) 'Restorative juvenile justice: in search of fundamentals and an outline for systemic reform', in G. Bazemore and L. Walgrave (eds) *Restorative Juvenile Justice: Repairing the Harm of Youth Crime.* Monsey, NY: Criminal Justice Press.

Beck, A., Harrison, P. and Adams, D. (2007) *Sexual Violence Reported by Correctional Facilities 2006.* Washington, DC: US Department of Justice, Bureau of Justice Statistics.

Bennett, J., Crewe, B. and Wahidin, A. (eds) (2008) *Understanding Prison Staff.* Cullompton: Willan Publishing.

Bergum, V. and Dossetor, J. (2005) *Relational Ethics: The Full Meaning of Respect.* Maryland: University Publishing Group.

Berzins, L. and Trestman, R. (2004) 'The development and implementation of dialectical behavior therapy in forensic settings', *International Journal of Forensic Mental Health*, 3(1): 93–103.

Best Practice in Alcohol and Other Drug Interventions Working Group (2000) *Evidence Based Practice Indicators for Alcohol and Other Drug Interventions.* Perth: Drug and Alcohol Office, Government of Western Australia.

Bewley-Taylor, D., Hallam, C. and Allen, R. (2009) *The Incarceration of Drug Offenders: An Overview.* London: International Centre for Prison Studies.

Bibas, S. (2007) 'Forgiveness in criminal procedure', *Ohio State Journal of Criminal Law*, 4: 329–48.

Bibas, S. and Bierschbach, R. (2004) 'Integrating remorse and apology into criminal procedure', *Yale Law Journal*, 114: 85–148.

Bilchik, S. (1998) *Guide for Implementing the Balanced and Restorative Justice Model.* Washington, DC: Office of Juvenile Justice and Delinquency Prevention.

Birgden, A. (2002) 'Therapeutic jurisprudence and "Good Lives": a rehabilitation framework for corrections', *Australian Psychologist*, 37(3): 180–6.

Birgden, A. (2004) 'Therapeutic jurisprudence and responsivity: finding the will and the way in offender rehabilitation', *Psychology, Crime and Law*, 10(3): 283–95.

Bland, R., Renouf, N. and Tullgren, A. (2009) *Social Work Practice in Mental Health*. Sydney: Allen and Unwin.

Bonta, J. and Andrews, D. (2007) *Risk-Need-Responsivity Model for Offender Assessment and Rehabilitation*. Ottawa: Public Safety Canada.

Bonta, J., Rugge, T., Scott, T., Bourgon, G. and Yessine, A. (2008) 'Exploring the black box of community supervision', *Journal of Offender Rehabilitation*, 47(3): 248–70.

Borowski, A. (1997) 'Working with juvenile offenders in correctional settings: practice with the involuntary client', in A. Borowski and I. O'Connor (eds) *Juvenile Crime, Justice and Corrections*. Melbourne: Longman.

Boys, A., Farrell, M., Bebbington, P., Brugha, T., Coid, J., Jenkins, R., Lewis, G., Marsden, J., Meltzer, H., Singleton, N. and Taylor, C. (2002) 'Drug use and initiation in prison: results from a national prison survey in England and Wales', *Addiction*, 97(12): 1551–60.

Braithwaite, J. (1989) *Crime, Shame and Reintegration*. Cambridge: Cambridge University Press.

Braithwaite, J. and Pettit, P. (1990) *Not Just Deserts: A Republican Theory of Criminal Justice*. Melbourne: Oxford University Press.

Brayford, J., Cowe, F. and Deering, J. (eds) (2010) *What Else Works? Creative Work with Offenders*. Cullompton: Willan Publishing.

Brown, D. and Wilkie, M. (eds) (2002) *Prisoners as Citizens*. Sydney: Federation Press.

Brown, J. (2004) 'Managing the transition from institution to the community: a Canadian parole officer perspective on the needs of newly released federal offenders', *Western Criminology Review*, 5(2): 97–107.

Bryant, C. (2008) *Understanding Bushfire: Trends in Deliberate Vegetation Fires in Australia*, Technical and Background Paper No. 27. Canberra: Australian Institute of Criminology.

Buchbinder, E. and Eisikovits, Z. (2008) 'Collaborative discourse: the case of police and social work relationships in intimate violence intervention in Israel', *Journal of Social Service Research*, 34(4): 1–13.

Buonanno, P. and Montolio, D. (2008) 'Identifying the socio-economic and demographic determinants of crime across Spanish provinces', *International Review of Law and Economics*, 28(2): 89–97.

Bureau of Justice Statistics (2008) *Census of State and Federal Correctional Facilities 2005*. Washington, DC: US Department of Justice.

Burgen, V. and Dossetor, J. (2005) *Relational Ethics: The Full Meaning of Respect*. Maryland: University Publishing Group

Burke, P. (2001) 'Collaboration for successful prisoner reentry: the role of probation and the courts', *Corrections Management Quarterly*, 5(3): 11–22.

Burke, P. (2008) *Transition from Prison to the Community Re-entry Handbook*. Washington, DC: United States Department of Justice National Institute of Corrections.

Burnett, R. (2007) 'The personal touch in ex-offender reintegration', paper presented to the Deakin University Third Annual Conference, *The Reintegration Puzzle: Fitting the Pieces Together*, Sydney, 7–8 May.

Burnett, R. and Maruna, S. (2004) 'So "prison works", does it? The criminal careers of 130 men released from prison under Home Secretary, Michael Howard', *Howard Journal*, 43(4): 390–404.

Butler, M. (2008) 'What are you looking at? Prisoner confrontations and the search for respect', *British Journal of Criminology*, 48(6): 856–73.

Byrne, F. and Trew, K. (2008) 'Pathways through crime: the development of crime and desistance in accounts of men and women offenders', *Howard Journal of Criminal Justice*, 42(2): 181–97.

Cameron, M. (2001) *Women Prisoners and Correctional Programs*, Trends and Issues in Crime and Criminal Justice No. 194. Canberra: Australian Institute of Criminology.

Cameron, A., Macdonald, G., Turner, W. and Lloyd, L. (2007) 'The challenges of joint working: lessons from supporting people health pilot evaluation', *International Journal of Integrated Care*, 7: 1–10.

Cameron, H. and Telfer, J. (2004) 'Cognitive-behavioural group work: its application to specific offender groups', *Howard Journal of Criminal Justice*, 43(1): 47–64.

Cammett, A. (2006) 'Expanding collateral sanctions: the hidden cost of aggressive child support enforcement against incarcerated parents', *Georgetown Journal on Poverty, Law and Policy*, 8(2): 313–39.

Carlson, J. and Thomas, G. (2006) 'Burnout among prison caseworkers and corrections officers', *Journal of Offender Rehabilitation*, 43(3): 19–34.

Carlton, B. (2007) *Imprisoning Resistance: Life and Death in an Australian Supermax*. Sydney: Institute of Criminology Press.

Carlton, B. (2008) 'Understanding prisoner resistance: power, visibility and survival in high-security', in T. Anthony and C. Cunneen (eds) *The Critical Criminology Companion*. Sydney: Hawkins Press.

Carnwell, R. and Carson, A. (2005) 'Understanding partnerships and collaboration', in R. Carnwell and J. Buchanan (eds) *Effective Practice in Health and Social Care: A Partnership Approach*. Maidenhead: Open University Press.

Carter, C. and Pycroft, A. (2010) 'Getting out: offenders in forestry and conservation work settings', in J. Brayford, F. Cowe and J. Deering (eds) *What Else Works? Creative Work with Offenders*. Cullompton: Willan Publishing.

Case, S. and Haines, K. (2009) *Understanding Youth Offending: Risk Factor Research, Policy and Practice*. Cullompton: Willan Publishing.

Cavadino, M. and Dignan, J. (2006) 'Penal policy and political economy', *Criminology and Criminal Justice*, 6(4) 435–56.

Chapman, D. (2003) *Sociology and the Stereotype of the Criminal*. London: Routledge.

Cherry, S. (2005) *Transforming Behaviour: Pro-Social Modelling in Practice*. Cullompton: Willan Publishing.

Child and Adolescent Mental Health Services (2008) *What You Need to Know About Self Harm and Getting Help*. Tasmania: Department of Health and Human Services.

Cianchi, J. (2009) 'Achieving and maintaining prison officer–prisoner relationships: Tasmanian perspectives from a time of culture change', unpublished Masters of Criminology and Corrections thesis, School of Sociology and Social Work, University of Tasmania, Hobart.

Clark, M. (2005) 'Motivational interviewing for probation staff: increasing the readiness to change', *Federal Probation*, 69(2): 22–8.

Coebergh, B., Bakker, L., Anstiss, B., Maynard, K. and Percy, S. (2001) *A Seeing 'I' to the Future: The Criminogenic Needs Inventory*. Wellington: New Zealand Department of Corrections.

Cohen, S. (1985) *Visions of Social Control: Crime, Punishment and Classification*. Cambridge: Polity Press.

Commission on English Prisons Today (2009) *Do Better, Do Less: A Report on the Commission on English Prisons Today*. London.

Commonwealth of Australia (2009) *Father Inclusive Practice Guide: A Tool to Support the Inclusion of Fathers in a Holistic Approach to Service Delivery*. Canberra: Australian Government Department of Families, Housing, Community Services and Indigenous Affairs.

Condon, L., Hek, G., Harris, F., Powell, J., Kemple, T. and Price, S. (2007) 'Users' views of prison health services: a qualitative study', *Journal of Advanced Nursing*, 58(3): 216–26.

Conolly, M. and Ward, T. (2008) *Morals, Rights and Practice in the Human Services: Effective and Fair Decision-making in Health, Social Care and Criminal Justice*. London: Jessica Kingsley.

Correctional Service of Canada (1998) *Pet Facilitated Therapy in Correctional Institutions*. Ontario: Correctional Service of Canada.

Correctional Service of Canada (2006) *Strategic Plan for Aboriginal Corrections 2006–07 to 2010–11*. Ontario: Correctional Service of Canada.

Correctional Service of Canada (2008) *Correctional Service of Canada 2007–2008 Performance Report*. Ontario: Correctional Service of Canada.

Correctional Service of Canada (2010) *Aboriginal Corrections*. Online at: www.csc-scc.gc.ca/text/prgrm/abinit/plan06-eng.shtml#6 (accessed 19 April 2010).

Corrective Services Ministers' Conference (2004) *Standard Guidelines for Corrections in Australia*. Corrective Services/Department of Justice in each state and territory.

Corrective Services Queensland (2008) *Queensland Corrective Services: Annual Report 2007–2008*. Brisbane: Corrective Services Queensland.

Coventry, G. and Westerhuis, D. (forthcoming) 'Preparation for freedom: Cyclone Larry and prison work'.

Crawley, E. and Crawley, P. (2008) 'Understanding prison officers: culture, cohesion and conflict', in J. Bennett, B. Crewe and A. Wahidin (eds) *Understanding Prison Staff*. Cullompton: Willan Publishing.

Crewe, J., Bennett, B. and Wahidin, A. (eds) (2008) *Understanding Prison Staff*. Cullompton: Willan Publishing.

Cunneen, C. and White, R. (2007) *Juvenile Justice: Youth and Crime in Australia*, 3rd edn. South Melbourne: Oxford University Press.

Day, A., Casey, S., Ward, T., Howells, K. and Vess, J. (2010) *Transitions to Better Lives: Offender Readiness and Rehabilitation*. Cullompton: Willan Publishing.

Day, A., Tucker, K. and Howells, K. (2004) 'Coerced offender rehabilitation – a defensible practice?', *Psychology, Crime and Law*, 10(3): 259–69.

Delaney, P. J., Fletcher, B. W. and Shields, J. J. (2003) 'Reorganizing care for the substance using offender – the case for collaboration', *Federal Probation*, 67(2): 64–8.

Del Vecchio, T. and O'Leary, K. (2004) 'Effectiveness of anger treatments for specific anger problems: a meta-analytic review', *Clinical Psychology Review*, 24: 15–34.

Denckla, D. (1999–2000) 'Forgiveness as a problem solving tool in the courts: a brief response to the panel on forgiveness in criminal law', *Fordham Urban Law Journal*, 27: 1613–19.

Denckla, D. and Berman, G. (2001) *Rethinking the Revolving Door: A Look at Mental Illness in the Courts*. New York: Centre for Court Innovation.

Devapriam, J., Raju, L., Singh, N., Collacott, R. and Bhaumik, S. (2007) 'Arson: characteristics and pre-disposing factors in offenders with intellectual disabilities', *British Journal of Forensic Practice*, 9(4): 23–7.

De Viggiani, N. (2007) 'Unhealthy prisons: exploring structural determinants of prison health', *Sociology of Health and Illness*, 29(1): 115–35.

Dolan, K., Khoei, E., Brentari, C. and Stevens, A. (2007) *Prison and Drugs: A Global Review of Incarceration, Drug Use and Drug Services*. Oxford: Beckley Foundation Drug Policy Programme.

Doley, R. (2003) 'Pyromania: fact or fiction?', *British Journal of Criminology*, 43: 797–807.

Douglas, T. (2009) 'Broadcasting behind bars', BBC News. Online at: http://news.bbc.co.uk/today/hi/today/newsid_8043000/8043258.stm (accessed 9 February 2010).

Drake, D. (2008) 'Staff and order in prison', in J. Bennet, B. Crewe and A. Wahidin (eds) *Understanding Prison Staff*. Cullompton: Willan Publishing.

Dryden, W. and Neenan, M. (2004) *Rational Emotive Behavioural Counselling in Action*, 3rd edn. London: Sage.

Duncan, S. (2009) *Reading Together*. Hobart: Tasmania Department of Justice, Tasmanian Prison Service.

Easteal, P. (1994) 'Ethnicity and crime', in D. Chappel and P. Wilson (eds) *The Australian Criminal Justice System: The Mid 1990s*. Sydney: Butterworths.

Ellwood, R., Murphy, K., Hanson, D., Hemingway, C., Ramsden, V., Buxton, J., Granger-Brown, A., Condello, L., Buchanan, M., Espinoza-Magana, N., Edworthy, G. and Hislop, T. (2009) 'The development of participatory health research among incarcerated women in a Canadian prison', *International Journal of Prisoner Health*, 5(2): 95–107.

Enayati, J., Grann, M., Lubbe, S. and Fazel, S. (2008) 'Psychiatric morbidity in arsonists referred for forensic psychiatric assessment in Sweden', *Journal of Forensic Psychiatry and Psychology*, 19(2): 139–47.

Evans, C. (2004) *A 'Pink Palace'? Risdon Prison, 1960–2004*. Hobart: Tasmania Department of Justice.

Fajnzylber, P., Lederman, D. and Loayza, N. (2002) 'Inequality and violent crime', *Journal of Law and Economics*, 45(1): 1–40.

Farrall, S. (2004) 'Social capital and offender reintegration: making probation desistance focused', in S. Maruna and R. Immarigeon (eds) *After Crime and Punishment: Pathways to Offender Reintegration*. Cullompton: Willan Publishing.

Farrow, K., Kelly, G. and Wilkinson, B. (2007) *Offenders in Focus: Risk, Responsivity and Diversity*. Bristol: Policy Press.

Federal Judicial Center (2003) *Handbook for Working with Defendants and Offenders with a Mental Illness*, 3rd edn. Washington, DC: Federal Judicial Centre.

Figley, C. (1995) *Compassion Fatigue: Coping with Secondary Stress Disorder in Those who Treat the Traumatized*. Bristol: Brunner Mazel.

Fleeman, W. (2003) *Pathways to Peace: Anger Management Workbook*, 3rd edn. Alameda, CA: Hunter House Inc.

Foucault, M. (1977) *Discipline and Punish: The Birth of the Prison*. Middlesex: Penguin.

Foucault, M. (1995) *Discipline and Punish: The Birth of the Prison*. New York: Vintage.

Fourgere, D., Kramarz, F. and Pouget, J. (2006) *Youth Unemployment and Crime in France*. Paris: Institute for the Study of Labour.

Fournel, P. (2009) 'Escape from the chain gang', *Guardian*, 4 June.

Freiberg, A. (2001) 'Problem-oriented Courts: Innovative Solutions to Intractable Problems?', *Journal of Judicial Administration*, 11(1): 8–27.

Freiberg, A. (2007) 'Non-adversarial approaches to criminal justice', paper presented at State Government of Tasmania Conference, *Court Mandated Diversion of Drug Offenders: The Development of Problem Solving Approaches in Tasmania*, 8 May, Hobart.

Fulkerson, A. (2001) 'The use of victim impact panels in domestic violence cases: a restorative justice approach', *Contemporary Justice Review*, 4(3–4): 355–68.

Furst, G. (2006) 'Prison-based animal programs', *Prison Journal*, 86(4): 407–30.

Gelsthorpe, L., Sharpe, G. and Roberts, J. (2007) *Provision for Women Offenders in the Community*. London: Fawcett.

Glaze, L. and Bonczar, T. (2008) *Probation and Parole in the United States 2007 Statistical Tables*. Washington, DC: US Bureau of Justice Statistics.

Glaze, L. and Maruschak, L. (2009) *Parents in Prison and Their Minor Children*. Washington, DC: US Department of Justice, Bureau of Justice Statistics.

Godly, S., Finch, M., Dougan, L., McDonnell, M., McDermeit, M. and Carey, A. (2000) 'Case management for dually diagnosed individuals involved in the criminal justice system', *Journal of Substance Abuse Treatment*, 18(2): 137–48.

Goldring, N. (2001) 'Drama therapy in Hermon Prison', *Innovations Exchange*, (9): 23.

Gordon, A. (2009) *Comorbidity of Mental Disorders and Substance Use: A Brief Guide for the Primary Care Clinician*. Canberra: Commonwealth of Australia.

Gorman, J. (2008) *How to Cope with Sleep Problems*. London: Mind.

Gosselin, L. (1982) *Prisons in Canada*. Montreal: Black Rose Books.

Gould, M. (2008) 'Redemption songs', *Guardian*, 10 December.

Goulding, D. (2007) 'Violence and brutality in prisons: a West Australian context', *Current Issues in Criminal Justice*, 18(3): 399–413.

Graham, H. (2007) *A Foot in the (Revolving) Door? A Preliminary Evaluation of Tasmania's Mental Health Diversion List*, Report for the Magistrates Court of Tasmania, Hobart.

Graham, S. and Burton, P. (2008) 'A model for integrated offender management and the post release options programme', unpublished paper, St Vincent de Paul Bethlehem House Homeless Men's Shelter, used with permission.

Grant, E. and Memmott, P. (2007/08) 'The case for single cells and alternative ways of viewing custodial accommodation for Australian aboriginal peoples', *Flinders Journal of Law Reform*, 10(3): 631–47.

Green, D. (2007) 'Risk and social work practice', *Australian Social Work*, 60(4): 395–409.

Green, S., Lancaster, E. and Feasey, S. (eds) (2008) *Addressing Offending Behaviour: Context, Practice and Values*. Cullompton: Willan Publishing.

Griswold, E. and Pearson, J. (2005a) 'Lessons from four projects dealing with incarceration and child support', *Corrections Today*, 67(4): 92–102.

Griswold, E. and Pearson, J. (2005b) 'Turning offenders into responsible parents and child support payers', *Family Court Review*, 43(3): 358–71.

Gursansky, D., Harvey, J. and Kennedy, R. (2003) *Case Management: Policy, Practice and Professional Business*. Sydney: Allen and Unwin.

Gussak, D. (2007) 'The effectiveness of art therapy in reducing depression in prison populations', *International Journal of Offender Therapy and Comparative Criminology*, 51(4): 444–60.

Gutheil, T. and Gabbard, G. (1993) 'The concept of boundaries in clinical practice: theoretical and risk management dimensions', in G. Adshead and C. Jacob (eds) (2009) *Personality Disorder: The Definitive Reader*. London: Jessica Kingsley Publishers.

Hagedorn, J. (ed.) (2007) *Gangs in the Global City: Alternatives to Traditional Criminology*. Urbana and Chicago: University of Illinois Press.

Hall, I., Clayton, P. and Johnson, P. (2005) 'Arson and learning disability', in T. Riding, C. Swann and B. Swann (eds) *The Handbook of Forensic Learning Disabilities*. Abingdon: Radcliffe Publishing.

Hall, J. (2007) *Intentional Fires and Arson*. National Fire Protection Association: Quincey, MA, United States.

Halliday, S., Burns, N., Hutton, N., McNeill, F. and Tata, C. (2008) 'Shadow writing and participant observation: a study of criminal justice social work around sentencing', *Journal of Law and Society*, 35(2): 189–213.

Halliday, S., Burns, N., Hutton, N., McNeill, F. and Tata, C. (2009) 'Street-level bureaucracy, interprofessional relations, and coping mechanisms: a study of criminal justice workers in the sentencing process', *Law and Policy*, 31(4): 405–28.

Hannah-Moffat, K. (2009) 'Gridlock or mutability: reconsidering "gender" and risk assessment', *Criminology and Public Policy*, 8(1): 209–20.

Hannah-Moffat, K. and Shaw, M. (eds) (2000) *An Ideal Prison? Critical Essays on Women's Imprisonment in Canada*. Nova Scotia: Fernwood Publishing.

Harlow, C. (2003) *Education and Correctional Populations*. Washington, DC: US Department of Justice, Bureau of Justice Statistics.

Harper, R. and Hardy, S. (2000) 'An evaluation of motivational interviewing as a method of intervention with clients in a probation setting', *British Journal of Social Work*, 30: 393–400.

Harris, M. and Pettway, C. (2007) *Best Practices Toolkit: Incarcerated Parents and Parenting Programs*. Ohio: Ohio Institute of Correctional Best Practices.

Hawkings, C. and Gilburt, H. (2004) *Dual Diagnosis Toolkit: Mental Health and Substance Misuse – A Practical Guide for Professionals and Practitioners*. London: Turning Point (UK) and Rethink.

Hayes, L. (1995) *Prison Suicide: An Overview and Guide to Prevention*. Massachusetts: National Institute of Corrections, US Department of Justice.

Healy, K. and Mulholland, J. (2007) *Writing Skills for Social Workers*. London: Sage.

Henry-Edwards, S. (2009) 'Getting SMART: enabling offenders in the NSW Department of Corrective Services to understand SMART Recovery', paper presented at Australian Institute of Criminology Conference, *Making a Difference: Responding to Need in Developing, Implementing and Evaluating Correctional Programmes*, Melbourne, 5–6 March.

HM Prison Service (2009a) *Performance Statistics for Prisons in England and Wales*. Online at: www.hmprisonservice.gov.uk/abouttheservice/prisonperformance/performancestatistics/ (accessed 17 November 2009).

HM Prison Service (2009b) *England and Wales Performance Standards*. Online at: www.hmprisonservice.gov.uk/resourcecentre/publicationsdocuments/index.asp?cat=105 (accessed 9 December 2009).

Hogeveen, B. (2006) 'Unsettling youth justice and cultural norms: the youth restorative action project', *Journal of Youth Studies*, 9(1): 47–66.

Home Office (2009) *Partnership Working Crime Reduction Toolkit*. Online at: www.crimereduction.homeoffice.gov.uk/toolkits/p00.htm (accessed 1 November 2009).

Hooper, J. (2007) 'Jailhouse frock: the Italian prison with designs on fashion', *Guardian*, 21 May.

Howells, K., Day, A., Williamson, P., Burner, S., Jauncey, S., Parker, A. and Haseltine, K. (2005) 'Brief anger management programs with offenders: outcomes and predictors of change', *Journal of Forensic Psychiatry and Psychology*, 16(2): 296–311.

Howerton, A., Burnett, R., Byng, R. and Campbell, J. (2009) 'The consolations of going back to prison: what "revolving door" prisoners think of their prospects', *Journal of Offender Rehabilitation*, 48(5): 439–61.

Hubband, N., McMurran, M., Evans, C. and Duggan, C. (2007) 'Social problem-solving plus psychoeducation for adults with personality disorder: pragmatic randomised control trial', *British Journal of Psychiatry*, 190: 307–13.

Hunter, N. and McRostie, H. (2001) *Magistrates Court Diversion Programme: Overview of Key Data Findings*. Office of Crime Statistics and Research. Online at: www.oscar.sa.gov.au/docs/information_bulletins/IB20.pdf (accessed 28 August 2007).

Institute for Criminal Policy Research (2009) *Statistics on Women and the Criminal Justice System*. London: Kings College and Ministry of Justice.

International Centre for Prison Studies (2004) *Guidance Note 9: Humanising the Treatment of Prisoners*. London: International Centre for Prison Studies.

International Centre for Prison Studies (2009) *World Prison Brief – Country Descriptions for United States of America, England and Wales, Scotland, Canada, Italy, Greece, Australia and New Zealand*. Online at: www.kcl.ac.uk/depsta/law/research/icps/worldbrief/ (accessed 13 November 2009).

Jacobson, J. and Edgar, K. (2007) *There When You Need Them Most: PACT's First Night in Custody Services*. London: Prison Reform Trust.

Jensen, K. and Gibbons, S. (2002) 'Shame and religion as factors in the rehabilitation of serious offenders', *Journal of Offender Rehabilitation*, 35(3): 209–24.

Jewkes, Y. (ed.) (2007) *Handbook on Prisons*. Cullompton: Willan Publishing.

Jiler, J. (2006) *Doing Time in the Garden: Life Lessons through Prison Horticulture*. California: New Village Press.

Jiler, J. (2009) 'Inmates harvest food, savings, education and jobs from jail gardens', *Great Lakes Echo*. Online at: http://greatlakesecho.org/2009/11/20/inmates-harvest-food-savings-education-and-jobs-from-jail-gardens/ (accessed 19 April 2010).

Johnson, L. (2007) 'Jail wall drawings and jail art programs: invaluable tools for corrections', *International Journal of Criminal Justice Sciences*, 2(2): 66–84.

Johnson, L. (2008) 'A place for art in prison: art as a tool for rehabilitation and management', *Southwest Journal of Criminal Justice*, 5(2): 100–20.

Just Detention International (2009) *Hope for Healing: Information for Survivors of Sexual Assault in Detention*. Los Angeles: Just Detention International.

Karmen, A. (2000) 'Poverty, crime, and criminal justice', in W. Heffernan and J. Kleinig (eds) *From Social Justice to Criminal Justice*. New York: Oxford University Press.

Karremans, J. and Lange, P. (2005) 'Does activating justice help or hurt in promoting forgiveness?', *Journal of Experimental Social Psychology*, 41: 290–7.

Kassinove, H. and Tafrate, R. (2002) *Anger Management: The Complete Treatment Guidebook for Practitioners*. California: Impact Publishers.

Kelley, M. (2009) 'A prisoner Tour de France', *Criminal Justice*. Online at: http://criminaljustice.change.org/blog/view/a_prisoner_tour_de_france (accessed 16 February 2010).

Kellogg, W. K. F. (2004) *Logic Model Development Guide*. Michigan: W. K. Kellogg Foundation.

Kelly, J., Goodwill, A., Keene, N. and Thrift, S. (2009) 'A retrospective study of historical risk factors for pathological arson by adults with mild learning disabilities', *British Journal of Forensic Practice*, 11(2): 17–23.

Kemp, R. (2008) 'My daddy is the man in the telly', *Guardian*, 1 November.

King, M. (2006) 'Afterword', in M. King and K. Auty (eds) *The Therapeutic Role of Magistrates' Courts*, E Law Special Series (1). Online at: http://elaw.murdoch.edu.au/special_series.html (accessed 1 August 2007).

King, M., Freiberg, A., Batagol, B. and Hyams, R. (2009) *Non-Adversarial Justice*. Sydney: Federation Press.

King, S. (2009) 'Reconciling custodial and human service work: the complex role of the prison officer', *Current Issues in Criminal Justice*, 21(2): 257–72.

Kirby, S. (2001) 'The development of a conceptual framework of therapeutic alliances in psychiatric nursing care delivery', in G. Landsberg and A. Smiley (eds) *Forensic Mental Health: Working with Offenders with Mental Illness*. New Jersey: Civic Research Institute.

Kistenmacher, B. and Weiss, R. (2008) 'Motivational interviewing as a mechanism for change in men who batter', *Violence and Victims*, 23(5): 558–70.

Kitchen, P. (2006) *Exploring the Link Between Crime and Socio-Economic Status in Ottawa and Saskatoon: A Small-Area Geographical Analysis*, report prepared for the Department of Justice Canada. Ottawa: Department of Justice.

Klaus, J. (1998) *Handbook on Probation Services: Guidelines for Probation Practitioners and Managers Publication No. 60*. Rome and London: United Nations Interregional Crime and Justice Institute.

Kopec, A. (1995) 'Rational emotive behavioural therapy in a forensic setting: practical issues', *Journal of Rational-Emotive and Cognitive-Behavior Therapy*, 13(4): 243–53.

Lacombe, D. (2008) 'Consumed with sex: the treatment of sex offenders in risk society', *British Journal of Criminology*, 48: 55–74.

Lamberti, J., Wiseman, R. and Faden, J. (2004) 'Forensic assertive community treatment: preventing incarceration of adults with severe mental illness', *Psychiatric Services*, 55(11): 1285–93.

LaVigne, N., Davies, E., Palmer, T. and Halberstadt, R. (2008) *Release Planning for Successful Reentry: A Guide for Corrections, Service Providers, and Community Groups*. Washington, DC: Urban Institute Justice Policy Centre.

Leahy, R. (2003) *Cognitive Therapy Techniques: A Practitioner's Guide*. London: Guilford Press.

Leonard, P., Shanahan, S. and Hillery, J. (2005) 'Recognising, assessing and managing offending behaviour in persons with an intellectual disability', *Irish Journal of Psychological Medicine*, 22(3): 107–12.

Leverton, M. (2009) 'Prisoners thrive on retail therapy', *Guardian*, 28 October.

Lewis, S., Raynor, P., Smith, D. and Wardak, A. (eds) (2006) *Race and Probation*. Cullompton: Willan Publishing.

Liau, A., Shively, R., Horn, M., Landau, J., Barriga, A. and Gibbs, J. (2004) 'Effects of psychoeducation for offenders in a community correctional facility', *Journal of Community Psychology*, 32(5): 543–58.

Liebling, A. (2004) 'The late modern prison and the question of values', *Current Issues in Criminal Justice*, 16(2): 202–19.

Liebling, A. and Arnold, H. (2002) *Measuring the Quality of Prison Life*, Home Office Research Findings 174. London: Home Office.

Liebling, A., Durie, L., Stiles, A. and Tait, S. (2005) 'Revisiting prison suicide: the role of fairness and distress', in A. Liebling and S. Maruna (eds) *The Effects of Imprisonment*. Cullompton: Willan Publishing.

Liebling, A., Price, D. and Elliott, C. (1999) 'Appreciative inquiry and relationships in prison', *Punishment and Society*, 1(1): 71–98.

Lifeline Australia (2005) *Toolkit for Helping Someone at Risk of Suicide*. Sydney: Lifeline Australia. Online at: www.lifeline.org.au/learn_more/media_centre/?a=14177 (accessed 19 April 2010).

Lifeline Australia (2009) *Toolkit: Overcoming Stress*. Sydney: Lifeline Australia.

Lipsey, M. and Cullen, F. (2007) 'The effectiveness of correctional rehabilitation: a review of systematic reviews', *Annual Review of Law and Social Science*, (3): 297–320.

Lowenstein, L. (2003) 'Recent research into arson (1992–2000): incidence, causes and associated features, predictions, comparative studies and prevention and treatment', *Psychiatry, Psychology and Law*, 10(1): 192–8.

Loxley, W. and Adams, K. (2009) *Women, Drug Use and Crime: Findings from the Drug Use Monitoring in Australia Program*. Canberra: Australian Institute of Criminology.

MacDonald, R. (2006) 'Social exclusion, youth transitions and criminal careers: five critical reflections on "risk"', *Australian and New Zealand Journal of Criminology*, 39(3): 371–83.

MacKenzie, D. (2000) 'Evidence-based corrections: identifying what works', *Crime and Delinquency*, 46(4): 457–71.

Maletzsky, B. and Steinhauser, C. (2002) 'A 25 year followup of cognitive behavioural therapy with 7,275 sexual offenders', *Behavior Modification*, 26(2): 123–47.

Marks, E. (1994) *Case Management in Service Integration: A Concept Paper*. New York: National Center for Children in Poverty, Columbia University School of Public Health.

Marshall, T. (1999) *Restorative Justice: An Overview*. London: Home Office, Research Development and Statistics Directorate.

Maruna, S. (2007) 'Public opinion: Shadd Maruna', *The Times Online*, 24 April. http://business.timesonline.co.uk/tol/business/industry_sectors/public_sector/article1693275.ece (accessed 3 February 2010).

Maruna, S. and Immarigeon, R. (eds) (2004) *After Crime and Punishment: Pathways to Offender Rehabilitation*. Cullompton: Willan Publishing.

Maruschak, L. (2008) *Medical Problems of Prisoners*. Washington, DC: US Department of Justice, Bureau of Justice Statistics. Online at: www.ojp.usdoj.gov/bjs/pub/html/mpp/mpp.htm (accessed 18 November 2009).

Mathiesen, T. (1990) *Prison on Trial: A Critical Assessment*. London: Sage.

Mawby, R. (2007) 'Public sector services and the victim of crime', in S. Walklate (ed.) *Handbook of Victims and Victimology*. Cullompton: Willan Publishing.

Mayhew, C. (2000a) *Preventing Client Initiated Violence: A Practical Handbook*. Canberra: Australian Institute of Criminology.

Mayhew, C. (2000b) *Preventing Violence Within Organisations: A Practical Handbook*. Canberra: Australian Institute of Criminology.

Mayhew, C. (2000c) *Violence in the Workplace – Preventing Armed Robbery: A Practical Handbook*. Canberra: Australian Institute of Criminology.

McCormack, J. (2007) *Recovery and Strengths Based Practice*. Glasgow: Scottish Recovery Network.

McDonough, J. and Burrell, W. (2008) 'Offender workforce development: a new (and better?) approach to an old challenge', *Federal Probation*, 72(2): 71–6.

McIvor, G. and Raynor, P. (eds) (2006) *Developments in Social Work with Offenders*. London: Jessica Kingsley.

McIvor, G., Kemshall, H. and Levy, G. (2002) *Serious Violent and Sexual Offenders in Scotland: The Use of Risk Assessment Tools in Scotland*. Edinburgh: Scottish Executive.

McMaster, K. (2004) 'Facilitating change through groupwork', in J. Maidment and R. Egan (eds) *Practice Skills in Social Work and Welfare: More than just Common Sense*. Sydney: Allen and Unwin.

McMurran, M. (2004) 'Assessing and changing motivation to offend', in W. Cox and E. Klinger (eds) *Handbook of Motivational Counselling: Concepts, Approaches and Assessments*. Chichester: John Wiley.

McMurran, M. and Wilmington, R. (2007) 'A Delphi survey of the views of adult male patients with personality disorders on psychoeducation and social problem-solving therapy', *Criminal Behaviour and Mental Health*, 17: 293–9.

McNeill, F. (2000) 'Defining effective probation: frontline perspectives', *The Howard Journal*, 39(4): 382–97.

McNeill, F. (2009a) *Towards Effective Practice in Offender Supervision*. Glasgow: Scottish Centre for Crime and Justice Research.

McNeill, F. (2009b) 'What works and what's just?', *European Journal of Probation*, 1(1): 21–40.

McNeill, F., Batchelor, S., Burnett, R. and Knox, J. (2005) *21st Century Social Work – Reducing Re-offending: Key Practice Skills*. Edinburgh: Scottish Executive.

McNeill, F. and Whyte, B. (2007) *Reducing Reoffending: Social Work and Community Justice in Scotland*. Cullompton: Willan Publishing.

Meadows, G., Singh, B. and Grigg, M. (2007) 'Looking forward', in G. Meadows, B. Singh and M. Grigg (eds) *Mental Health in Australia: Collaborative Community Practice*, 2nd edn. South Melbourne: Oxford University Press.

Meek, R. (2007) 'Parenting education for young fathers in prison', *Child and Family Social Work*, 12(3): 239–47.

Mellor, T. (2002) 'Integrated offender management: changing the way we work with offenders in New Zealand', paper presented at *Probation and Community Corrections: Making the Community Safer* conference, Perth, 23–24 September.

Mendel, E. and Hipkins, J. (2002) 'Motivating learning disabled offenders with alcohol related problems: a pilot study', *Journal of Learning Disabilities*, 30: 153–8.

Mental Health First Aid (2007) *Guidelines for Supporting a Person Who has Experienced a Traumatic Event*. Online at: www.mhfa.com.au/documents/guidelines/8187_MHFA_adulttrauma_guidelines.pdf (accessed 19 April 2010).

Merrington, S. and Hine, J. (2001) *Probation Work with Offenders*. London: Home Office.

Michalowski, R. and Carlson, S. (1999) 'Unemployment, imprisonment and social structures of accumulation: historical contingency in Rusche-Kirchheimer hypothesis', *Criminology*, 37(2): 217–50.

Miller, W. (1996) 'Motivational interviewing: research, practice and puzzles', *Addictive Behaviours*, 21(6): 835–42.

Ministerial Advisory Committee on AIDS, Sexual Health and Hepatitis (2008) *Hepatitis C Prevention, Treatment and Care: Guidelines for Australian Custodial Settings*. Canberra: Australian Government Department of Health and Ageing.

Ministry of Health (NZ) (2006) *Results from the Prisoner Health Survey 2005.* Wellington: Ministry of Health, New Zealand.

Ministry of Justice (UK) (2009a) *Offender Management Caseload Statistics 2008.* London: Ministry of Justice.

Ministry of Justice (UK) (2009b) *Intensive Help for Vulnerable People: Applying Case Management Models in the Justice System Research Summary 8/09.* London: Ministry of Justice, United Kingdom.

Ministry of Women's Affairs (2006) *The Status of Women in New Zealand: New Zealand's Sixth Report on its Implementation of the United Nations Convention on the Elimination of all Forms of Discrimination against Women.* Online at: www.mwa.govt.nz/news-and-pubs/publications/international/cedaw-report.html (accessed 16 November 2009).

Moller, L., Stover, H., Jurgens, R., Gatherer, A. and Nikogosian, H. (2007) *Health in Prisons: A WHO Guide to the Essentials in Prison Health.* Copenhagen: World Health Organisation Regional Office for Europe.

Morash, M. (2009) 'A great debate over using the Level of Service Inventory – Revised (LSI-R) with women offenders', *Criminology and Public Policy*, 8(1): 173–82.

Morrissey, J., Meyer, P. and Cuddeback, G. (2007) 'Extending assertive community treatment to criminal justice settings: origins, current evidence and future directions', *Community Mental Health Journal*, 43(5): 527–44.

Moulds, J. (2008) 'Inside job: media training is giving the women inside Downview Prison a new outlook', *Guardian*, 7 May.

Muller, D. (2008) *Offending and Re-Offending Patterns of Arsonists and Bushfire Arsonists in NSW.* Canberra: Australian Institute of Criminology.

Murdoch, J. (2006) 'The impact of the Council of Europe's "Torture Committee" and the evolution of standard setting in relation to places of detention', *European Human Rights Law Review*, 159.

Musser, P., Semiatin, J., Taft, C. and Murphy, C. (2008) 'Motivational interviewing as a pre-group intervention for partner-violent men', *Violence and Victims*, 23(5): 539–57.

Nadesu, A. (2009) *Reconviction Patterns of Released Prisoners: A 60-month Follow-up Analysis.* Wellington: Policy, Strategy and Research, Department of Corrections New Zealand.

NCETA (National Centre for Education and Training in Addiction) (2005) *Stress and Burnout: A Prevention Handbook for the Alcohol and Other Drugs Workforce.* South Australia: Flinders University.

Nelson, M. and Trone, J. (2000) *Why Planning for Release Matters.* New York: State Sentencing and Corrections Program, Vera Institute of Justice.

New South Wales Department of Corrective Services (2008) *Throughcare.* Online at: www.203.202.1.170/Information/Publications/Throughcare/Throughcare.pdf (accessed July 2009).

New South Wales Ombudsman (1996) *Report of the Inquiry into Juvenile Detention Centres.* Sydney: Office of the Ombudsman.

Newbold, G. (2008) 'Another one bites the dust: recent initiatives in correctional reform in New Zealand', *Australian and New Zealand Journal of Criminology*, 41(3): 384–401.

Nicholl, C. (2001) *Implementing Restorative Justice: A Toolbox for the Implementation of Restorative Justice and the Advancement of Community Policing*. Washington, DC: Office of Community Oriented Policing Services, US Department of Justice.

O'Donohue, D. (2004) 'Using constructive challenge during intervention', in J. Maidment and R. Egan (eds) *Practice Skills in Social Work and Welfare: More than just Common Sense*. Sydney: Allen and Unwin.

O'Dwyer, E. (2010) 'Inside stories', *The Age Newspaper Good Weekend*, 13 February: 29–32.

Office of the Deputy Prime Minister (2002) *Reducing Re-offending by Ex-prisoners*. London: Social Exclusion Unit, ODPM.

Ogloff, J. and Davis, M. (2004) 'Advances in offender assessment and rehabilitation: contributions of the risk-need-responsivity approach', *Psychology, Crime and Law*, 10(3): 229–42.

Ore, T. and Birgden, A. (2003) 'Does prison work? A view from criminology', *Policy*, 19(2): 62–3.

Ormerod, E. (2008) 'Companion animals and offender rehabilitation – experiences from a prison therapeutic community in Scotland', *Therapeutic Communities*, 29(3): 285–96.

Osher, F., Steadman, H. and Barr, H. (2002) *A Best Practice Approach to Community Re-entry from Jails for Inmates with Co-occurring Disorders*. New York: National GAINS Centre.

O'Toole, S. and Eyland, S. (eds) (2005) *Corrections Criminology*. Sydney: Hawkins Press.

Palmer, D. and Collard, L. (1993) 'Aboriginal young people and youth subcultures', in R. White (ed.) *Youth Subcultures: Theory, History and the Australian Experience*. Hobart: National Clearinghouse for Youth Studies.

Papps, K. and Winkelmann, R. (2000) 'Unemployment and crime: new evidence for an old question', *New Zealand Economic Papers*, 34(1):

Parks, G. (2007) 'New approaches to using relapse prevention therapy in the criminal justice system', *Corrections Today*, 69(6): 46–9.

Payne, J. (2006) *Specialty Courts: Current Issues and Future Prospects*, Trends and Issues in Crime and Criminal Justice No. 317. Canberra: Australian Institute of Criminology.

Pearson, J. (2004) 'Building debt while doing time: child support and incarceration', *American Bar Association Judge's Journal*, 1(43): 5–12.

Penal Reform International (2001) *Making Standards Work: An International Handbook on Good Prison Practice*. London: Penal Reform International and the Netherlands Ministry of Justice.

Pennsylvania Coalition Against Rape (2006) *Meeting the Needs of Prison Rape Victims: A Technical Assistance Guide for Sexual Assault Counselors and Advocates*. Pennsylvania Coalition Against Rape:

Peters, R. and Osher, F. (2004) *Co-occurring Disorders and Specialty Courts*, 2nd edn. New York: National GAINS Centre.

Pettus-Davis, C., Scheyett, A., Hailey, D., Golin, C. and Wohl, D. (2009) 'From the "streets" to "normal life": assessing the role of social support in release planning for HIV-positive and substance involved prisoners', *Journal of Offender Rehabilitation*, 48(5): 367–87.

Phillips, S., Burns, B., Edgar, E., Mueser, K., Linkins, K., Rosenheck, R., Drake, R. and Herr, E. (2001) 'Moving assertive community treatment into standard practice', *Psychiatric Services*, 52(6): 771–9.

Pomeroy, E., Kiam, R. and Green, D. (2000) 'Reducing depression, anxiety and trauma of male inmates: an HIV/AIDS psychoeducational group intervention', *Social Work Research*, 24(3): 156–67.

Popovic, J. (2006) 'Meaningless vs meaningful sentences: sentencing the unsentenceable', paper presented at the *Sentencing: Principles, Perspectives and Possibilities* conference, National Judicial College of Australia and the ANU College of Law, Canberra, 10–12 February 2006.

Porporino, F., Fabiano, E. and Robinson, D. (1991) *Focusing on Successful Reintegration: Cognitive Skills Training for Offenders*. Ontario: Correctional Service of Canada.

Pratt, J. (2008a) 'Scandinavian exceptionalism in an era of penal excess, part 1: the nature and roots of Scandinavian exceptionalism', *British Journal of Criminology*, 48(2): 119–37.

Pratt, J. (2008b) 'Scandinavian exceptionalism in an era of penal excess, part 2: does Scandinavian exceptionalism have a future?', *British Journal of Criminology*, 48(3): 275–92.

Priday, E. (2006) 'New directions in juvenile justice: risk and cognitive behaviourism', *Current Issues in Criminal Justice*, 17(3): 343–59.

Pryor, S. (2001) *The Responsible Prisoner: An Exploration of the Extent to which Prison Removes Responsibility Unnecessarily and an Invitation to Change*. London: HM Inspectorate of Prisons.

Randerson, J. (2008) 'Jailbirds creating eco-havens in prison', *Observer*, 21 September.

Raynor, P. (2002) 'Community penalties: probation, punishment, and "what works"', in M. Maguire, R. Morgan and R. Reiner (eds) *The Oxford Handbook of Criminology*, 3rd edn. Oxford: Oxford University Press.

Reilly, P. and Shopshire, M. (2002) *Anger Management for Substance Abuse and Mental Health Clients: A Cognitive Behavioural Therapy Manual*. Rockville, MD: Centre for Substance Abuse Treatment, Substance Abuse and Mental Health Services.

Reiman, J. (1998) *The Rich Get Richer and the Poor Get Prison*. Boston, MA: Allyn and Bacon.

Rempel, M., Fox-Kralstein, D., Cissner, A., Cohen, R., Labriola, M., Farole, D., Bader, A. and Magnani, M. (2003) *The New York State Adult Drug Court Evaluation*. New York: Centre for Court Innovation.

Reuters (2008) 'Women in Milan jail want a break – into fashion', online at: www.reuters.com/article/idUSL2210696720070726 (accessed 19 April 2010).

Reuters (2009) 'What could possibly go wrong?', online at: www.reuters.com/article/idUSTRE54O38O20090525 (accessed 16 April 2010).

Riminton, H. (2007) '"Thriller" prisoners prepare to make "electric dreams" come true', CNN, 5 September. Online at: www.cnn.com/2007/WORLD/asiapcf/09/04/dancing.prisoners/index.html#cnnSTCText (accessed 3 February 2010).

Rinehart, T., Laszlo, A. and Briscoe, G. (2001) *Collaboration Toolkit: How to Build, Fix and Sustain Productive Partnerships*. Washington, DC: US Department of Justice, Office of Community Oriented Policing Services.

Robinson, D. (1995) *The Impact of Cognitive Skills Training on Post-Release Recidivism among Canadian Federal Offenders*. Ontario: Correctional Service of Canada.

Roman, C., Moore, G., Jenkins, S. and Small, K. (2002) *Understanding Community Justice Partnerships: Assessing the Capacity to Partner*. Washington, DC: Urban Institute Justice Policy Centre and the National Institute of Justice.

Rome, A., Morrison, L., Duff, J., Martin, J. and Russell, P. (2002) *Integrated Care for Drug Users: Principles and Practice*. Edinburgh: Scottish Executive.

Rooney, R. (ed.) (2009) *Strategies for Work with Involuntary Clients*, 2nd edn. New York: Columbia University Press.

Rosenfeld, B., Galietta, M., Ivanoff, A., Garcia-Mansilla, A., Martinez, R., Fava, J., Fineran, V. and Green, D. (2007) 'Dialectical behavior therapy for the treatment of stalking offenders', *International Journal of Forensic Mental Health*, 6(2): 95–103.

Ross, S. (2005) 'Bridging the gap between prison and the community: post-release support and supervision', in S. Eyland and S. O'Toole (eds) *Corrections Criminology*. Sydney: Hawkins Press.

Rottman, D. and Casey, P. (1999) 'Therapeutic jurisprudence and the emergence of problem-solving courts', *National Institute of Justice Journal*, 12(14): 240.

Rynne, J., Harding, R. and Wortley, R. (2008) 'Market testing and prison riots: how public-sector commercialization contributed to a prison riot', *Criminology and Public Policy*, 7(1): 117–42.

Sainsbury Centre for Mental Health (n.d.) *Personality Disorder: A Briefing for People Working in the Criminal Justice System*. London: Sainsbury Centre for Mental Health.

Sainsbury Centre for Mental Health (2009) *Briefing 39: Mental Health Care and the Criminal Justice System*. London: Sainsbury Centre for Mental Health.

Sandifer, J. (2008) 'Evaluating the efficacy of a parenting program for incarcerated mothers', *Prison Journal*, 88(3): 423–45.

Saunders, P. and Billante, N. (2003) 'Does prison work?', *Policy*, 18(4): 3–8.

Schwartz, J. and Barry, C. (2005) *A Guide to Preparing for and Responding to Prison Emergencies*. Washington, DC: US Department of Justice, National Institute of Corrections.

Scottish Executive (2005) *Social Focus on Deprived Areas 2005*. Edinburgh: Scottish Executive National Statistics Publication.

Scottish Prison Service (2009) *Scottish Prison Service Annual Report and Accounts 2008–09*. Edinburgh: Scottish Prison Service.

Seno, A. (2008) 'Dance is a part of rehabilitation at Philippine prison', *New York Times*, 15 January.

Seymour, A. (2001) *The Victim's Role in Offender Reentry: A Community Response Manual*. Washington, DC: Office for Victims of Crime, US Department of Justice.

Sharma, R., Reddon, J., Hoglin, B. and Woodman, M. (2008) 'Assessment of the long term benefits of life skills programming on psychosocial adjustment', *Journal of Offender Rehabilitation*, 47(1/2): 121–37.

Sheehan, R. and Flynn, C. (2007) 'Women prisoners and their children', in R. Sheehan, G. McIvor and C. Trotter (eds) *What Works with Women Offenders?* Cullompton: Willan Publishing.

Shepherd, G., Boardman, J. and Slade, M. (2008) *Making Recovery a Reality*. London: Sainsbury Centre for Mental Health.

Shinkfield, A. and Graffam, J. (2009) 'Community reintegration of ex-prisoners: type and degree of change in variables influencing successful reintegration', *International Journal of Offender Therapy and Comparative Criminology*, 53: 29–42.

Shivy, V., Wu, J., Moon, A. and Mann, S. (2007) 'Ex-offenders reentering the workforce', *Journal of Counseling Psychology*, 54(4): 466–73.

Siegert, R., Ward, T., Levack, W. and McPherson, K. (2007) 'A Good Lives Model of clinical and community rehabilitation', *Disability and Rehabilitation*, 29(20–21): 1604–15.

Singh, L. (2010) 'Prison takes the lead in assistance dogs project', media release, 11 February, Department of Corrections, Tasmanian Government: Hobart.

Skinner, N. and Roche, A. (2005) *Stress and Burnout: A Prevention Handbook for the Alcohol and Other Drugs Workforce*. Adelaide: National Centre for Education and Training in Addiction.

Slattery, P. (2000/2001) 'Kids locked up', *Education Links* (61/62): 56–60.

Smart, C. (1976) *Women, Crime and Criminology: A Feminist Critique*. London: Routledge and Kegan Paul.

SMART Recovery Australia (2009) *What is SMART Recovery?* Online at: www.smartrecoveryaustralia.com.au/aboutsmart.html (accessed 7 December 2009).

Smith, B. (2002) *An End to Silence: A Prisoner's Handbook for Identifying and Addressing Sexual Misconduct*, 2nd edn. Washington, DC: American University, Washington College of Law.

Smith, P., Cullen, F. and Latessa, E. (2009) 'Can 14,737 women be wrong? A meta-analysis of the LSI-R and recidivism for female offenders', *Criminology and Public Policy*, 8(1): 183–208.

Smith, R., Grimshaw, R., Romeo, R. and Knapp, M. (2007) *Poverty and Disadvantage among Prisoner's Families*. York: Joseph Rowntree Foundation.

Solomon, A., Osbourne, J., LoBuglio, S., Mellow, J. and Mukamal, D. (2008a) *Life After Lockup: Improving Reentry from Jail to the Community*. Washington, DC: Urban Institute Justice Policy Centre.

Solomon, A., Osbourne, J., Winterfield, L., Elderbroom, B., Burke, P., Stroker, R., Rhine, E. and Burrell, W. (2008b) *Putting Public Safety First: 13 Parole Supervision Strategies to Enhance Reentry Outcomes*. Washington, DC: Urban Institute Justice Policy Centre.

South, C.R. and Wood, J. (2006) 'Bullying in prisons: the importance of perceived social status, prisonization, and moral disengagement', *Aggressive Behaviour*, 32(5): 490–501.

Sprott, J. and Doob, A. (1998) 'Understanding provincial variation in incarceration rates', *Canadian Journal of Criminology*, 40: 305–22.

Statistics Canada (2005) *Adult Correctional Services in Canada 2003–2004*. Ottawa: Statistics Canada.

Steering Committee for the Review of Commonwealth/State Service Provision (2008) *Report on Government Services, Vol. 1: Education, Justice, Emergency Management*. Melbourne: Productivity Commission.

Stewart, D. (2008) *The Problems and Needs of Newly Sentenced Prisoners: Results from a National Survey*. London: Ministry of Justice.

Strelan, P., Feather, N. and McKee, I. (2008) 'Justice and forgiveness: experimental evidence for compatibility', *Journal of Experimental Social Psychology*, 44: 1538–44.

Strimple, E. (2003) 'A history of prison inmate–animal interaction programs', *American Behavioral Scientist*, 47(1): 70–8.

Stump, E., Beamish, P. and Stellenberger, R. (1999) 'Self-concept changes in sex offenders following prison psychoeducational treatment', *Journal of Offender Rehabilitation*, 29(1/2): 101–11.

Sykes, G. (1958) *The Society of Captives: A Study of a Maximum Security Prison*. Princeton, NJ: Princeton University Press.

Tata, C., Burns, N., Halliday, S., Hutton, N. and McNeill, F. (2008) 'Assisting and advising the sentencing decision process: the pursuit of "quality" in pre-sentence reports', *British Journal of Criminology*, 48: 835–55.

Tavares, C. and Thomas, G. (2008) *European Statistics in Focus: Crime and Criminal Justice*. Luxembourg: Office for the Official Publications of the European Communities.

Taylor, J., Thorne, I., Robertson, A. and Avery, G. (2002) 'Evaluation of a group intervention for convicted arsonists with mild and borderline intellectual disabilities', *Criminal Behaviour and Mental Health*, 12: 282–93.

Taylor, K. and Blanchette, K. (2009) 'The women are not wrong: it is the approach that is debatable', *Criminology and Public Policy*, 8(1): 221–9.

Taxman, F., Yancey, C. and Bilanin, J. (2006) *Proactive Community Supervision in Maryland: Changing Offender Outcomes*. Maryland: University of Maryland and Virginia Commonwealth University.

Teevan, S. and Gorman, J. (2008) *How to Cope with Panic Attacks*. London: Mind.

Teodorescu, A. (2009) 'Prison drama an escape for Romanian inmates', *Romanian News Watch*, 30 November.

Tracy, S. (2004) 'Dialectic, contradiction, or double bind? Analyzing and theorizsing employee reactions to organizational tension in corrections', *Journal of Applied Communications Research*, 32(2): 119–46.

Trevethan, S., Moore, J. and Rastin, C. (2002) *A Profile of Aboriginal Offenders in Federal Facilities and Serving Time in the Community*. Ontario: Correctional Service of Canada.

Trotter, C. (1996) 'The impact of different supervision practices in community corrections: cause for optimism', *Australian and New Zealand Journal of Criminology*, 29(1): 29–46.

Trotter, C. (2006) *Working with Involuntary Clients: A Guide to Practice*, 2nd edn. Sydney: Allen and Unwin.

Trupin, E., Stewart, D., Beach, B. and Boesky, L. (2002) 'Effectiveness of a dialectical behavior therapy program for incarcerated female juvenile offenders', *Child and Adolescent Mental Health*, 7(3): 121–7.

Uggen, C., Manza, J. and Behrens, A. (2004) '"Less than the average citizen": stigma, role transition and the civic reintegration of convicted felons', in S. Maruna and R. Immarigeon (eds) *After Crime and Punishment: Pathways to Offender Reintegration*. Cullompton: Willan Publishing.

Uggen, C., Van Brakle, M. and McLaughlin, H. (2009) 'Punishment and social exclusion: national differences in prisoner disenfranchisement', in A. Ewald and B. Rottinghaus (eds) *Criminal Disenfranchisement in an International Perspective*. New York: Cambridge University Press.

United Kingdom National Strategy for Neighbourhood Renewal (2000) *Report of Policy Action Team 8: Anti-social behaviour*. London: Home Office.

United Nations (2005) *Human Rights and Prisons: Manual on Human Rights Training for Prison Officials*. New York: Office of the United Nations High Commissioner for Human Rights.

United Nations Office on Drugs and Crime (2008a) *Tenth United Nations Survey on Crime Trends and Operations of Criminal Justice Systems 2005–2006*. Vienna: United Nations Office on Drugs and Crime.

United Nations Office on Drugs and Crime (2008b) *Handbook on Prisoner File Management*. New York: United Nations.

United Nations Office of Drugs and Crime (2009) *Handbook on Prisoners with Special Needs*. New York: United Nations.

Vess, J. (2006) 'Preparing practitioners for assessing and managing risk', in K. McMaster and L. Bakker (eds) *Will They Do It Again? Assessing and Managing Risk*. Lyttleton: Hall McMaster and Associates.

Vetere, A. and Cooper, J. (2001) 'Working systemically with family violence: risk, responsibility and collaboration', *Journal of Family Therapy*, 23: 378–96.

VicHealth (n.d.) *The Partnerships Analysis Tool: For Partners in Health Promotion*. Melbourne: VicHealth.

Vinson, T. (2004) *Community Adversity and Resilience: The Distribution of Social Disadvantage in Victoria and New South Wales and the Mediating Role of Social Cohesion*. Sydney: Ignatius Centre, Jesuit Social Services and University of New South Wales.

Walgrave, L. (1999) 'Community service as a cornerstone of a systemic restorative response to (juvenile) crime', in G. Bazemore and L. Walgrave (eds) *Restorative Juvenile Justice: Repairing the Harm of Youth Crime*. Monsey, NY: Criminal Justice Press.

Walmsley, R. (2008) *World Pre-Trial/Remand Imprisonment List*. London: International Centre for Prison Studies, Kings College.

Walmsley, R. (2009) *World Prison Population*, 8th edn. London: International Centre for Prison Studies, Kings College.

Walters, S., Clark, M., Gingerich, R. and Meltzer, M. (2007) *Motivating Offenders to Change: A Guide for Probation and Parole*. Washington, DC: US Department of Justice, National Institute of Corrections.

Ward, T. (2009) 'Dignity and human rights in correctional practice', *European Journal of Probation*, 2(1): 110–23.

Ward, T. and Birgden, A. (2007) 'Human rights and correctional clinical practice', *Aggression and Violent Behaviour*, 12(6): 628–43.

Ward, T. and Brown, M. (2004) 'The Good Lives Model and conceptual issues in offender rehabilitation', *Psychology, Crime and Law*, 10(3): 243–57.

Ward, T., Day, A. and Casey, S. (2006) 'Offender rehabilitation down under', *Journal of Offender Rehabilitation*, 43(3): 73–83.

Ward, T. and Maruna, S. (2007) *Rehabilitation: Beyond the Risk Paradigm*. New York: Routledge.

Ward, T. and Stewart, C. (2003) 'The treatment of sex offenders: risk management and good lives', *Professional Psychology, Research and Practice*, 34(4): 353–60.

Webb, R. and Vulliamy, G. (2001) 'Joining up the solutions: the rhetoric and practice of interagency cooperation', *Children and Society*, 15: 315–32.

Western Australia Department of Corrective Services (2008) *10th Anniversary of Work Camps in Western Australia*, commemorative booklet, Western Australia Department of Corrective Services.

White, R. (1999) 'On prison labour', *Current Issues in Criminal Justice*, 11(2): 243–8.

White, R. (2002) 'Early intervention models, community change and workplace environments', *Youth Studies Australia*, 21(4): 16–23.

White, R. (2008a) 'Class analysis and the crime problem', in T. Anthony and C. Cunneen (eds) *The Critical Criminology Companion*. Sydney: Federation Press.

White, R. (2008b) 'Prisoners, victims and the act of giving', *Parity*, 21(9): 18–19.

White, R. (2009) 'Indigenous youth and gangs as family', *Youth Studies Australia*, 28(3): 47–56.

White, R. (2010) 'When prisoners leave: offenders, victims and the post-release process', in S. Shoham, P. Knepper and M. Kett (eds) *International Handbook of Victimology*. New York: Taylor and Francis.

White, R. and Coventry, G. (2000) *Evaluating Community Safety – A Guide*. Melbourne: Victoria Department of Justice.

White, R. and Coventry, G. (2008) 'Prisoners, work and reciprocal reintegration', in C. Cunneen and M. Salter (eds) *Proceedings of the 2nd Australian and New Zealand Critical Criminology Conference* (refereed papers). Sydney: University of NSW, Crime and Justice Research Network.

White, R. and Heckenberg, D. (2006) *Post-Release Options Project Final Workshop Report*. Hobart: School of Sociology and Social Work, University of Tasmania.

White, R. and Mason, R. (2003) *An Evaluation of the 'Inside Out' Prison Program*. Hobart: Criminology Research Unit, University of Tasmania.

White, R. and Perrone, S. (2010) *Crime, Criminality and Criminal Justice*. South Melbourne: Oxford University Press.

White, R. and Tomkins, K. (2003) *Issues in Community Corrections: Briefing Paper No. 2*. Hobart: Criminology Research Unit, School of Sociology and Social Work, University of Tasmania.

Whitehead, D. (2006) 'The health promoting prison (HPP) and its imperative for nursing', *International Journal of Nursing Studies*, 43: 123–31.

Williams, D. (2005) 'Prisoner rehabilitation, Italian style', *Washington Post*, 14 March, page A13.

Williamson, P., Day, A., Howells, K., Burner, S. and Jauncey, S. (2003) 'Assessing offender readiness to change problems with anger', *Psychology Crime and Law*, 9(4): 295–307.

Willis, M. (2008) *Reintegration of Indigenous Prisoners: Key Findings*, Trends and Issues No. 364. Canberra: Australian Institute of Criminology.

Wilson, D., Bouffard, L. and MacKenzie, D. (2005) 'A quantitative review of structured, group oriented cognitive behavioral programs for offenders', *Criminal Justice and Behavior*, 32(2): 172–204.

Winick, B. (2000) 'Applying the law therapeutically in domestic violence cases', *UMKC Law Review*, 69(1): 1.

Winick, B. (2003) 'Problem solving courts and therapeutic jurisprudence', *Fordham Urban Law Journal*, 30: 1055–93.

Witvliet, C., Worthington, E., Root, L., Sato, A., Ludwig, T. and Exline, J. (2008) 'Retributive justice, restorative justice and forgiveness: an experimental psychophysiology analysis', *Journal of Experimental Social Psychology*, 44: 10–25.

Woodside, M. and McClam, T. (2006) *Generalist Case Management: A Method of Human Service Delivery*, 3rd edn. Belmont: Thomson Brooks Cole.

World Health Organisation (2000) *Preventing Suicide: A Resource for Prison Officers*. Geneva: Department of Mental Health, World Health Organisation.

Wortley, R. (2002) *Situational Prison Control: Crime Prevention in Correctional Institutions*. Cambridge: Cambridge University Press.

Wright, M. (2002) 'The court as last resort: victim-sensitive, community-based responses to crime', *British Journal of Criminology*, 42(3): 654–67.

Zurhold, H., Stover, H. and Haasen, C. (2004) *Female Drug Users in European Prisons – Best Practice for Relapse Prevention and Reintegration*. Hamburg: Centre for Interdisciplinary Addiction Research.

# Index

Note: the letter 'b' after a page number refers to a box; the letter 'f' to a figure; 't' to a table.